D1238258

John Bracchetta and Joyce Mills in Eugene Feist's
Building Blocks

The Off-Broadway Theater

by

Julia S. Price

GREENWOOD PRESS, PUBLISHERS
WESTPORT, CONNECTICUT

Library of Congress Cataloging in Publication Data

Price, Julia S
  The off-Broadway theater.

    Reprint of the ed. published by the Scarecrow
Press, New York.
    Bibliography: p.
    1. Theater--New York (City) 2. American drama
--20th century--History and criticism. 3. Drama--
History and criticism. I. Title.
PN2277.N5P7 1974   792'.09747'1   73-8256
ISBN 0-8371-6972-0

Originally published in 1962 by The Scarecrow Press, Inc.,
New York

Reprinted with the permission of The Scarecrow Press, Inc.

Reprinted in 1974 by Greenwood Press,
a division of Williamhouse-Regency Inc.

Library of Congress Catalogue Card Number 73-8256

ISBN 0-8371-6972-0

Printed in the United States of America

I dedicate this work to my dearly beloved grandmother, Julia Hegedus Szeman, whose memory remains a constant inspiration to her family.

Preface

Off-Broadway, Avant Garde to Commercial Theater, With
Emphasis on the New Play by the American Playwright..

One is always seeking exciting theater; a theater that
disturbs, challenges, provokes; a theater that arouses the
hearts of men in our time. Today, in an era of conform-
ity, new productions are usually far from experimental.
Only as the leaders of our contemporary theater---writers,
producers, directors, playwrights---show a real desire to
create boldly, to experiment with new forms, can we hope
for the emergence of a truly modern theater. This requires
a genuinely responsive audience; one that can go beyond the
established patterns of today's commercialized stage. Both
the dramatist and the audience must be in quest of the novel
in theatrical productions. The artist must also be techni-
cally expert through diligent practice of his art to successfully convey his new ideas. A pioneering spirit Off-Broadway will indeed prove rewarding.

Between 1905-1961 Off-Broadway introduced new forms
of theater as well as new interpretive talents to America.
These new experimental forms have gradually been assimi-
lated into the commercial Broadway theater. Broadway
theater has developed its creative imagination through its
association with Off-Broadway.

In compiling a chronological study of the Off-Broadway
theater one may group plays into tentative relationships
which indicate a freshness of composition in the treatment
of the material or in the originality of the thematic approach.

The American playwright has revealed true growth in his dramatic presentations Off-Broadway---his plays have brought an indigenous theater which reflects the true culture of our American way of life. The Off-Broadway dramatist projects the ideals, quests and needs of the people who make up his audience. The Off-Broadway playwright may communicate to his audience with compassion and understanding.

In any theatrical experience of value the audience should be stimulated and an intellectual rapport established between playwright and audience which extends the limitations of ordinary dramatic presentation. The playwright must project values intelligible to his particular audience. Off-Broadway is unique in that it has an understanding audience which comprehends new horizons of thought and for whom the playwright is better able to write to the utmost limit of his talents.

Fine American interpretive talents have appeared on Off-Broadway---actors, scenic artists, lighting designers. However, the true contribution of Off-Broadway to theater is the new drama written by American playwrights which has developed off the Broadway limits. With the changing Off-Broadway scene in which the repertory theater is often more important than the American theater of the creative new playwright, the writer who needs to be heard is losing an important outlet.

What has changed Off-Broadway and what are the indications of its future growth? The answers to these difficult questions are best indicated by the study of its history with specific attention concentrated on the new playwright. The reason for fewer original productions Off-

Broadway becomes evident in this study of the productions of the past fifty years.

Off-Broadway has given the American audience exceptional drama by new American playwrights, revivals of great classics of the theater, revivals of hits of the commercial Broadway theater and has presented European dramas which have won acclaim in other countries. However, the real hope of any creative enterprise is to inspire its own artists to produce their individual contributions, which may transcend the established models and pioneer original forms.

The Off-Broadway stage, unlike the established American theater, has always given glimpses of new, bold, horizons. Its five recognizable periods may be designated as: Off-Broadway theater in its early period to the 1920's, Off-Broadway in the 1930's, Off-Broadway in the 1940's, Off-Broadway of 1950-1955, Off-Broadway of 1955-1960.

Theater Off-Broadway was established in the 1900's and reached its first fervent outburst of creativity in the 1920's. In its early period it was concerned primarily with the communication of new drama to a select and receptive audience. New techniques of production were employed for the best presentation of the emerging new forms of dramatic expression of the time.

The Provincetown theater of the 1930's, although not classified as a legitimate producing unit, contributed immensely not only to Off-Broadway but to Broadway theater as well. This and other Off-Broadway theaters of the time attracted a wide audience of people of differing social and cultural backgrounds.

After the introduction of Off-Broadway in 1905 and the

ix

fervor of activity in the 1920's and 1930's, the "renaissance" movement after the second World War was a truly inspired phase which brought many writers to the Off-Broadway scene. Some of these playwrights are now established in other media but their first real recognition was Off-Broadway. Although Off-Broadway initiates new talents in writing, it has not always been able to sustain that which it developed because of its financial insecurity.

Since 1952, a new trend has evolved. Off-Broadway has gradually reduced the production of original plays because financial and professional requirements have become increasingly prohibitive. Off-Broadway, admirably qualified to present new drama, could continue to produce more original plays. Many of the original scripts presented Off-Broadway after the second World War, both published and unpublished, would form an excellent repertoire for a creative theater. Off-Broadway today is on the whole, so concerned with meeting production costs that the demand for an American advanced guard theater is being denied. There are exceptions in which certain theaters have been extremely successful in producing a new playwright but their activity is not sustained.

Off-Broadway has become an excellent revival theater. Indigenous theater is often sacrificed to European or library productions which has been proven popular and which guarantee a safe investment to the producer. Much of the commercial formula has been applied to productions Off-Broadway. The financial problem leads producers to turn away from the untried or unusual script.

Off-Broadway theater must meet the demand for creative drama. Off-Broadway will continue to develop as long

x

as the emergence of new theatrical talent gives the movement impetus through presentation of original plays and the use of creative methods of production. Many interests both internal and external have contributed to the development of the Off-Broadway theater---new production methods, foreign artistic influences and the lower cost of production as compared to the scale on Broadway. Off-Broadway is extending its boundaries beyond New York into the very heart of America by the tours of some of its productions.

Off-Broadway theater presents the best drama of many cultures but it could produce more of the best of the dramatic works of our own new playwrights. Off-Broadway with its ever broadening base will remain the most exciting of theaters as long as young artists with courage continue to display and develop their talents in an established theater which stimulates creativity and imagination.

I would like to express my thanks to all those who made possible this study of Off-Broadway theater:

Mr. George Freedley of the New York Public Library Theater Collection, who initiated my interest in the topic and whose staff has been a constant source of information in my research; Mrs. Elizabeth Barrett and Mr. William Carson who encouraged me in my enterprise; Mrs. Irene Roncsak, my mother, and Mr. John Szeman, my grandfather, who underwrote the work and who were a constant source of comfort when it was needed. I also wish to thank all of my friends who gave me .encouragement and understanding during the long composition of this work.

Table of Contents

Preface; Off-Broadway, Avant-Garde To Commercial
Theater, With Emphasis On The New Play
By The American Playwright   vii

I.   Off-Broadway in the 1920's   1
     Progressive Stage
     Provincetown
     Washington Square Players
     Cherry Lane Theater

II.   Off-Broadway in the 1930's   15
     Little Theater Tournament
     Provincetown Productions
     Theater of Action

III.   Off-Broadway in the 1940's   34
     During the War Years
     Renaissance Off-Broadway Since 1947
     Productions of New Plays, Starting in 1946
     Originals Only
     Significant Producing Groups

IV.   Off-Broadway 1950-1955-A Study of the Original
Plays   43

V.   Theater Prospectus and Analysis of Some Interesting
Plays Produced in the Fifties   76
     Haven in the Dark by Paul Nord
     Aegean Fable by Bill Long
     A Double Bill
         A Switch in Time by Lola Pergament
         I Believe in Rubble by Deric Riegen
     Sandhog by Earl Robinson and Waldo Salt
     A Time of Storm by Sheldon Stark
     Sign of Winter by Ettore Rella

Production Off-Broadway

VI.   Main Production Trends Off-Broadway from
1950-1960   97

Main Producing Units
   The Phoenix Operation
   Circle-in-the-Square
   Cherry Lane Theater

Impetus for the New Play Off-Broadway

   Producing Units Formed Solely to Produce
   the New Play
      Abbey Theater
      Dramatist Workshop
      New Playwrights
      Originals Only
      The Cricket Theater

   Living Theater
   Drama Desk
   New Dramatist's Committee

The Present Repertory Stage Off-Broadway

Finances of Off-Broadway

VII. Financial Aspects of the Off-Broadway Theater   112
      The Actor
      The Scene Designer
      The Stage Hands Union
      The House
      Off-Broadway's Approach to the Producing
        Problem
            Theater League---1949
            Theater League---1955
      The Financial Situation and the American Play-
      wright in the Off-Broadway Scene
      Off-Broadway and the Producer
      Financial Outline for 1960

VIII. Off-Broadway, 1955-1960   135

Views of Current Off-Broadway Leaders

IX. Views of Current Off-Broadway Leaders   175
      Jerry Tallmer
      Leo Garen
      Ted Mann
      Gene Frankel

Kip Hastings
James Spicer
Judith Malina

Bibliography of Plays

New and Revival Off-Broadway Plays, 1950-1960   192

Index   254

Chapter I

Off-Broadway in the 1920's
Progressive Stage
Provincetown
Washington Square Players
Cherry Lane Theater

Off-Broadway has a history of exciting theater. The germination of the Off-Broadway theater came through imaginative artists who found a purpose in their new theater which went beyond their own need for expression. They established a stage which worked with the society and artists of its time and was a true indigenous theater. In its early days this stage gave a voice to inspired talents of the theater.

In the early part of the century the native drama on Broadway was at an impasse. Most theatrical presentations were mediocre romantic comedy. The establishment of a new theatrical movement was greatly needed.

As early as 1905, Julius Hopp had organized a Progressive Stage Society in New York City for the presentation of radical plays.

> One cannot decide which was the stronger in Hopp, the passion for the theater or the passion for social reform. We find him continually confusing the two, now using the theater as a means of disseminating radical ideas, now organizing progressive societies for the support of new plays. Hopp belongs to the school of those who would impose on the theater of America the systems of the Continent.[1]

1

Hopp modelled his Progressive Stage Society after a
type of theater in Germany of that period. This theater
was established to free drama to meet the needs of the people and heralded the influx of European plays so much in
vogue Off-Broadway in the middle of the twentieth century.

> But Hopp organized the Progressive Stage Society, the
> Wage Earners' Theater, the Educational Theater for
> schools, The Theater League, and he had a hand in
> Reicher's The Modern Stage, in each appealing to the
> people as to a great beleagured mass to solidify their
> interest in support of radical plays...Before anyone
> else he had seen that the present system of organiza-
> tion of the theater is wrong and had started to recon-
> struct that system.[2]

The first signs among artists of dissatisfaction with
the commercial theater became evident at this time. Broadway had for years before the First World War presented
"entertainment." It "went on its merry way, attempting to
live up to its appellation of the Great White Way and dis-
pensing entertainment to an eager public..."[3] Such Shows as
George White's Scandals and the Ziegfield Follies, together
with many melodramas and sentimental comedies were the
standard theater fare. "It was, on the whole, a pleasant
world of escape and make-believe that was presented on the
stage, a conventional and Freudless universe, not much
more adult than the movies of a later age. and just about as
sentimental."[4]

Off-Broadway theater was at first almost exclusively
devoted to the original play. The decade beginning in 1910
brought the first burgeoning of an Off-Broadway movement
supporting the new dramatist. The now legendary Provincetown theater with its playwright genuis, Eugene O'Neill,
brought a new dramatic form to the romantic Broadway theater. Interestingly, Broadway at that time produced revivals

and presented European plays as well as its romantic fare.
Off-Broadway, meantime, devoted almost exclusive attention
to the production of advanced American play forms.

The birth of the Off-Broadway theater may be most di-
rectly attributed to the Provincetown playhouse, which gave
recognition to such talents as Eugene O'Neill and Robert
Edmond Jones. O'Neill more than any other single person
may be regarded as the dramatic genuis who gave the group
its impetus and lasting fame. His works to this day fire
the dramatic imagination, even on Broadway.[5]

A number of artistically inclined personalities were
summering at Provincetown, Massachusetts, in 1915. John
Reed kept open house. George Cram Cook and Susan Glaspell were in Provincetown, together with Wilbur Daniel
Steele, Hutchins Hapgood, E. J. Ballantine, David Carb,
the Zorachs, Joseph O'Brien and Robert Edmond Jones...
"With so many arts represented, drama was the natural
meeting-ground, the inevitable medium of expression."[6]

The first plays were given at Hutchins Hapgood's house,
and the first Provincetown program read:

> 1915 Summer
> Wharf Theater
> Provincetown, Massachusetts
>
> Constancy by Keith Boyce
> Suppressed Desires by George Cram Cook
> 　　　　and Susan Glaspell
> Change Your Style by George Cram Cook
> Contemporaries by Wilbur Daniel Steele[7]

The Wharf theater was built in 1916 and seated 200,
only about 150 of them comfortable. Season tickets were
sold for $4.00 and that season included ten performances.[8]
Provincetown programs listed a new production every three
weeks.[9] Subscriptions provided a constant audience.

The first New York seasons of the Provincetown were

offered at thirty-nine Macdougal Street from 1916-1918. The
Playwright's Theater was formed on the parlor floor-the
home of the Provincetown Players under the supervision of
George Cram Cook until 1917.

The Constitution provided for a membership divided
into (1) Active Members, who were engaged in the production and the administration of the club-theater, (2) Associate
members, who were the season ticket holders, and (3) Club
Members who were persons interested in the work of the
Provincetown Players'.[10]

The prospectus declared:

> The present organization is the outcome of a group of
> people interested in the theater, who gathered spon-
> taneously during two summers at Provincetown, Mass-
> achusetts, for the purpose of writing, producing and
> acting their own plays. The impelling desire of the
> group was to establish a stage where the playwrights
> of sincere, poetic, literary and dramatic purpose could
> see their plays in action and superintend their produc-
> tion without submitting to the commercial manager's
> interpretation of public taste. Equally it was to afford
> an opportunity for actors, producers, scenic and cos-
> tume designers to experiment with a stage of extremely
> simple resources---it being the idea of the Players
> that elaborate settings are unnecessary to bring out the
> essential qualities of a good play.[11]

It was announced that, with the exception of two
salaried officers who would devote their entire time to the
work, the members would give their services without compensation. The members divided themselves in two groups--
while one group of ten or twelve were acting in a play, the
other group was rehearsing.

At first only one-act plays were done.[12] George
Cram Cook's The Athenian Women given in April, 1918, was
the first full-length play. The adherence to the one-act form

during the first years was the result of no conscious decision.[13]

O'Neill's first full-length Provincetown play, Beyond
the Horizon, was produced in 1920 and "revealed both the
author's dramatic growth and Broadway's receptiveness to
the new drama"[14] ..."and a significant victory for the art
theater as well when it was awarded the Pulitzer Prize."[15]

The group disbanded some time after their eminently
successful presentation of The Emperor Jones, which was
taken on Broadway, to reconsider their aims and purposes.
After a year's inactivity they reopened in October, 1923.
Jig Cook and Susan Glaspell, the former leaders, were still
away, deep in their own work and the new life they had
found in Greece.

Unfortunately, George Cram Cook died in Delphi on
January 14, 1924.[16] Subsequently the group split in 1925.[17]
The "Triumvirate" established itself at the Greenwich Village Theater and took the name of the Experimental Theater, Incorporated. The triumvirate consisted of Macgowan,
critic, who became director and asked O'Neill, playwright,
and Robert Edmond Jones, artist, to act as associate directors.

Although the enterprise was described in the opening
prospectus as a theater which would not compete with Broadway, the directors showed a lively appreciation of professional standards and made plans for using professional talent whenever possible.

In regard to this O'Neill issued a statement in answer
to press criticism on Irvin S. Cobbs' All God's Chillun:

> ...we are not a public theater. Our playhouse is
> essentially a laboratory for artistic experiment. Our
> aims are special. We are not seeking to rival the

> theater uptown, we make no attempt to cater to the
> taste of a general public. Our audience is intentionally
> a restricted one. Admitting (which we do not) that we
> are responsible to anyone outside our own organization,
> it is by our subscriber's alone we can with any reason
> be held to account.[18]

Meanwhile, the old timers who remained at Provincetown Playhouse at 133 Macdougal St., who called themselves the Arcadia Revisited Group, were directed by James
Light and M. Eleanor Fitzgerald. They issued prospectus
stating that they planned to follow the old principles, signed
by:

James Light	Cleon Throckmorton
Eugene O'Neill	Harold McGee
M. Eleanor Fitzgerald	Pauline H. Turkel
	Stella Hanau[19]

On December 14, 1929, when Winter Bound closed,
the theater on Macdougal St. closed with it.[20] So ended
the first major theater movement Off-Broadway. It was
dedicated mainly to the presentation of new drama by A-
merican playwrights. Its list of plays are an outstanding
monument to creative American dramatic talent. Among
them were The Ancient Mariner by Stark Young, All God's
Chillun and The Emperor Jones by Eugene O'Neill.[21]

In 1915, the Washington Square Players were established. This was another important step in the formation of Off-Broadway. This group influenced from its first
days the Broadway scene.[22]

They produced experimental one-act plays beginning
in the Autumn of 1914. Scenery was by Robert Edmond
Jones. The capacity of the theater was about 40 people at
$.25 a seat.[23]

> The Players are the outgrowth of a little group that
> used to foregather in Washington Square, radicals, so-
> cialists, progressives, artists, writers and plain men

and women---Here was the guild of artists whose en-
thusiasms took the place of the cold organization by
commercial compact of the regular theater.[24]

The Washington Square Players sponsored two kinds
of plays in particular: new American plays and the best ex-
amples of the recent drama of Europe. They used the one-
act play form out of necessity but it proved itself, both in
furthering the scope of the authors and actors and in the
comparative cheapness of production.[25]

Ticket prices rose to $2.00 although they began in
October 4, 1915, in the Bandbox Theater with admission at
$.50 and a rental of $8,000.[26] Upon their move to the
Comedy Theater near Broadway the rental of $32,000.
raised ticket rates.[27]

A group of subscribers placed into the hands of the
company a fund amounting to $10,000. a season which pro-
vided little more than $1,500. per production. The rest of
the expenses had to be paid from box office receipts.[28]
Nevertheless, backed by a subscription audience it could
experiment and offer a variety of European and American
plays. Later this playhouse became the now illustrious
Theater Guild which advocates the same principles on
Broadway.

An interesting Off-Broadway theater appearing at this
time was that of Stuart Walker, whose Portmanteau Theater
was founded in 1915-16. It gave its first performance at
Christadora House (a social settlement).

The Portmanteau Theater was a portable, collapsible
theater that could be taken apart and packed up at three
hour's notice.[29] It was the first children's theater in New
York.[30] Among plays presented was Two Fans and A
Candlestick by Mary MacMillan. The Theater presented
such parable plays of Lord Dunsany as The Gods of the

Mountain, The Golden Doom, and King Argimines and the
Unknown Warrior. Later plays like Oscar Wilde's Birthday
of the Infanta and Stevenson's Gammer Gurton's Needle were
given. This provided a variety of rarely produced plays,
although the only original plays were for children.

Regular prices were $.50 to $2.00, but children's
matinees ran $.25 to $.50. The actors were young professionals who played for a nominal sum.[31]

A theater which is still known is the Neighborhood Playhouse. Although an adjunct of the Henry Street Settlement,
it was designed not as a social experiment but to serve the
needs and the interests of people in the area.

It was founded in the middle 1920's by Alice and Irene
Lewisohn and evolved from festivals with the children of the
Settlement. They called it the "theater of experience" formulated with the "echoes subconscious in their young players."[32] At the basis of the theater is "service of the neighborhood." The "larger share of the work of the theater is
given over to productions of a local appeal."[33]

The theater was built for "a cost of $150,000. which
included the ground."[34] A maximum of fifty cents was
charged for tickets and each play was done for five weeks, or
ten times. After five weeks of plays they had an equal
period of children's festivals. The theater, holding 450,
could bring in between $160. and $190. "This gave an income for each play production covering ten performances of
about $1500."[35] There was no advertising but "newspaper
men understand that if they come there are seats ready for
them."[36]

Plays performed from 1915-1917 included Tethered
Sheep by Robert Gilbert Welsh, Wild Birds by Violet Pearn,
The Price of Coal by Harold Brighouse, Red Turf by

Rutherford Mayne, and Isaac Percy's Early Morning After Burial and Sisters.[37]

Pausing to reconsider further development in 1927, the Neighborhood Playhouse incorporated "to develop and to exhibit...productions embodying new or unusual forms of expression in the drama, the dance, music, and the decorative arts either separately or in correlation."[38] The Neighborhood Playhouse is still in operation presenting new plays by new playwrights.

Other theaters of this time included the Little Theater founded by Ames which opened on March 11, 1912. It was a commercial theater, but the size of the theater made the cost of the tickets prohibitive. Ames wished to present only the best plays in the best fashion, but found it impossible to attract a large enough audience at $2.50 per ticket.[39]

In 1917 the East and West Players were founded with a program of Yiddish plays. They began production in the Educational Alliance auditorium on East Broadway, the center of intellectual life or the East Side.[40] It cost $.25 to $1.00 to see the plays.[41] It presented, among others, He and She by Isaac L. Percy, Colleagues by Zalmon Libin, Night by Sholom Asch, and Percy Hirshbein's The Stranger.[42] Since it appealed to a theater-conscious audience which appreciated its cultural literature, the theater flourished and had a constant audience.

The Bramhall Theater was erected by a Mr. Davenport on his estate near Stamford in 1912. His theater was dedicated to new American plays and he became a playwright himself because he needed truthful plays. As an outgrowth of his first enterprise, he built a theater on 27th Street in New York in 1915, which was a model for tiny theater buildings.[43]

The Brooklyn Repertory Theater, established in 1917, presented plays in the auditorium of the Brooklyn Y.M.C.A. It is still active, mainly producing revivals.[44]

Another group established in 1917 was The Negro Players under the management of Emilie Hapgood and the direction of Robert Edmond Jones. It presented three one-act plays about Negroes by Ridgely Torrence, the American poet---The Riders of Dreams, Simon, the Cyrenian, and Granny Maumee. This was the first time Negroes had appeared in plays about Negroes.[45]

The Morningside Players started in the Fall of 1916 with an ambitious presentation of The Iron Cross by Elmer Reizenstein. They were made up of people from Columbia University and vicinity.[46]

The Cherry Lane Theater opened in 1924, converted at a cost of $15,000. from a 105-year old box factory. The opening production was Saturday Night by Robert Fresnell, and audiences were charged $5.00 a seat. By 1926, the group was losing money and disbanded.[47]

The Cherry Lane house was not abandoned, however. Among the plays of a second group called The Cherry Lane Players, Inc., was Wild Birds by Dan Totheroh, a new author. Wild Birds was presented in the Spring of 1928.[48]

The groups mentioned in this section were all dedicated to a new dramatic expression. All operated on modest budgets. The content of the play, not its commercial potential, was the deciding factor in its production. From this arose a vital theater which has changed theater history in America.

In the early twentieth century many theaters came into being Off-Broadway. The actors and designers who worked

in them advanced in their own fields through their association with new and original plays---many by American play--
wrights. (The term "original" is used in an avant-garde
sense: plays which reach for new frontiers in dramatic
form.)

Without oppressive financial costs and with the services
of many people who gave willingly of their time, often without recompense, the new plays searched for truthfulness –
a primary goal of art. Broadway still continued, at this
time, to do romantic plays like Romance by Edward Sheldon,[49] Good Gracious Annabelle by Clare Kummer,[50] and
Why Marry? by Jesse Lynch Williams.[51] Off-Broadway,
meanwhile, tried to present plays appealing to many different audiences not reached by Broadway. By presenting
plays for neighborhood groups as well as the intelligensia,
Off-Broadway was fulfilling its purpose as a progressing
American theater.

Notes

1. Dickinson, Thomas H., The Insurgent Theater, New
    York, B. W. Huebsch, 1917. p. 61.

2. Ibid., p. 63

3. Edmond M. Gagey, Revolution in American Drama, New
    York, Columbia University Press, 1947. p. 1.

4. Ibid., p. 4

5. Deutsch, Helen Hanau, Stella, The Provincetown, A
    Story of the Theater, New York, Farrar & Rinehart,
    1931, p. 102.

6. Ibid., p. 6-7.

7. Ibid., p. 199.

8. Mackay, Constance D'Arcy, The Little Theater In the
    United States, New York, Henry Holt & Company,

c. 1917. p. 46.

9. Ibid., p. 49.

10. Ibid., p. 38.

11. Ibid., p. 17-18.

12. Ibid., p. 51.

13. Ibid., p. 26.

14. Gagey, Edmond M., op. cit., p. 45.

15. Ibid., p. 46.

16. Deutsch, Helen & Hanau, Stella, op. cit., p. 125.

17. Ibid., p. 136.

18. Ibid., p. 109.

19. Ibid., p. 138.

20. Ibid., p. 185-6.

21. Ibid., p. 128.

22. "Off-Broadway," Newsweek, March 14, 1955, 45:95-8.

23. Mackay, Constance D'Arcy, op. cit., p. 28.

24. Dickinson, Thomas, H., op. cit., p. 172.

25. Ibid., p. 183.

26. Dickinson, Thomas H., op. cit., p. 177.

27. Ibid., p. 178.

28. Ibid., p. 181.

29. Mackay, Constance D'Arcy, op. cit., p. 39.

30. Dickinson, Thomas H., op. cit., p. 160.

31. Mackay, Constance D'Arcy, op. cit., p. 42-3.

32. H. Ingersoll, "Neighborhood Playhouse," Theater Arts, 13: 764-9, October, 1929.

33. Dickinson, Thomas H., op. cit., p. 166.

34. Ibid., p. 165.

35. Ibid., p. 168.

36. Ibid., p. 170.

37. Mackay, Constance D'Arcy, op. cit., p. 60.

38. Ingersoll, H., op. cit., p. 764-9.

39. Dickinson, Thomas H., op. cit., p. 156.

40. Mackay, Constance D'Arcy, op. cit., p. 62.

41. Ibid., p. 65.

42. Ibid., p. 63.

43. Dickinson, Thomas H., op. cit., p. 212.

44. Mackay, Constance D'Arcy, op. cit., p. 68.

45. Ibid., p. 69.

46. Ibid., p. 71.

47. "Decline and Fall of the Empire, Rescue of the Cherry Lane," The Drama, A Monthly Review, Published Eight Time A Year From October to May; Theodore Ballou Hinckley, Editor; Sponsored by Drama League of America, November, 1952; Reprinted in Theater Arts, 36:16, November, 1952.

48. "The Roaring Twenties," Special Exhibition, Museum of the City of New York, Fifth Avenue, 103rd & 104th St., June 23, 1959.

49. Mantle, Burns and Sherwood, Garrison P., The Best Plays of 1909-1919, and the Year Book of the Drama in America, New York, Dodd, 1943. p. 118.

50. _Ibid._, p. 281.

51. _Ibid._, p. 315.

Chapter II

Off-Broadway in the 1930's
Little Theater Tournament
Provincetown Productions
Theater of Action

In the 1930's Off-Broadway presented theater of political and moral consciousness. This theater was developed
for an audience of diversified social and cultural backgrounds. With the depression, people turned to the stage
for answers to their pressing problems.

In the 1930's, the Off-Broadway stage became ideal for
the presentation of highly controversial ideas. It became a
people's theater which was not interested merely in entertainment or commercial success. The theaters did intend to
meet the expenses of production; but a profit was an unanti-
cipated bonus.

Although many of these plays dealt with vital problems,
the people involved were interested in artistic production.
The social milieu of the day led to the appearance of a type
of theater Off-Broadway which was sometimes classified as
the "agit-prop" theater; one which demands immediate action on social problems. The "agit-prop" drama was a
fighting form of expression which attempted active participa-
tion in the lives of its people.

Provincetown, particularly in the person of Eugene O'
Neill, had left its mark upon Broadway in the 1920's. The
social climate of the 1930's brought a new outburst of theatrical awareness to this already historic theater. Broadway

had changed since the first World War. Off-Broadway and
Broadway sought answers to the problems which faced society at this time.

> At the start the postwar playwrights shared the spirit
> of disillusioned questioning that pervaded the fiction
> and poetry of the "lost generation..."In drama it
> generally took the form of debunking the pretensions
> and ideals of middle-class culture...The moral revolu-
> tion, greatly accelerated by the First World War, was
> now reinforced by a systematic study of Freud, with
> the result that the ethical code of the Frohman-Belasco
> era was promptly relegated to the movies...[1]

At the beginning of the depression in the early 1930's,
the Broadway "record of revivals," was "quite startling."
It seemed that "a third as many old plays were revived as
there were new plays produced."[2] Most of them had been
produced just a few years earlier for the first time. A
major factor in their revival was the fact that tickets to
"some of them were sold at prices little higher than the
government tax, with a majority of them at $1.00 and
less." Others, which often were the best, at "no more
than $1.50."[3] The depression had affected Broadway finan-
cially as well as artistically.

One of the greatest influences of the time was the
establishment of the Federal Theater in 1935. By 1938
some "twenty new plays and revivals were staged or sponsored by WPA theater, including four successes sufficiently
outstanding to excite comment..." One was a story of
Lincoln's youth called Prologue to Glory, written by E. P.
Conkle of the University of Iowa.[4]

Among the plays performed by the Federal Theater
were Hauptmann's The Weavers, Ghosts by Ibsen, Chiarelli's
The Mask and the Face, Chlumberg's Miracle at Verdun, Ander-

son's Gods of the Lightning, Peters and Sklar's Stevedore, Bein's Let Freedom Ring, Odet's Awake and Sing, Katajev's Squaring the Circle, and Saul's and Lantz's The Revolt of the Beavers.[5] The "production of vital new plays is one of the Federal Theater's important functions..."[6]

The Federal theater was an outgrowth of the art theater. Many of its members had worked Off-Broadway. Like Off-Broadway, the Federal theater was interested in the mass of people and their problems and needs.

Typical of current Broadway drama was Tobacco Road, then in its fifth year on Broadway and threatening to break the record of 2,532 performances set by Anne Nichol's Abie's Irish Rose.

In 1939, The Playwright's Producing Company was organized to encourage original writing on Broadway. It was composed of Robert Sherwood, Maxwell Anderson, Sidney Howard, S. N. Behrman, and Elmer Rice, who banded together for the purpose of producing their own plays. Tho first production was Sherwood's Abe Lincoln in Illinois.[8]

Some playwrights on Broadway did present advanced works but most still wrote to popular standards. Typical Broadway plays were June Moon by Kaufman-Larder and As Husbands Go by Crothers--an especially popular playwright.[9] This type of drama did not significantly explore any of the issues of the day. The theater in the thirties was somewhat sobered by Nazi agression in Europe "which compelled the playwrights to adopt a positive stand in defending democracy, and even war."[10]

While Broadway could not but help being somewhat affected by the times, it was Off-Broadway which presented the issues of the thirites most forcefully.

At the Cherry Lane Theater on December 3, 1930, the

Dramawrights presented Ivan Sokoloff's, The Passion of
Judas. This is one of the earliest plays of the 1930's. It
offered the theory that Judas Iscariot got into all of his en-
tanglements because he couldn't control his love life. Sad
to say, the playwright was not given credit for any "intention to entertain as well as enlighten." Following the unsuccessful The Passion of Judas was Experience, a play
with music. [11]

Other producing groups of the '30's were at the New
School for Social Research; the Roof of the Hotel Sutton,
330 East 56th St.; the Lighthouse Little Theater; Sutton Theater; Ibsen Theater; the Recital 63rd St. Theater which housed
the Living Theater; Heckscher Theater; the Chanin Building
Theater and the Bronx Project Theater. [12]

The Bronx Theater Guild was an active producing group
of the 1930's which gave its patrons..." the opportunity to
witness high-grade new plays amid surroundings at once
artistic and cozy at popular prices." They presented
H.H.H., an "uproarious comedy," featuring Sidney Strovo
and a cast of 20. [13]

The playhouses which presented Yiddish drama were
quite active during the thirites. These included the Folks
Theater, Downtown National Theater, Public Theater and the
Second Avenue Theater. [14]

Eva LeGallienne's Civic Repertory Theater produced
many plays around 1930. This was an exceptional theater.
Although it was not exactly Off-Broadway, it had the same
credo in regard to the presentation of the new, unusual
play. The nucleus of the group included Egon Brecher,
Josephine Hutchinson, Harold Moulton, Sayre Crawley,
Robert Ross, Alma Kouger, Leona Roberts, Paul Leyssac,
Donald Cameron, J. Edward Bromberg and Jacob Ben-Ami. [15]

The Civic Repertory lasted for five years.[16] LeGallienne began the company in 1926. In the Autumn of 1927,
she was awarded the Pictorial Review Prize of $5,000, as
the American woman making the most distinctive contribution to the field of art, letters, science, industry and
social progress during that year.[17]

She clearly stated her reasons for forming the theater.

I turned my back on Broadway because it had nothing
to give me but money and I had nothing to give it. It
was a great relief to the managers I had deviled to put
on the kind of shows I wanted. As I felt that price was
keeping away the kind of people I wanted, I decided on
a $1.50 top price. But I couldn't get a theater on
Broadway. I was told it would lower standards...
But we needed a subsidy to carry on. So I went to the
people. Every town in Europe of any size supports as
a matter of course a repertory theater. Why shouldn't
we, in America, who are supposed to decide things for
ourselves? I found that members at $1.00 a year
would do it."[18]

These words may well echo the criteria of many of
the Off-Broadway theaters of the day. Off-Broadway wanted
something Broadway could not offer in the way of creative
drama and also wanted to broaden its appeal.

At the Craig Theater on May 12, 1931, a very interesting event took place. This was the 9th annual Little
Theater Movement Tournament.

One of the plays was Charles O'Brien Kennedy's The
Mighty Nimrod. The play was reported as being "well-
acted, expertly directed, and funny enough to stand a chance
as a regular Broadway attraction after a few talky spots
have been eliminated." It was a spoof about everything
from prohibition to Al Capone and the famed "Coolidge me-
chanical horse..."

The winning play of the tournament was If Booth Had

Missed, given by the Morningside Players of Columbia.[19]
The Theater Arts Monthly cup was awarded to the Morningside Players as was the $1,000. offered by the French Pub-
lishing Company for the best original play.[20]

New plays were constantly being given during the 1930's
at the Provincetown Playhouse. Most of these were original plays by Americans. Among them was Crescendo, a
play about flaming youth,[21] and Black Diamond, a play
which included a lynching,[22] neither of which received glow-
ing reviews.

However, on January 31, 1933, The Magnanimous
Lover by St. John Ervine, Ghost Bereft by Jane Barlow,
and One Day More by Joseph Conrad were presented at the
Provincetown Theater in what sounds like an interesting program.[23]

Raw Meat by Richard Lockridge presented at the Provincetown on March 22, 1933, was called "prodigiously better than the recent presentations..." It was a satirical
farce "laughing at the big game hunters so often in the roto-
gravures."[24]

One of the most amazing productions Off-Broadway at
this time was Precedent by I. J. Golden, staged by Walter
Hart. It was given on April 13, 1931 at the Provincetown.
An interesting feature of the production is that most of the
critics reviewed it. Brooks Atkinson said "when there is
something unusual to be said and heard the Provincetown is
still a good forum."[25]

The play was called "obviously partisan in its appeal."
It seems that the producers intended that Governor Rolf of
California would be influenced by the play and open the
doors of the dungeon of a certain "Mr. Mooney." Golden,
the author of Precedent was a St. Louis attorney, who,

horrified by the inequities visited upon Mooney, quit the law
temporarily to embrace the stage as an instrument of justice more puissant than the bar. Unversed in the subtle
technicalities of three-act entertainment he barged in with
the "staccato method" of an amateur. Precedent, therefore,
is "one of those dab-dramas wherein the author, when he
finds himself in a cul-de-sac, rings the curtain down and
begins anew--after a lapse of five minutes." It left one
"wishing that Mr. Galsworthy had told it instead of Mr.
Golden."[26].

Richard Lockridge stated that "the Provincetown Theater...was reclaimed for the drama of social protest...[27]
The production was considered a sincere and forceful one,
causing such a furor in regard to the Billings-Mooney case
that Gilbert W. Gabriel remarked:

> I didn't know Off-Broadway had come that far to
> warrant being written about. I guess Off-Broadway has
> come of age.[28]

When some critics stated that the group was inexperi-
enced, the actors of Precedent raised a loud cry and estimated that their experience included 162 years of stock and
82 years of touring.[29]

Precedent moved uptown to the Bijou theater on Broadway in May of 1931, six weeks after the original opening.
The comment was made that instead of suffering by its
change to a Broadway theater, Precedent had gained in
speed, in precision, and in expertness with better backstage
facilities. The concensus as to its merit and as to the
talents of its cast had changed:

> Fortunately it remains as simple and unassuming as
> it was at the beginning and gives the same sense of
> letting ugly facts speak out for themselves in their
> own dynamic way. And fortunately, too, its cast
> remains unchanged.

The play was recommended to anyone "seriously interested either in the theater or in justice. In its stark, grim
and relentless way, it is one of the most affecting productions the season has mothered."[30]

After the resounding success of Precedent, many social
dramas were produced at the Provincetown. On October 22,
1931, No More Frontier was presented. It was by new playwright, Talbot Jennings, who wrote the type of play the Provincetown "was originally intended to encourage." Dr. Jennings who came to the theater by way of the University of
Idaho, service with the field artillery in France, Harvard,
and Professor Baker's Yale Workshop, "has something to
say, and all things considered, says it with eloquence."[31]

Coastwise by H. A. Archibald and Don Mullally was presented at the Provincetown on November 30, 1931. It is
the story of a British Columbia prostitute who marries and
straightens out a British gentleman but refuses to return to
England with him. Although not too well received as a play,
the cast included Shirley Booth and Richard Stevenson.[32]

Black Souls by Annie Nathan Meyer was presented at the
Provincetown in 1932. It dealt with the Negro problem in
the South. The play was directed by James Light,[33] a
familiar name since the founding of the Provincetown theater.

On May 11, 1932, Albert Maltz and George Sklar's
Merry-Go-Round was presented at the Provincetown. It
moved uptown to the Avon theater.[34] It was the first play
by these two Columbia graduates who were to be heard from
a great deal later. At the time they wrote this play they
were in George Pierce Baker's course at Yale. The play
was said to be an "exciting and brutal melodrama" about
big town politics.[35] The flashing moving headline so much

in use by the Federal Theater later, was introduced between the quickly wandering scenes of the Meyerhold-Pisca-
tor style.[36]

After Merry-Go-Round moved to the Avon Theater, it
was closed by the mayor. The theater was not allowed to
reopen, supposedly because "its license had expired." As
Richard Lockridge stated "this insistence of the latter (the
license commissioner) on the license law in the case, and
only in the case, of a play which is abusive of politicians
is welcome to his naivete. He might even put this naivete
on exhibition and charge admission."[37] This statement im-
plied that the license commissioner's protest only made it
apparent that the play was undesirable because of its ex-
posure of a corrupt political system.

Perhaps the most interesting theater Off-Broadway at
this time was the worker's theater. The creation of this
theater could only have come about in a period of heightened
social consciousness. It was devoted exclusively to the
problems of the working class and shaped by its members.

In the beginning phases of the worker's theater, language was a barrier and the plays were presented to a very
limited audience. This kept the theater from enriching our
American culture. Later, some of these theaters such as
the Artef, the Jewish Worker's Theater and the Ukranian
Dramatic Circle were to play an important part in the
dramatic renaissance of the 1930's.[38]

The Workers Drama League was "formed in New York
in 1926..."[39]

But the Workers Drama League came forward with a
new and revolutionary conception. Worker's drama...
should concern itself primarily with the lives and problems of the workers themselves, their hardships, their
strikes their aspirations. The League's most successful

production was Karl Wittfogel's satire, <u>The Biggest</u>
<u>Boob in the World</u>, translated from the German by
Upton Sinclair and adapted by Michael Gold...[40]

In the winter of 1930-31, when unemployment relief
was just starting, an amateur worker's theater, called the
Workers Laboratory Theater, "dramatized and presented a
theme that meant life and death to millions. Their first
play was <u>Unemployed</u>..."

> The principle of the early worker's theater demanded
> that a dramatic solution be offered in each play and
> was at the same time an adequate social solution, valid
> in the outer world.

<u>Unemployed</u>, following this thesis, offered the audi-
ence of unemployed a "way out." The solution offered was
that "we must organize; organization is our weapon, says
the leading player."[41]

> But the central principle which had to be established
> concerned the relation between the new workers theater
> and the type of theater then prevailing in the United
> States---the bourgeois theater; the theater whose pro-
> ductions reflected the viewpoint of the upper and middle
> classes at the time. Disgusted with the triviality and
> decadence of the typical Broadway drama, with the lack
> of concern with the workers and farmers and their
> problems of hunger and insecurity, some of the leaders
> of the workers theater believed the old theater should
> be completely ignored.[42]

The <u>Workers Theater</u> magazine critically followed
the work productions of this theater.[43]

Mordecai Gorelik formed the Theater Collective, a
worker's theater, in 1931, which was the first permanent
Off-Broadway group of the 1930's.[44]

The Civic Repertory Theater on 14th St. presented
<u>Peace on Earth</u> by Albert Maltz and George Sklar on Novem-
ber 29, 1933, as the initial offering of the Theater Union,
Inc., The play was described as a propaganda piece for

peace. Eva LeGallienne had by this time left the 14th St. Theater.[45]

The ground work for Theater Union's success was prepared for by the previous 3 years labors of the League of Worker's Theaters.[46]

Peace on Earth[47] carries "furthest to the left the play against war."

> For locale our left playwrights have taken the most seemingly peaceful place on earth: a New England college town. But when they analyze this scene, we see it in the light of the economic forces that dominate it...A young American college professor...When he finds behind this scene, not the peace and freedom he believed in, but war...a war for profits manifesting itself nationally in industrial...conflict, and internationally in world conflict, and when he tries to use his American birthright of freedom to tell the truth as he sees it, his martyrdom begins.[48]

Professor Peter Owens is drawn into the social conflict unwillingly because of a strike of union men who know the soap which they supposedly are transporting is really munitions and for whom Owens speaks.[49] In the resulting controversy Owens is accused of shooting one of the men in the assembly hall.[50]

As Owens awaits execution in the death cell he hears the announcement of war claiming an innocent ship was blown up...[51]

> The response of audiences to the different elements and incidents of the play was fresh proof of what theater can mean when it is an illuminating projection of matter vital to men's lives. A vigorous portrayal of the American scene and the American temper, in relation to the most important of world problems, Peace on Earth stands as another milestone in the history of American drama.[52]

Ben Blake was one of the founders of this "new thea-

ter movement" established at the Provincetown playhouse
called the Theater Union, Inc., which was "shaking the
foundations of Broadway." Blake had written The Awakening of the American Theater.[53] The Theater Union gained
a following in New York after its beginning with Peace on
Earth, and the move to 14th Street. This production was
followed by Sailors of Cattaro and Stevedore, both of which
were highly praised. They attracted large crowds and increasingly favorable attention from the "capitalist press."[54]

The Sailors of Cattaro, by Friedrich Wolf, is based
on a mutiny in the Austrian fleet stationed in the Bay of
Cattaro. Its chief characters are real. These men were
shown by court-martial records to have been shot near
Cattaro as the "ringleaders of a revolt that began as a mutiny to stop the war, but soon took on a social revolutionary
character."[55] Wolf quoted as his text the words of Lenin
"that once a revolution is begun it must be carried through..."
At first this goal is lost and immediate, individual desires
substituted. The leader at the crisis in the action refused
to resort to "autocratic rule." To the playwright this
failure to discriminate between "democratic theory and
revolutionary practice represents not only the crux of his
play, but the crux of the dissension which divides the revolutionary forces of the world today."[56]

> A play that represents as effectively as does this one
> the problem that is, in one form or another, now
> troubling the entire world, must be regarded as vital.[57]

Perhaps the best of the American plays presented at
the Theater Union was Stevedore by Paul Peters and George
Sklar, which was "a protest against racial discrimination in
the South, a plea for closer cooperation between white and
black workers."

> A false charge of rape---at the start of the play---
> leads to a wholesale roundup of Negroes, including
> Lonnie, a stevedore with a rebellious temper. Later
> his labor activities bring on a second arrest on the
> same charge, but he escapes...When the gang threatens
> to attack and burn the houses in the Negro quarter,
> Lonnie persuades his companions to defend themselves.
> Reinforced at the last minute by a white organizer and
> some of his union men, the Negroes win the pitched
> battle that ensues though Lonnie himself is killed.[58]
> Although the play's action and characterization are on
> the level of melodrama, its very simplicity and obvious-
> ness help to make it effective as propaganda.[59]

Other manifestations of the worker's theater included
the Park Theater which on May 27, 1935, presented a
drama entitled The Young Go First by Peter Martin, George
Scudder and Charles Friedman. It was a "Drama of Theater of Action," formerly called the Worker's Laboratory
Theater. Settings were by Mordecai Gorelik.[60]

The tone of the Theater of Action, in plays such as
The Young Go First, was one which waxed fretful, fevered
and pettish with the order of things in general, but it lacked
the gusty forcefulness which the Group Theater managed to
call forth in its dramatic protests. Theater of Action lacked
Mr. Odet's earthy humor, which it at best pallidly imitated.
"Even a sympathetic audience found it hard to accept the
naive suggestion that the government camps are such salt
mines of human exploitation as the authors suggest, altho
its members were patently more than anxious to do so."[61]

It was decided in 1935 to replace the League of
Worker's Theaters by a broad national organization that
would be "representative of the entire American theater..."
In January, 1935, the New Theater League was formed---
"For a mass development of the American theater to its
highest artistic and social level; for a theater dedicated to

the struggle against war, fascism and censorship."[62]

   This type of manifesto and these dramas of the
Theater of Action and the New Theater League may have
been attributed wrongfully to the Federal Theater. The
establishment of these wrong associations may have caused
the Federal Theater's unfortunate demise. The Federal
Theater, set up by act of Congress as part of the Works
Progress Administration on April 8, 1935,[63] used the
talents of unemployed theater people during the depression
until it was disbanded by act of Congress on June 30,
1939.[64] Although Federal Theater did have a large audience and responded to their needs, it is unfortunate that it
was regarded as revolutionary theater.

   The leftist drama Off-Broadway had its affect on
Broadway theater, particularly with the situation of the
Group theater on Broadway and its foremost playwright,
Clifford Odets.

> Leftist drama, not normally seasoned with humor, was
> enlived in the 1937-1938 season by the success of two
> musical plays---Marc Blitzstein's The Cradle Will Rock
> and (Labor Stage, Inc.) Pins and Needles. The former,
> written for production by the Federal Theater but
> deemed dangerously controversial by Washington, was
> put on by John Houseman and Orson Welles as the
> first offering of the Mercury Theater.[65]

   The revue, Pins and Needles, produced by the
acting organization of the International Ladies' Garment
Workers' Union with music and lyrics by Harold J. Rome
and sketches by Marc Blitzstein and Arthur Arent, gave
many topics satirical or burlesque treatment, such as
"Mussolini's prizes for prolific motherhood, the four (later
five) little angels of peace, and even so domestic an institution as the Vassar daisy chain."[66]

   While Off-Broadway and the rest of the world seethed

with the problems of unemployment and social disorders,
Broadway concentrated mainly upon the development of a
higher style of comedy. Most of the comedy had the "bois-
terous, realistic, completely unromantic spirit of typical
Broadway comedy."

> Whatever its failings, it kept its humor and its sanity
> at a time when civilization seemed to be going to
> smash under the impacts of depression and war. Its
> impudent escapism is admirably expressed in the
> Pulitzer Prize You Can't Take It With You (1936) by
> Moss Hart and George S. Kaufman.[67]

Notes

1. Gagey, Edmond M., Revolution in American Drama,
   New York, Columbia University Press, 1947. p. 121.

2. The Best Plays of 1932-33 And the Year Book of the
   Drama in America; Edited by Burns Mantle; New York,
   Dodd, 1933. p. 3.

3. Ibid.

4. The Best Plays of 1937-38 and the Year Book of the
   Drama in America; Edited by Burns Mantle; Dodd, New
   York, 1938. p. 3.

5. Block, Anita; The Changing World in Plays and Theater;
   Boston, Little, Brown, 1939; p. 415.

6. Ibid., p. 416.

8. The Best Plays of 1937-38 And the Year Book of the
   Drama In America; Edited by Burns Mantle; New York,
   Dodd, Mead and Company; 1938. p. 3.

9. The Best Plays of 1932-33 And the Year Book of the
   Drama in America; loc. cit.

10. Gagey, Edmond M., op. cit., p. 121.

11. "Dramawrights Stage 'Passion of Judas'; Make High
    Promise for Next Production at Cherry Lane, 'Experi-
    ence,'" New York Telegram, Dec. 3, 1930; Off-Broad-

way Clippings, through 1954; Theater Collection, New
York Public Library.

12. "Stage; U.S.: N.Y.:" Off-Broadway Clippings, through
1954; Theater Collection; New York Public Library.

13. "Sidney Stravo, Director, Announces Removal of the
Bronx Theater Guild to the Tremont Theater," New
York Times, Sunday, Jan. 12, 1930; Off-Broadway
Clippings, through 1954; op. cit.

14. "Stage: U.S.: N.Y.: "Off-Broadway Clippings, through
1954; op. cit.

15. Hutchens, John; "Curtain Going Up, Broadway in Prospect;" 1930; Off-Broadway Clippings, through 1954;
op. cit.

16. Steinberg, Mollie B.; The History of the Fourteenth
Street Theater, New York; Dial, 1931. p. 92.

17. Steinberg, Mollie B.; op. cit.; p. 93.

18. Steinberg, Mollie B.; op. cit.; p. 91.

19. The Herald-Tribune; May 26, 1931; Off-Broadway Clippings, through 1954; Theater Collection; New York Public Library.

20. The Herald Tribune; May 12, 1931; op. cit.

21. Hathaway, D.L. "Review---Provincetown Playhouse,"
Off-Broadway Clippings, through 1954; op. cit.; November 11, 1932.

22. "Provincetown Playhouse," Off-Broadway Clippings,
through 1954; op. cit.; February 23, 1933.

23. Brown, John Mason; New York Evening Post; January 3,
1932; Off-Broadway Clippings, through 1954; op. cit.

24. Lockridge, Richard; New York Sun; March 23, 1933;
Off-Broadway Clippings, through 1954; op. cit.

25. Atkinson, Brooks; N. Y. Times; April 14, 1931; Off-
Broadway Clippings, through 1954; op. cit.

26. "Provincetown Theater;" April 14, 1931; Off-Broadway Clippings, through 1954; op. cit.

27. Lockridge, Richard; New York Sun; April 15, 1931; Off-Broadway Clippings, through 1954; op. cit.

28. Gabriel, Gilbert W.; "Jehovah on a Soap Box;" New York American; April 15, 1931; Off-Broadway Clippings, through 1954; op. cit.

29. Hammond, Percy; Herald-Tribune; April 15, 1931; Off-Broadway Clippings, through 1954; op. cit.

30. Brown, John Mason; "Two on the Aisle;" N.Y. Evening Post; May 28, 1931; Off-Broadway Clippings, through 1954; op. cit.

31. The Herald Tribune; November 1, 1931; "Off-Broadway Clippings, through 1954;" op. cit.

32. Atkinson, J. Brooks; N. Y. Times; December 1, 1931; "Off-Broadway Clippings, through 1954;" op. cit.

33. Waldorf, Wilella; 'A New Play Dealing with the Negro Problem In the South, Opens At the Provincetown;' The Evening Post; March 30, 1932; "Off-Broadway Clippings through 1954;" op. cit.

34. Atkinson, J. Brooks; N. Y. Times; May 11, 1932; "Off-Broadway Clippings, through 1954;" op. cit.

35. Atkinson, J. Brooks; 'Big Town Politics in an Exciting and Brutal Melodrama at the Provincetown;' N.Y. Times; April 23, 1932; "Off-Broadway Clippings, through 1954;" op. cit.

36. N. Y. Post; April 23, 1932; "Off-Broadway Clippings, through 1954;" op. cit.

37. Lockridge, Richard; N. Y. Sun; May 9, 1932; "Off-Broadway Clippings, through 1954;" op. cit.

38. Blake, Ben; The Awakening of the American Theater; Tomorrow, 303 Fourth Ave., New York City; 1935; p. 9.

39. Ibid., p. 10.

40. Ibid., p. 11.

41. Ibid., p. 19.

42. Ibid., p. 22.

43. Ibid., p. 24.

44. Stage: U.S.: N.Y.: "Off-Broadway Clippings, through 1954;" Theater Collection; New York Public Library.

45. N. Y. Times, "Off-Broadway Clippings, through 1954;" November 30, 1933; op. cit.

46. Blake, Ben; op. cit.; p. 40.

47. Ibid., p. 34.

48. Block, Anita; op. cit.; p. 337.

49. Ibid., p. 341.

50. Ibid., p. 349.

51. Ibid., p. 350.

52. Ibid., p. 351.

53. Houghton, Norris; "Worker's Theater,"; Advance from Broadway, 19,000 Miles of American Theater; Harcourt, Brace and Company; New York; Copyright, 1941; p.271.

54. Ibid., p. 272.

55. Block, Anita; op. cit.; p. 210.

56. Ibid., p. 211.

57. Ibid., p. 212.

58. Gagey, Edmond M.; op. cit.; p. 160.

59. Ibid., p. 161.

60. "Drama of Theater of Action;" N. Y. Herald Tribune;

May 28, 1935; "Off-Broadway Clippings, through 1954;" op. cit.

61. Brown, John Mason; N. Y. Eve. Post; May, 1935; "Off-Broadway Clippings, through 1954;" op. cit.

62. Blake, Ben; op. cit.; p. 52.

63. Flannagan, Hallie; Arena A History of the Federal Theater; Duell, Sloane & Pearce; New York; 1940.

64. Ibid., p. 365.

65. Gagey, Edmond M.; op. cit.; p. 161.

66. Ibid., p. 162.

67. Gagey, Edmond M.; op. cit.; p. 229.

Chapter III

Off-Broadway in the 1940's
During the war years
The renaissance Off-Broadway, since 1947
Productions of new plays, starting in 1946
Originals only
Significant producing groups

With the advent of the 1940's, the Broadway stage
was devoted to comedy. Plays were more frivolous and the
box office was larger.

There were some serious plays such as Robert E.
Sherwood's There Shall Be No Night, about the Russian in-
vasion of Finland, and Maxwell Anderson's Key Largo. However, comedy, perhaps because of the great duress in which
the world found itself, was the mainstay.

One of the most popular plays was Life With Father
by Russel Crouse and Howard Lindsay. Saroyan's The Time
of Your Life was one of the greater achievements of the
comedy stage. [1]

World War II brought a halt to most theater activities
Off-Broadway from 1940-1945. After the Second World War
many of the G.I.'s returned with high enthusiasm to begin a
new theater movement Off-Broadway. This movement was
vigorous and the number of productions phenomenal.

At the same time, Broadway was affected by the war
and presented many war plays but more than ever there was
box office for escapist drama. Broadway presented musicals
such as The Day Before Spring [2] by Alan Jay Lerner and
comedies like A Sound of Hunting by Harry Brown and The

34

Next Half Hour by Mary Chase.[3]

    Home of the Brave by Arthur Laurents is a play
Broadway could be justly proud to have done.[4] Another
noteworthy event was the formation of the American Repertory Theater by Eva LeGallienne and Cheryl Crawford,
which produced plays such as Henry VIII, What Every
Woman Knows and John Gabriel Borkman.[5]

    During the war years the important Off-Broadway
endeavor was the formation of the Experimental Theater in
1941. It was started by the Dramatists' Guild and Equity,
under the direction of the late Antoinette Perry. This theater aided the new playwright by awarding various scholar-
ships, prizes, and opportunities for experimental production.[6]

    The playwright was given special attention Off-Broad-
way in the 1940's. It was a time of many productions of
new plays. In 1946, the Associated Playwrights, Inc., composed of ten authors who attended the Theater Guild's playwriting seminar, gave a series of experimental productions
at the Grand Street Playhouse. Among them were Winners
and Losers by Nicholas Biel, The Deputy of Paris by
Edmund B. Hennefeld, and Our Lan' by Theodore Ward.[7]

    The post-war renaissance movement Off-Broadway
had many new producing groups such as the Playcrafters.
They presented an original play in December, 1946, Love
Comes First, by Pascal Biancardo and Jeff Kerrigan. A
group called The Playwrights Theater gave Save the Pieces
by Leon Morse. Modern Art, headed by veterans, started
a season February 7, with the new play, Sauerkraut Seeds,
by Erwin Peter Faith. Modern Stage Company gave We
Will Dream Again, a comedy by Giuseppe de Gioa, on
April 11. New plays were presented at the Provincetown

Playhouse, too, such as It's Your Move by Jerry Stevens,
The Man Who Never Lived by Madison Goff and Personal
Island by Pauline Williams. [8]

A group called New Stages produced a highly successful version of Sartre's The Respectful Prostitute on Bleecker
Street in 1947. [9] This play went on Broadway in 1948, in
conjunction with an original Off-Broadway play by an American author. Thus an original play from Off-Broadway crept
onto Broadway as a rider to a European play. As its curtain raised for the Broadway production of The Respectful
Prostitute, New Stages used the 1947 production of the Six
O'Clock Theater, Richard Harrity's Hope Is A Thing With
Feathers. [10]

Another group, Originals Only, was in almost contin-
uous operation from November, 1949 on. They started in
March, 1948, with the original plan of being a "laboratory
for writers to hear their own writings." Starting with a
"concert" reading open to the public, scripts with a "public
appeal later were given production." [11]

Originals Only presented such plays as Dream House
by Tom Hill in 1949, Dakota by Tom Hill, and The Warrior's
Return by Jules Koslow in 1950. [12]

A play often produced in college theaters, Too
Many Thumbs by Robert Hivnor, an American playwright,
was presented by Off-Broadway, Inc., at the Cherry Lane
Theater in July, 1949. Unfortunately, it lost all the money
they had on a previous production of Gertrude Stein's Yes
Is For A Very Young Man. The company included very
good actors in the persons of Kim Stanley and Nehemiah
Persoff. [13]

James Dyas, today producer-director of the Red

Barn Theater in Saugatuck, Michigan, began his work Off-
Broadway in 1947 with Laura by Vera Caspary. In 1950,
Dyas won an award as the best Off-Broadway director for
his production of Trouble in July, [14] which opened on December 6, 1949, and was an adaptation by Owen Steele of
Erskine Caldwell's novel. It was felt it "might have a
chance on Broadway."[15]

This was a very interesting statement in light of
future developments. It seemed to indicate a new dollars
and cents orientation of Off-Broadway theater, which was
beginning to look toward profits and successful box office
rather than for purely dramatic value. Playwrights and
directors with Broadway standards were beginning to take
over. The stage with something to say for an audience
different from the commercial theater was being challenged.
Off-Broadway was beginning to be seen as a good thing by
investors.

One successful play producing group still reminiscent
of the 1930's was the politically oriented Peoples' Drama.
It had a resounding success with Nat Turner in 1950, a
play about the Negro revolutionist of 1831.[16]

Blackfriars Theater presented a new play in October,
1950, Shake Hands With the Devil, by Robert C. Healey.
In the same year, the Footlight Players, put on a new play
by Stacey Hull, And So They Perish, at the Hudson Guild.[17]

Off-Broadway flourished during the post-war period.
Show Business reported that 159 Off-Broadway groups were
operating in 1948. By 1949 the number had reached 264.[18]

Production costs on Broadway continued to skyrocket
during the post-war period. The popularity of the musical
comedy stage had, with its attendant large casts and extra-
vagant scenery, brought Broadway production budgets to

fabulous sums. In 1944, <u>Seven Lively Arts</u> represented an
investment of $300,000. Opening night tickets sold for
$24.50 and included free champagne. <u>Billion Dollar Baby</u>
represented an investment of $250,000.[19]

However, musicals are not the exception. Legitimate
theater since 1940 has been a very expensive and insecure
investment.

> ...Margaret Webster has called (the prevailing Broad-
> way system), a market for best-sellers only. The
> extreme centralization of American drama in New York
> has brought about an increasingly unhealthy financial
> situation, which is reflected in abnormally high costs of
> production. Whereas in the Belasco era a play could
> be put on for $5,000. or less, the present average is
> about $50,000. for an ordinary one-set play, with
> musical shows, as we have seen, coming closer to
> $250,000. For a relatively simple stage set alone the
> producer must invest in the neighborhood of $5,000.
> Union regulations, often arbitrary and irrational, have
> helped to boost costs heavenward. An acute shortage
> of theaters on Broadway has not only impeded the ar-
> rival of new productions but has permitted the owners
> to require a weekly guarantee of $3,000. to $3,500.,
> making it impossible for a play to continue that is not
> an immediate hit...
> Since sixty percent or more of Broadway productions
> are failures, the theater business in New York has be-
> come more than ever a gamble. One can scarcely
> blame many producers and their angels for playing
> safe to the best of their ability by selecting scripts by
> known dramatists on tried and true subjects with definite
> promise of popular appeal, but the result has been to
> discourage the production of serious and experimental
> plays. At the same time the increase in costs has
> forced the price of theater goers, an evil that is
> aggravated when a smash hit comes along. Immediately,
> the agencies and speculators take over and seats vanish
> from the box office, leaving the theater the property of
> the carriage trade and of visiting salesmen from out of
> town.[20]

From the situation described above a very great
need for continued Off-Broadway theater becomes apparent.

Off-Broadway in the 1940's provided an inexpensive stage
where one could present challenging works. Some groups
produced with an eye to the box office, but most were sincere in their desire for an unusual drama different from
that offered on Broadway.

European dramas began to become very popular even
in the 1940's. Robert Ramsey's On-Stage group for example presented many "fine and unusual productions" such as
Yerma by Lorca and Pirandello's Henry IV. They also presented an original one-act play, This Way To Me, which
"revealed the group at its very best."[21]

Another event of note in 1949 which contributed to
the flourishing Off-Broadway theater which was to come in
the 1950's, was the ruling by Equity allowing its people to
work Off-Broadway, some for as little as $5.00 a week.[22]
This introduced a professional production level which Off-
Broadway had not always previously attained.

This influx of professional talent has tended to re-
duce the experimental in favor of the commercial, with
known names in the productions.

The Equity agreement with Off-Broadway was worked
out in September, 1949. It was an adaptation of the "contract which has been used successfully in the Los Angeles
area for the past ten years."

> This contract permits professional members of any
> branch of the Four A's (Actor's Equity Association
> divisions) up to and including 49% of the cast, to work
> with non-members. Non-members must, however, ob-
> tain Work Permits from Actor's Equity Association.[23]

No actual pay scale had been determined at that time,
but on December 6, 1950, a meeting of the Council of
Actors' Equity Association extended the contract until
March 31, 1950.[24]

In 1949, another pioneering event took place when
the first Off-Broadway Theater League was formed to work
out financial problems. This was the group which asked
Equity to drop its ban. This accomplished, they tried to
attain such other desirable goals as an improved real estate situation and joint ticket distribution.[25]

In 1948 and 1949, during the post-war insurgence of
the Off-Broadway theater, little attention was paid to it as
a money maker. It was not until 1950 that Off-Broadway
became involved in genuine commercial enterprise.[26]

As Off-Broadway entered the arena of financial enterprise, the Off-Broadway theater as an experimental stage
went into a decline. With the half-century mark Broadway
realized Off-Broadway's importance to its continued supply
of talent. Off-Broadway became less and less experimental.
The theater of the continent and Broadway revivals engaged
more of the efforts of Off-Broadway. This gave the Off-
Broadway theater of the 1950's the strange position of being
Broadway theater gone Off-Broadway. The 1940's was a
period of fervent activity and transition which ushered in
the more professionally oriented Off-Broadway theater of
today. But the original play which merits production is
still of prime importance Off-Broadway and the 1950's
brought to this stage many new exciting and creative talents.

Notes

1. The Best Plays of 1939-40 and the Year Book of the
   Drama In America, Edited by Burns Mantle, New York,
   Dodd, 1940, p.v.

2. The Best Plays of 1945-46 And the Year Book of the
   Drama In America, Edited by Burns Mantle, New York,
   Dodd, 1946, p. i.

3. Ibid., p. 7.

4. Ibid., p. 75.

5. Ibid., p. 4.

6. Gagey, Edmond M.; Revolution in American Drama,
   New York, Columbia University Press, 1947. p. 274.

7. The Best Plays of 1946-47, And the Year Book of the
   Drama In America; Edited by Burns Mantle, New York,
   Dodd, 1947, p. 485.

8. Ibid., p. 493.

9. "Off-Broadway," Newsweek, March 14, 1955; 45:95-8.

10. The Burns Mantle Best Plays of 1948-1949 And the Year
    Book of the Drama in America, Edited by John Chap-
    man, New York, Dodd, 1949; p. 428.

11. "Originals Only Revises Operations to Concentrate on
    Labor-story for Writers," Show Business; Monday,
    October 31, 1955; p. 1.

12. The Burns Mantle Best Plays of 1949-1950 And the Year
    Book of the Drama in America; Edited by John Chap-
    man; New York, Dodd, 1955; p. 382.

13. Kane, Lawrence;'Five Minutes from Broadway," Thea-
    ter Arts; December, 1949.

14. "Who's Who," Red Barn Theater program; Saugatuck,
    Michigan; 11th Season; p. 12.

15. "Owen Steele's Adaptation of Erskine Caldwell's Novel,"
    Variety; Dec. 7, 1949; "Off-Broadway" Clippings,
    through 1954, Theater Collection; New York Public
    Library.

16. Kane, Lawrence; op. cit.

17. The Burns Mantle Best Plays of 1949-1950 And the
    Year Book of the Drama in America, op. cit., p. 387.

18. Ibid., p. 382.

19. Gagey, Edmond M.; op. cit.; p. 265.

20. Ibid., p. 272.

21. Stern, Harold; "Off-Broadway;" Actor's Cues Show
    Business; Vo. 9. No. 3; Tuesday, January 18, 1949,
    p. 1.

22. The Burns Mantle Best Plays of 1949-1950 And the
    Year Book of the Drama in America, op. cit., p. 382.

23. "Agreement for Off-Broadway Group," Equity, Official
    Organ of the Actor's Equity Association; September,
    1949; (Volume XXXIV---No. 9); p. 18.

24. "Off-Broadway Contract Extended," Equity, Official
    Organ of the Actor's Equity Association; October,
    1949; Volume XXXV---No. 1; p. 19.

25. "Off-Broadway Theater League Sets Up Working Com-
    mittees to Expand Scope," Actor's Cues Show Busi-
    ness; Tuesday, August 2, 1949; p. 1.

26. "Off-Broadway Grows; Becomes Big Biz," Actor's
    Cues Show Business; Volume X---No. 6; Monday,
    February 6, 1950; p. 1.

Chapter IV

Off-Broadway 1950-1955-a study of the original
plays

It is difficult to locate copies of new plays by American authors produced Off-Broadway. Most of these plays
were never published and, consequently, unless the author
or the agent who handles the play can be located, it is impossible to obtain the work. Some authors have even lost
their own copies. One great service of the New York Public
Library is its provision of manuscripts of produced plays
which are submitted by playwrights to the manuscript division of the Theater Collection.

It is difficult to find original American plays produced Off-Broadway in 1950. However, Haven in the Dark
by Paul Nord, which was later to be a 1954 Off-Broadway
production, was being considered by Eddie Dowling in 1950
for a Broadway production.

Ninth Life by Sidney E. Porcelain, presented Off-
Broadway in 1950-51, is a charming one-act play written in
a stylized manner resembling Molière. It exudes an atmosphere of learning and mystery and was turned into what
must have been a very effective TV show, especially with
its surprise ending reminiscent of the best of Hitchcock.
The plot revolves around a scientist, his wife and his friend,
who is the wife's lover. Expounding the idea that man, like
cats, has nine lives, the scientist, who thinks he has three
lives left, asks the friend to shoot him as a final test of the
theory. When the scientist dies, his wife reveals that,

43

unknown to her husband, she had tried to poison him twice previously.[1]

Because there are so few available American plays, some of the foreign plays, new to American audiences, should be considered. An outstanding one in this group was Ubu Roi by Alfred Jarry, which was produced by the coura- geous and enterprising Living Theater of Judith Malina and Julian Beck. The Living Theater has done much to further the works of American playwrights who write poetic drama. The Living Theater feels that it is not a lack of good scripts which causes concern since they have many American plays they would like to produce. The real problem is that they have no chance to do so.[2]

This is diametrically opposed to the views held by leaders of other producing units Off-Broadway, who feel that there are too few good original scripts other than those of name playwrights.[3] Of course, Broadway is not too often in the market for poetic drama unless it is the writings of a Christopher Fry or the allegedly poetic theater of a Max- well Anderson, both of whom may be regarded as romantic playwrights.

Ubu Roi is the farcical but tragic account of future events. During Jarry's tragic lifetime the play was produced at the Theater de L'Oeuvre in Paris with Gemier in the title role in December, 1896. "It caused an uproar, was violently booed and violently applauded."[4] The play is a vigorous attack on Jarry's detested petit bourgeois. Ubu Roi with his wife are certainly, by any set of standards, two of the most unethical people who ever existed. Their success is due to their complete disregard of honor or fair dealing. They turn against each other when there is a revolution which threatens them as individuals. The com-

plete irony of the story is that in order to save their lives
they flee from Poland to arrive at a land of safety somewhere in the European Western world to which Jarry be-
longed.

The story's setting is Poland, where Ubu ruthlessly
destroys the existing system and becomes the supreme
authority in all matters of state. Although this is inherent-
ly an account of vicious despotism, it is so presented that
sometimes the humor is carried too far and becomes dis-
gusting. This is a provoking and timely play despite the
more than half a century since its first production.[5]

Another play of a different type presented in 1950
was the British import, Miranda, by Peter Blackmore.
There seems to be little reason for this play's production
Off-Broadway other than that it did play in England and in
this perhaps assured the producer that he would have a
success here. The thin plot is highly fanciful. Miranda is
a fascinating mermaid who saves a middle-aged surgeon's
life during his vacation in France. He is intrigued by her
and to get her into his London apartment passes her off
to his wife as a paralyzed patient. After the appropriately
comical situations provoked by Miranda, who manages to
entrance all of the men introduced to her, she is discovered to be a mermaid and exits through the window to her
home, the sea. Left alone, the surgeon's wife significantly calculates the months before the mermaid will arrive at
her destination "somewhere very lovely in May."[6] This
play was considered by Broadway producers.

Although during the 1949-1950 season some 264 plays
were supposed to be running Off-Broadway, possibly more than
than 60 others existed but failed to submit data,[7] there are
no manuscripts available of these plays. The only source

of information is the reviews, to be found mostly in Show
Business. These reviews do give a picture of constant
production of original plays, some of which were successful.

One original play, about ani-semitism in Hungary in
1882-1883, The Burning Bush, adapted by Noel Langley,[8]
was presented at the Dramatic Workshop of Erwin Piscator.
The Workshop is still running a playwright's series and a
Saturday night showing of many new plays, including some
by Americans. The Dramatic Workshop also did There Is
No End by Anthony Palma,[9] an American writer.

A controversial play performed by the Abbe Practical
Workshop, Bldg. 222, was about the mental ward of a na-
val hospital.[10]

Another work at this time by "Theater 108" was
Homecoming by Horton Foote which opened March 13, 1950.
It depicted "the hopeless infatuation of a small town doctor
for a former sweetheart, now turned prostitute! The review was ecstatic and described the production as so "pene-
tratingly" written, "beautifully" directed and acted, that it
"should insure a long and profitable career for 'Theater
108.'" However, "Theater 108" is not among our current
Off-Broadway groups.

The Longitude 49 company on May 22, 1950, presented one of the "rarities of the American theater, a
social drama with a wide popular appeal." The play was
written and directed by Herb Tank.[12]

Edwin Justus Mayer's Children of Darkness was produced by the Triangle Players of the West Side YMCA. The
production was lauded and Mayer's script stood up "amazing-
ly well." It was said to have "some of the cleverest dialogue to be found in contemporary drama."[13] The Last Love
of Don Juan, also by Mayer was presented Off-Broadway in

1954.

One group dedicated to the encouragement and presentation of creative writing Off-Broadway was not faring
so well at this time. The review of Originals Only's play,
A Chair for Lorna, at the Stephen-Wallace studio said as
"a group dedicated to the encouragement of original creative
writing they certainly haven't had much to work with."[14]
Finally, this commendable group which presented one failure
after another was successful in 1950 with Etched in Granite
by Ivan Becker.

It was not felt that the play was brilliant but rather
that it showed what producer "Tom Hill's minions can do
once given the opportunity to sink their histrionic teeth into
something." The play was concerned with a social problem
which many described as being peculiarly American, the
matriarchal aspects of our society.[15]

One drama presented Off-Broadway in 1950 which
it was hoped would go on Broadway in the traditional formula, was Christopher Columbus Brown by Horace W.
Stewart, otherwise known as Nick O'Dennis of stage and
screen fame. Reviewers felt it to be a "highly entertaining and
spirited Off-Broadway" production.[16]

Social dramas have always seemed to fare well Off-
Broadway and in the case of Nat Turner by Paul Peters,
the social aspects are well handled without descending into
the emotional pitfalls of type of play. It was presented at
the People's Drama Playhouse on December 18, 1950, directed by Gene Frankel. The play "treats with dignity and
sensitivity and without a trace of hysteria, the story of the
Negro who led one of the abortive slave uprisings in the
South prior to the Civil War." It was called a play which
"treated the theater as an adult institution."[17]

The Cherry Lane Playhouse at its inception was interested in dealing with original drama, but has since become almost exclusively a revival theater. Such unsuccessful plays as A Season in Hell by Rae Dalvin may have contributed to the demise of original play producing groups at the Cherry Lane, one of which was the Gregor Players in 1950. Season in Hell received very unfavorable notices.[18] The Cherry Lane Theater is perhaps one of the most picturesque to be found anywhere in Manhattan. Located in a right angle street which blocks the high buildings of New York from view, it is in a quaint street with old colonial buildings, exuding an atmosphere of the late 1900's. The cafes are ideally situated next to the theater and are as provocative as the street.

The 1950-1951 season included many interesting productions. Unfortunately the scripts cannot be obtained.

The five Off-Broadway plays to be discussed for the 1950-1952 season are notable because of the slick quality of three of them. This quality would suggest possible Broadway production. One did receive Broadway presentation and is now in the manuscript department of Samuel French: Dear Barbarians, a comedy by Lexford Richards. This is a fast-moving script which uses the techniques of Broadway situation comedy, but that did not quite ring the cash register. Alexander, the hero of the comedy, is a "barbarian" because he is a "taker."

Dear Barbarians is a light, sophisticated comedy about the view of marriage inspired in the younger generation by the unhappiness in the marriages of their parents. This leads this generation to prefer to discover the faults of those they love before marriage and not after.[19] It could have been inspired by Bertrand Russell's Marriage

<u>and Morals.</u>

    <u>The Lion Hunters</u> by Tad Mosel, presented during the 1951-1952 season, is an interesting commentary on a phase of society reminiscent of the <u>demi-monde</u> of Dumas fils. Mosel has since been successful in television, but he did not desert the theater. In 1960-1961 an adaptation of his play based on James Agee's Pulitzer prize novel, <u>A Death in the Family,</u> was produced on Broadway. Ted Hutto of the William Morris Agency, who manages Mosel, described this Broadway play, <u>All the Way Home,</u> a year before its production, as the "most beautiful play he has read."[20]

    Until the very last lines of The <u>Lion Hunters,</u> it seems to be about a Pal Joey type. However, all of the loveable traits to be found in Joey are missing. Ted, the "kept man" of this piece, is a lethal animal. As a too-good looking boy who goes to New York to get into show business, he takes instead the more profitable life of preying on old rich women. When he finally marries a stable girl, Celia, it becomes apparent that he only married her in order to escape the mature women to whom he had been chained, and not, as he had professed, in order to lead a decent life. He is not able to face the hard road of respectability and leaves his wife for an heiress. This is a stark picture of a world wherein the people who exhibit a veneer of accomplishment are shown as so many vultures, almost in the fashion of Becque. The predators in turn are hunted by those upon whom they prey, who display them as trophies.

    The characterizations are often too superficial, especially that of Ted who is treated as a megalomaniac rather than as a man with a magnetism which leads others to devote their lives to his comfort.[21]

There's Always A Murder by Ken Parker is a slick
mystery similar to television's Mr. and Mrs. North series.
Later, Parker did become a successful TV writer. Parker
had once leased an apartment in which there had been a
murder in the bathtub. Embroidering upon the situation,
Ken Parker initiated a newlywed show business couple into
this gruesome setting. The play has been presented by
high school and community theater groups all over the country. The first production was directed by the author under
the title, Four Flights Up on January 6, 1948, at the Provincetown Playhouse.[22]

Parker has had a diversified career as an actor,
as reviewer for the Arena Guild of America in their publication, Arena News,[23] and as producer at the Jan Hus Theater.[24]

Of the other two productions of the year, Dark
Legend by Helene Frankel was a psychological drama based
on the book by Dr. Frederic Werthan, an authority on juvenile delinquency. A theme of this kind would be difficult to
produce under most circumstances. Miss Frankel reports
that there has been an interest in making the play into a
film, but that Dr. Wertham does not feel that it should be
filmed because of professional considerations.

The plot concerns a beautiful but completely uneduca-
ted Sicilian woman who married at fifteen and was brought to
America by her husband. After her husband's death she
goes from his funeral into the arms of a lover, by whom
she has a child. Her son by her first husband has always
loved his mother to such a morbid extent that after her
lover has left her and the mother attempts to remarry, the
emotional shock completely deranges him.[25] The play was
awarded a prize by the National Theater Conference in 1951.

Bill Long's <u>Aegean Fable</u> is delightful. It is about
the antics of the Greek philosopher, Thales, who in order
to demonstrate that he is not irresponsible and can make as
much money as the materialists of the world, succeeds in
turning the affairs of the world topsy-turvy, but nonetheless proves his point. (see p.   ) It was presented at
Originals Only on May 27, 1951,[26] and was considered "no
great shakes as a play, but it does expose its creator as a
writer of promise."[27]

Although no copy of <u>Starfish</u> by William Noble, presented in the 1951-1952 season is obtainable, Noble reported
that the play was being given on the West Coast and was
produced in a theater in Germany. According to Noble his
script had never been performed Off-Broadway but was presented in a community theater near New York City. He and
James Herlihy later had a hit on Broadway, <u>Blue Denim</u>,[28]
made into a movie in 1959.

Three of the plays produced during 1952-1953 were
quite light. <u>Three in One</u> by Ken Parker followed his usual
style. The plays were taken from his television work,
which included "A Cup of Tea" and "Star-Minded." Although
the production was meant to offer a new form of staging
which required only limited settings, emulating a television
production, the plays were far from being experimental
and probably fare better in front of the television camera.

"A Cup of Tea" which is called a play of the super-
natural, is an interesting twist on a confidence game prac-
ticed by a tea leaf reader.[29] The second, "Star Minded,"
is the old story of the cure of the inveterate movie fan
when her movie idol proves less fascinating than the lasting
devotion of her husband.[30]

<u>Faith and Prudence</u> is a play any high school group

Mary Westland (as Prudence Clark) and Anne Marie Lee (as Julie Anne Peck) in a scene from "FAITH AND PRUDENCE," a three act farce comedy by Lottie Michelson, as presented at the Blackfriars' Theater in New York, October 13, 1952.

or community theater could do. There is a great deal of humor in it. It even employs a male mannequin who comes to life in a less gruesome way than Percy MacKayes' The Scarecrow. This mannequin is much too instrumental in the situation and even though he is not the protagonist, he becomes almost a deus ex machina. This play is, finally, well-made. The protagonists are very interesting and loveable characters, which may be reason enough for its production.

The plot concerns the inveterate bachelor and the timid but accomplished and sweet spinster. Because of an inclination of Boyle, the seafaring bachelor, to go to sleep upon drinking and the inability of Prudence to hold her liquor, they get into a situation which precipitates marriage arrangements. Prudence's marionette causes Boyle to suspect her honor and the marriage is almost called off. Boyle ultimately awakens to the realization that Prudy is worth fighting for against all rivals.[31]

Hey, You! is a delightful sketch set to music and dance. Poetic in form, it covers the plight of the lonely young man who is lost in a world which denies him a place. He is a member of the "lonely crowd."

The setting is a subway station and the man in the ticket cage, though begging for attention, is ignored. He prevents a robbery and the BMT gives him a medal for his bravery. Everyone again leaves, uninterested in him after the event, but he pleads that he has "poems to tell...songs to sing." It is a very poignant sketch and one hopes that the collaborators, one of whom is a dentist, will write more.[32]

Noone by Gil Orlovitz is one of those plays which leave a clinical taste and an incomplete comprehension

of the events of the drama. It is a highly oedipal drama
which involves a man who not only puzzles his psychia-
trists but is allowed to mystify the audience. An inmate
escapes from a mental hospital and is sought by the police
until found with his mother who has been mentally ill for
years, gradually destroying everyone around her.
Orlovitz himself classified the play as "educational material."[33]

One of the most successful Off-Broadway productions of 1953 was End As a Man which began as a novel.
The Calder Willingham play opened Off-Broadway and later
went uptown and was subsequently filmed. It concerned
varieties of hellraising at a Southern military academy.[34]
It was apparent that director Jack Garfein had "trained
his sights on aping the slick product of Times Square."[35]

In the 1953-1954 season Off-Broadway had gone
from "little theater" to "big business." According to
Burns Mantle some Off-Broadway went on Broadway. This
was the case with The Girl on the Via Flaminia. It did
exceptionally well at the Circle-in-the-Square during that
group's formative period.

The Girl on the Via Flaminia was produced in 1953
by London-born American dramatist, Alfred Hayes. It is
exceptional in its move uptown.[36] It was a dramatization
of Hayes' popular war novel by the same name.

The play is written in the style of the popular I-
talian films of that period. The central figures are an A-
merican soldier who wants someone to love and an Italian
girl who after the war, as happened to many of the Italian
women, must sacrifice her honor in order to obtain the
basic necessities of life. Unlike some of the girls in Italy
of the time, she is unable to adjust herself to this moral

degradation and at the curtain has left to throw herself into
the Tiber.

This is a war story which at the time had a large
audience. It is a deeply human story with an overt sensa-
tional appeal. It dealt with a problem very close to the
aftermath of war.

In the 1953-1954 season, Off-Broadway presented as
two of its most interesting plays A Time of Storm by Sheldon Stark, which was a predecessor of the Crucible, also
about the Salem witch-trials of 1693, and Haven in the Dark
by Paul Nord, which has a similarity in its style to Pirandello.

A Time of Storm, while not as dramatic or theatrical a work as the Crucible, explored human values more
thoroughly. Whereas the wife and the husband in the Crucible never quite became real humans, the character of
Nathaniel the husband, Mercy the wife, and Sarah, the
daughter, are completely portrayed here. The horror of
homes without love makes even the brutalities of the witch
trials seem minor. Perhaps this play was not as effective
in that the plot was divided among its several themes, while
Miller concentrated upon the effects of the trials upon the
innocents accused of witchcraft and the demoniacal behavior
of the girl accusers. Sheldon Stark delved into the reasons
that girls like Sarah eventually turn into heartless killers.
Sarah's mother only married Nathaniel for security and
never gave her love to anyone. The play is further weak-
ened by a third sub-plot involving two lovers, Cadmus and
Melinda, who try to save Nathaniel. Despite these short-
comings, A Time of Storm is a powerful dramatic work.
Its last act has strength and the curtain scene is intensely
effective. It was given at the Greenwich Mews Theater on

February 26, 1954.[38]

Paul Nord's <u>Haven in the Dark</u> is an experimental
play which is a psychological study which explores the truth
of reality with an approach modeled on that of Pirandello.
(see p.   )

<u>The Death of Odysseus</u> by Lionel Abel is an interest-
ing short vignette based on the legend. The play was first
produced by John Bernard Myers in association with the
Artist's Theater at the Amato Opera Theater in New York
on November 3, 1953.

The paradox of Odysseus's death is fully exploited
in the drama. Odysseus is revealed as a man too clever to
die until he discovers that to continue to live demands the
sacrifice of one of his children. At first, betraying them
for his own self preservation, he leads his sons to battle
among themselves rather than die himself, but he is ultimately a father and true to his instincts as such. To save
his son he gives his life. Although the dialogue is not
particularly inspired, the situation leads to some amusing
high spots.[40]

<u>Madam, Will You Walk</u>? was Sidney Howard's last
play. It was performed on the road shortly after his death
but never brought to Broadway. Its New York debut was at
the Phoenix Theater on December 1, 1953.

The plot is another variation on the Faust theme.
An Irish spinster, through her association with the Prince
of Darkness, attempts to bring happiness again into our tense
lives. She falls in love with a taxi cab driver who is also
a dancer and decides to begin her evangelism by the reestab-
lishment of vaudeville. There is great opposition to her
eccentric behavior and her guardians threaten to commit her,
but all ends well, and she dances into the arms of the man

The first production of Paul Nord's "Haven in the Dark,"
Werdman Studio, 1949. l. to r. Libby Steiger, Lois Brown,
Gordon Sterne, Donald Stuart. Standing: Lynn Lee.

she has discovered and loves, as the curtain falls.

The essence of the play as stated by Dr. Brightlee, the "Animating Force," is that Miss Coyle "becomes part of a larger design long since prepared. And prepared in the holy conviction that man must be reawakened to the realization---which has grown dim to him---of his own importance above that of every other fact in the universe."[41]

As Joseph Wood Krutch stated "when Howard treats Faust, the tale becomes not heavier but tighter than usual... Howard was not serious about the precise role of the devil...But he was very serious about people, about goodness, happiness, joy, and the ways of the world which defeat them."[42]

Late Arrival by Charles Oxton, presented at the Blackfriar's Guild, is again the type of play which any community theater, even some high school groups, would feel perfectly free to present. The plot explores the transition of an intelligent girl from adolesence to maturity during a family crisis. Barbara, a college coed, upon discovering that her mother is pregnant feels that her acquaintances will laugh at her and ridicule her family. Barbara painfully matures to the realities of life. She accepts her new brother when he is finally brought home and at the same time enters into a more wholesome relationship with down-to-earth people.

This is the American family formula with just enough unhappiness to upset the equilibrium, but it is not a situation which will be upset for too long.[43] It is hard to see what attraction this had for the "intellectual" Off-Broadway audience.

The Emperor's Clothes by George Tabori, although not a very effective drama, was first produced on Broadway

where it failed. At a time when despotism and totalitarian-
ism persist such a drama reveals the human values which
are undergoing trial. The reviewer, however, felt that the
play was "too melodramatic, too articulate a stage piece,
to be more than infrequently exciting theater."[44]

The professor, Elek, was the most interesting and
well-developed character. He has been reduced to a shell
of a man by the police state in which he lives, but ultimately regains the initiative which he once possessed by
accepting responsibility for his son's actions even when doing so means sacrificing himself at the hands of the state.
At the drama's conclusion although he is physically beaten,
he has found his strength as a man through his regained
moral convictions.[45]

Bullfight, one of the more successful Off-Broadway
plays, was presented at the Theater de Lys on January 12,
1954. The action of this play by Leslie Stevens takes place
in and around the village of Concepcion del Oro in Zacate-
cas, Mexico.

It is a passionate, fierce drama of love and pride.
The Salamanca family name is inherited by two brothers
both drawn to the bull ring by family tradition, although
both lack the abilities of the matador. The elder, Domingo
del Cristobal Salamanca, proves avaricious and cowardly.
After dishonouring the family both in the ring and in A-
merica, he returns to bring shame to the peasant sister
of the girl his brother has married. Then finally through
his quest for fame he drives his brother Esteban to his
death in the bull ring.

The play exudes the fire of the Mexican life, with
a set suggesting a bull ring, in accordance with the central
theme. The bright passionate colours used are yellow,

orange, and red, and the apron stage jutted twelve feet
into the orchestra.

Guitars were used in the background and the crowd
became an antiphonal chorus to the story of passion which
builds to a climax of modern tragedy. As Domingo brings
the ears of the bull which killed his brother as a final
tribute at the brother's funeral, the tribute becomes a
futile gesture from the lost. The scene is underscored by
an emotional funeral mass.[46]

Stevens has since written a successful Broadway
play, Marriage-Go-Round, which has also been filmed.
Another play of his, Pink Jungle, was scheduled for Broadway but never made it.

On Thursday, May 6, 1954, after a week of paid
previews, Eugene Feist's Building Blocks was presented by
Two by Four Productions, a group mainly from Carnegie
Tech., at 83 East Fourth Street, in a modified arena playhouse.

Although it starts slowly and the introductory scenes
are contrived, it progresses into a well-paced, intriguing
play. Throughout there are some inept scenes but Feist
has a "knack of exposing his people's thoughts in subdued
half-sentences that link together and achieve the kind of
intimate rapport that alone justifies in-the-round production."[47]

It is the story of two young people; the girl apparent-
ly mature beyond her years and a boy who achieves maturity through his responsibilities as a husband and a parent.
The boy enters the Air Force without revealing his marriage. He goes AWOL, but later decides to return and
take his punishment. Susan goes home and finishes college.
In the last scene the boy now an Air Force cadet on leave

to see his family, offers a toast to his son as the curtain falls.[48]

The dialogue, which is "Mr. Feist's forte,"[49] crackles in a smooth, uninterrupted flow. Building Blocks is the sensitively characterized account of a "man who comes of age through his love for a woman; the play relies on characterization rather than plot."[50]

It ran a total of 30 performances until the expiration of both theater lease and license. Feist was the managing director of the New Theater in Nashville, Tennessee which gave very interesting productions, including writers like Anouilh. In Nashville, Feist directed 24 plays including his adaptation of Armand Salacrou's Archipel Lenoir which he called Relative Strangers. At present he is working with the directing and the playwriting units of Actors Studio.

The Girl from Samos, by Ida Ehrlich, reconstructed from Menander's fragment, was presented at the Labor Temple on November 15, 1954.[51] This play of the 1954-1955 season is not truly original, but it is a delightful adaptation worthy of attention.

The plot, true to Menander plot constructions in which are found the noble slave, abandoned children, and regained identities, is appealing through its insight into the character of ancient Greece. It is unfortunate that the performance was reported as below par and not up to the excellent script.[52]

Verse drama in the 1954-1955 season was high on the list of productions but, unfortunately, most works of merit even in this field were foreign imports like The Dreaming Dust by Denis Johnston or In April Once, a wonderful play by William Alexander Percy. One American

verse drama, I Believe in Rubble by Deric Riegen, is an
extremely outspoken play. The title indicates its thesis,
that only through the periodic demolition of old and decadent
civilizations are advancements made possible. The man who
sees the world without illusion is sought by both sides of
rival totalitarianistic systems, but his word is only heeded
when in the chaos wrought by conflict the world must depend
upon wisdom in order to develop a new order.[53] It was the
subject of a University of California Master's thesis in
1953. (see p.)

Two revues were presented at the Phoenix in the
1954-1955 season, one of which, The Golden Apple by John
LaTouche and Jerome Moross was of special merit. Its
budget was one to which Off-Broadway groups of the usual
variety do not aspire, but compared to Broadway budgets,
cheap at $75,000. It was considered the season's "most
individual musical" and was taken on Broadway.[54]

Based on the Homeric version of the Trojan Wars,
the action takes place in the state of Washington between
1900 and 1910. The period was chosen because America at
this time was just beginning to feel its growing pains.[55]

Phoenix '55, with sketches by Ira Wallach, had a
successful run. The sketches would be suitable for TV but
have little significance as literature. They range from the
do-it-yourself man who removes his own appendix to the
woman who wins $50,000. in a baking contest by using the
recipe on the side of the sponsoring company's flour box.[56]

Two particularly significant dramas with plots touching upon a similar social problem are Teach Me How to Cry
by Patricia Joudry, presented by LPS Productions at Theater de Lys on April 5, 1955, and Sing Me No Lullaby by
Robert Ardrey, given at the Phoenix on October 4, 1954.

Teach Me How to Cry explores small town bigotry.
It is not recommended for an audience which goes to the
theater for a pat on the back, as it portrays a perhaps too
revealing portrait of American provincialism, too close to
all of us to be lightly shrugged away as mere drama.

Melinda, the illegitimate daughter of a simple seam-
stress, is saved from her closeted existence when she
meets a newcomer to her home town, Will Henderson, the
son of an unsuccessful traveling salesman. The hypocritical
mores of the town eventually assert themselves against their
love and the malice of the solid citizenry is exerted in
attempts to drive them apart. Because Will beats one of
his fellow high school students for implying that Melinda
isn't "nice," he is expelled and he and his family are forced
to leave town. However they overcome the prejudices surrounding them and two young lives are saved.[57]

The Show Business 14th Annual Awards of 1955
judged this as the best new play Off-Broadway, and Nancy
Marchand in the cast as the best supporting actress.[58] It
was later bought by Hollywood and filmed.

Sing Me No Lullaby by Robert Ardrey and The Emperor's Clothes by George Tabori have a great similarity
in their theme. Both are comments on the extreme social
and moral pressures brought to bear upon the individual in
our time.

Sing Me No Lullaby unfolds the story behind the reunion of a 1930's University of Illinois class. Mike Hertzog,
a brilliant scientist, is about to desert his land because security measures have made him an enemy of the United
States. Ben Callinger, who has been a quitter since his
defeat in a political election in his youth, is brought
through Mike's crisis to a realization for the need to fight

so that men like Mike can live in a world which is too
afraid or too ignorant to speak out for them. Ben reenters
politics but not without the knowledge that Mike Hertzog contributed to his own tragedy. Men like Mike, who as a
youth insisted that one had to take sides have contributed to
the idea of total commitment. The world had come finally
to agree with Mike.[59]

Elek Odrey, the professor who is the hero of The
Emperor's Clothes, is punished by a society which he, too,
has helped to shape and which he helped lead, as he led his
son, to a perversion of truth---a truth that must be either
black or white. However, Elek does not steal away into the
night as Mike does in Sing Me No Lullaby. Instead he gets
back his youthful strength by accepting the responsibility for
the weakness of his son, and the world which he had helped
to make.

Sandhog, a musical produced by the Phoenix theater,
is based upon Theodore Dreiser's short story "St. Columba
and the River." It is social commentary on the Irish im-
migrants who built the Holland tunnel. The play, by Earl
Robinson and Waldo Salt, was produced November 23, 1954,
at the Phoenix Theater and could effectively be presented to a
select audience. The characterizations tend to be super-
ficial but this is compensated for by the rapid tempo of
the scenes and the pulsing rhythm of the ballads.

Johnny, an ambitious immigrant, assumes grave
responsibilities for himself and for his Irish countrymen.
His love for Katie, his wife, and their devotion to each other
draws poignancy from the dangerous work of building the
tunnel. It is a play reminiscent of the Federal Theater,
particularly with the irony expressed in the concluding lines
when Johnny says:

Boys, I poured a short one to celebrate this great
occasion. The opening of the tunnel and the dawn of a
new period of unemployment. [60]

Annie's Son, by Harold Cobin, investigates the plight
of a young New York boy whose ne'er-do-well father reenters the dope traffic after being released from prison and
ruins the boy's future. All the mother's plans and struggles
to build a respectable life for her son are frustrated. [61]

The Terrible Swift Sword by Arthur Steuer was presented by the Phoenix Theater's "New Directions" series in
November of 1955. The script is reminiscent of Calder
Willingham's End As a Man. It explored the unsavory aspects of human relationships in a military academy. The
brutality the hero endures as retaliation for his abusive
questioning of authority, shapes him into a man. This does
not prevent the theme of the play from being horrifying in
its picture of human beings distorted into vicious robots by
an inflexible system. [62]

The Last Love of Don Juan by Edwin Justus Mayer,
whose title explains its subject, was presented at the Rooftop Theater. It is a farce overlaid with philosophy which
almost succeeds in smothering the play. Mayer could not
decide whether he was writing a play or a treatise.

The play recounts the employment of Don Juan to
overcome the frigidity of the new princess in a seventh
century Spanish town. This latest princess of the realm has
brought economic disaster because she will not employ her
charms to draw merchants to the town. Don Juan, after
duly conquering the princess, is greatly disillusioned upon
discovering that she has had an uncouth cook in the palace
as her lover from the beginning.

After this great disillusionment of Don Juan's life,

Don Quixote, who is included in the cast of illustrious characters, presents the philosophy to which Don Juan ultimately
turns.   The final message seems to be that in the pursuit of
illusions alone is there any truth to be discovered.[63]

The play was reviewed as "a travesty that travesties
nothing, a morality which it would pay well not to examine
too carefully."[64]

A delightful satire on the international scene, A
Switch In Time, by Lola Pergament was presented at the
Greenwich Mews Theater as part of "2 for Fun," a community project sponsored by the Village Presbyterian Church and
the Brotherhood Synagogue.   The other play was Chekhov's
The Anniversary.   This is the type of fun which Off-Broadway could produce more frequently.

The play hinges upon the hypothetical world situation
instituted by the sudden transposition of the USSR and Canada
by some experimentally minded space creatures who propose
to the Earthlies a "spherical experience in great alterna-
tives."[65]   The ensuing contradictory situation makes enemies
of friends and necessitates negotiations with former enemies.
Show Business called it the "Best Off-Broadway play, acting
and direction of the season."[66]   It is the type of satirical
spoof which is a delight to discover and ideal for Off-Broadway.

Robert Hivnor is the author of another arresting play,
The Ticklish Acrobat, which can be recommended to any
little theater group.   It was produced first by John Bernard
Meyers in association with the Artist's Theater at the Amato
Opera Theater on March 8, 1954.[67]

Those who have seen a production of Too Many
Thumbs by Hivnor, will note the parallelism between it and
The Ticklish Acrobat.   Hivnor taught for many years at the

GREENWICH MEWS THEATRE

141 West 13th Street

FIRE NOTICE: The exit indicated by a red light and sign nearest to the seat you occupy is the shortest route to the street. In the event of fire please do not run — WALK TO THAT EXIT.

EDWARD CAVANAGH, FIRE COMMISSIONER.

THE GREENWICH MEWS THEATRE
presents

2 For Fun

Directed by JACK SYDOW

Settings by Sonia Lowenstein — Costumes by Louise Evans
Lighting and Sound by Jerry Balash

A community project sponsored by the Village Presbyterian Church and the Brotherhood Synagogue

 ## 1. THE ANNIVERSARY
by ANTON CHEKHOV

THE CAST
(In Order of Appearance)

Kuzma Nicholayevich Khirin	CHARLES RANDALL
Andrey Andereyevich Shipuchin	WILLIAM EDMONSON
Bank Clerk	JIM CLARK
Tatiana Alexeyevna Shipuchina	ELLEN HOLLY
Nastasya Fyodorovna Merchutkina	RUTH VOLNER
Leader of the Deputation	FREDRIC MARTIN
Member of the Deputation	ELI RILL, BUSH HUNTER

TIME: 1900 — Russia — The Provincial Mutual Bank.

 ## 2. A SWITCH IN TIME
by LOLA PERGAMENT

THE CAST

Narrator, James Chap, Dr. Lyman Cosmon	JIM CLARK
Mona Bona, Mrs. Rise Yomar	RUTH VOLNER
Jack Shackles, Senator Yukon Terp	WILLIAM EDMONSON
Abo, George Bathrone	CHARLES RANDALL
Zog, Associated Press Man	FREDRIC MARTIN
Hamilton V. Hamilton	ELI RILL
Naida Gisben, Sharon Guilders	ELLEN HOLLY

TIME: Almost Any Time

PRODUCTION STAFF

Artistic Director	LILY TURNER
Administrative Coordinator	STELLA HOLT
Press Representative	LOLA PERGAMENT
Stage Manager	JIM CLARK
Production Assistants	JUDITH STRAND, GEORGE BORKIN, ANJA ROTERS

The Greenwich Mews Theatre is founded on the basic belief that there is only one race — the human race. "2 For Fun" therefore, is cast without regard to color — the fitness of the actor or actress for the part being the only criterion observed.

67

University of Minnesota and Too Many Thumbs, a satire on
Darwinism, was produced at the Cherry Lane Theater.

The protagonist of The Ticklish Acrobat is a young,
wealthy archaelogist, who in his search for the meaning of
life demolishes a small town in Dalmatia level by level. As
he dismantles the town his scientific discoveries reveal,
first, a Moorish palace; then, an European fort and dungeon;
and the dawn of the settlement as the site of a Greek temple.
The city issspared being completely razed by an American
girl with whom he has fallen in love. She is courageous
and through her the archaelogist realizes that it is better to
leave standing the temple built for the worship of love, even
Grecian love, than to destroy man's creations in a meaning-
less search for a possibly unattainable scientific truth.[68]

Another inspiring play of the season was The Immortal
Husband by James Merrill, produced by John Bernard
Myers and directed by Herbert Machiz in association with
The Artist's Theater at the theater de Lys in New York on
February 14, 1955. The Artist's Theater was established
to bring poets, painters, composers and professional actors
to work together for a fresh expression in drama. It was
established to prove that literature can be theater.[69]

The Immortal Husband is a "modern reconstruction of
the myth of Tithonus and Aurora, who persuaded Zeus to
give her lover immortality but failed to ask for eternal
youth." Tennessee Williams has called the play, "pure
poetry plus theater, a rare and magical combination."[70] The
play established Merrill as a "playwright of major potential-
ities," and it "joins that small company of plays...with
which...the American theater must come to terms."[71]

Off-Broadway has the ability to introduce meaningful
plays---from the drama of social consciousness to the revue

such as The Golden Apple. Many of these original dramas .
Broadway could not or would not produce. Many of the suc-
cessful plays Off-Broadway between 1950 and 1955--like
Summer and Smoke by Williams and Dear Barbarians by
Richards---were earlier unsuccessful on Broadway.

Such plays as The Golden Apple require large budgets
for Off-Broadway, which only a subsidized theater like the
Phoenix could produce. As a subsidized theater, the Phoenix can compete with Broadway productions, even vying for
new plays.

Other Off-Broadway theaters presented new low budget
plays. Social problem and political plays, an Off-Broadway
tradition such as Teach Me How to Cry, The Emperor's
Clothes (first produced on Broadway) and Sing Me No Lullaby
were produced. Because of their jarring and perhaps too
sensitive material, they would have been skeptically received
by Broadway producers. These are fine plays for the special Off-Broadway audience in search of fresh, stimulating
ideas. These plays establish a standard Off-Broadway must
continue to maintain.

Sandhog, an example of the drama of social significance,
answers "the need for a revolution to the dictatorship of the
box office so that the theater may be released to all the
people."[72]

Psychological plays which attempt to bring about better
understanding among people are typified by Noone, Dark
Legend and The Terrible Swift Sword. Such dramas are
often presented Off-Broadway. Sometimes, however, they
disintegrate into shocking, clinical analyses and consequently
defeat their purpose.

Poetic drama can be produced in the Off-Broadway
setting better than anywhere else. Writers such as Deric

Riegen, Gertrude Stein and William Carlos Williams not
only can be produced Off-Broadway, but can be produced
with sensitivity and understanding.

Many plays of community theater appeal are introduced
Off-Broadway, such as Faith and Prudence, Late Arrival,
There's Always A Murder, and A Switch in Time.

If we do not give American playwrights a stage, we
can expect them to turn their creative efforts to another
literary form.[73] We need a drama which will answer "the
need for a new creativeness" so that the stage may "re-
assert its identity alongside of the cinema and the radio."[74]

Notes

1. Porcelain, Sidney E., MS. "Ninth Life," dated Aug.
    4, 1959, from Mr. Porcelain, 111 East 26th St.,
    N. Y. 10, New York, produced 1950-1951.

2. Spicer, James, Interview, Living Theater, 530 Sixth
    Ave. NYC, 6/18/59.

3. Fraenkel, Gene and James Spicer, Interviews, Ibid.,
    Gene Fraenkel Dramatic Workshop, 115 MacDougal St.,
    6/22/59.

4. Jarry, Alfred, Ubu Roi, trans. by Barbara Wright,
    (Published by Gaberbocchus Press, London, Distributed
    in the United States by New Directions, First published
    in 1951), p. VI.

5. Ibid., pp. 9-164.

6. Blackmore, Peter, Miranda, (published by H. F. W.
    Deane and Sons, Ltd., London, Distributed by the
    Walter H. Baker Company, Boston, Massachusetts),
    Copyright, 1948, pp. 7-67.

7. Chapman, John, editor; The Burns Mantle Best Plays
    of 1949-1950 and the Year Book of the Drama in Amer-
    ica, (Published by Dodd, Mead and Company), New
    York, 1955, p. 382.

8.   "The Burning Bush," Actors Cues Show Business,
       (Vol. X---No. 2), Wednesday, Jan. 10, 1950, p. 6.

9.   Stern, Harold, "Reviews," Actors Cues Show Business,
       (Vol. X---No. 9), Monday, February 27, 1950, p. 6.

10.   Stern, Harold, "Reviews," Actors Cues Show Business,
       (Vol. X---No. 7), Monday, February 13, 1950, p. 7.

11.   Stern, Harold, "Reviews," Actors Cues Show Business,
       (Vol. X---No. 11), Monday, March 13, 1950, p. 6.

12.   Op. cit., (Vol. X---No. 20), Monday, May 22, 1950,
       p. 6.

13.   Stern, Harold, "Reviews," (Vol. X---No. 24), Monday,
       June 19, 1950, p. 5.

14.   Stern, Harold, "Reviews," (Vol. X---No. 28), Mon-
       day, July 10, 1950, p. 6.

15.   Stern, Harold, "Reviews," (Vol. X---No. 30), Monday,
       July 24, 1950, p. 5.

16.   Stern, Harold, "Reviews," Actors Cues Show Business,
       (Vol. X---No. 42), Monday, Oct. 16, 1950, p. 5.

17.   Stern, Harold, "Reviews," (Vol. X---No. 51), Mon-
       day, Dec. 18, 1950, p. 5.

18.   Stern, Harold, "Reviews," (Vol. X---No. 51), Mon-
       day, December 18, 1950, p. 6.

19.   Richards, Lexford, MS. "Dear Barbarians," in the
       Samuel French, Inc., Manuscript Collection, 25 West
       45 St., New York 36, 6/7/59.

20.   Hutto, Ted, Interview 6/7/59, at William Morris
       Agency, 1740 Broadway, New York City.

21.   Mosel, Tad, MS. "The Lion Hunters," read 6/7/59,
       in the Priscilla Morgan Manuscript file of the William
       Morris Agency, 1740 Broadway.

22.   Parker, Ken, There's Always A Murder, copyright,
       1951, Samuel French, Inc., pp. 10-126.

23.   "Reviews," Show Business, (Vol. XIII---No. 27),
       Monday, July 6, 1953, p. 7.

24.   "Reviews," Show Business, (Vol. XII---No. 50),
       Monday, Dec. 8, 1952, p. 6.

25.   Fraenkel, Helene, MS, "Dark Legend," produced
       March 24, 1952 at the President Theater, from the
       author 6/23/59, Old Mill Isle, Westport, Conn.

26.   Long, Bill, MS. "Aegean Fable," copyright 1949 by
       author, in Theater Collection, New York Public
       Library, New York City.

27.   Stern, Harold, "Reviews," Show Business, (Vol.
       XI---No. 22), May 28, 1951, p. 7.

28.   Noble, William, telephone conversation on 6/5/59.

29.   Parker, Kenneth T., Parker's Television Plays, A
       Collection of Eight Plays Written for Stage and Tele-
       vision, "A Cup of Tea," Copyright, 1954, (Publish-
       er: The Northwestern Press, Minneapolis), pp. 21-
       39.

30.   Ibid., "Star-Minded," pp. 93-114.

31.   Michelson, Lottie, MSS. "Faith and Prudence," in
       the Theater Collection, New York Public Library.

32.   Meranus, Norman, Dr. & June Carroll, MS. "Hey
       You!" (originally "A Dime for Two Nickels"), pre-
       sented at Provincetown Playhouse, 1952; from Dr.
       Meranus, 109 N. Main St., Herkimer, N. Y., 6/15/59.

33.   Orlovitz, Gil, MSS. "Noone," copyright by Gil Orlovitz
       September, 1950, copy from author 6/12/59, 403 W.
       21 St., N. Y. 11, N. Y.

34.   Kronenberger, Louis, editor; "Off-Broadway," The
       Burns Mantle Yearbook, The Best Plays of 1953-
       1954, (Published by Dodd, Mead and Company, New
       York, 1957), p. 356.

35.   Stewart, Robert J., "Reviews," Show Business,
       (Vol. XIII---No. 38), Monday, September 21, 1953, p. 7.

36.   Cordell, Richard A. and Lowell Matson, editors; The

Off-Broadway Theater, Seven Plays; Alfred Hayes,
The Girl on the Via Flaminia, Random House, New
York, Copyright, 1959, pp. 5-73.

37.   Frankel, Gene, Interview with 6/22/59, Gene
        Frankel Dramatic Workshop, 115 MacDougal St.

38.   Stark, Sheldon, MSS, "Time of Storm," produced
        February 25, 1954, in manuscript division of Daniel
        Hollywood Associates, 101 W. 55 St., obtained
        6/13/59, New York City.

39.   Nord, Paul, MSS, "Haven in the Dark," produced
        March 4, 1954 at Originals Only Playhouse, New
        York, in Theater Collection, New York Public Library.

40.   Abel, Lionel, The Death of Odysseus, in Five Plays
        for a New Theater, Copyright 1956, pp. 3-27.

41.   Howard, Sidney, "Madam, Will You Walk?", Thea-
        ter, Arts, Volume XLI, No. 2, February, 1957, p.53.

42.   Krutch, Joseph Wood, "Sidney Howard Storyletter,"
        Theater Arts, Volume XLI, No. 2, February, 1957,
        p. 92.

43.   Oxton, Charles, Late Arrival, (Published by Samuel
        French, Inc., London, Toronto, Copyright, 1955
        (Revised version, by Charles Oxton, pp. 7-124.

44.   Greenberg, Ed, "Reviews," Show Business, Vol.
        XIII---No. 44, Monday, November 2, 1953, p. 7.

45.   Tabori, George, The Emperor's Clothes, (Published
        by Samuel French, Inc., London, Toronto), Copy-
        right, 1953 (Acting Edition, by George Tabori) pp.
        7-95.

46.   Stevens, Leslie, Bullfight, a play in three acts,
        (Samuel French, Inc.), copyright 1959 by Leslie
        Stevens, pp. 5-95.

47.   L.D.K., "Theaters: 'Building Blocks'," Women's
        Wear Daily, Wednesday, May 12, 1954; p. 90.

48.   Feist, Eugene, MSS, "Building Blocks," a play in
        three acts, pp. 1-29.

49.   Stewart, Robert, Show Business, 5/17/54, Clippings
       from Eugene Feist.

50.   Clippings from Eugene Feist, Variety, 6/2/54.

51.   Ehrlich, Ida Lublenski, The Girl from Samos,
       (Published by Everyman's Theater, 152 W. 42nd St.,
       NYC), Copyright 1955 by Ida Lublenski Ehrlich, pp.
       3-50.

52.   Stewart, Robert, "Reviews," Show Business, Vol.
       XIV---No. 47, Monday, November 29, 1954, p. 6.

53.   Riegen, Deric, MSS, I Believe In Rubble as produced
       first at Yale University in 1952, 6/12/59.

54.   Kronenberger, Louis, editor; op. cit., p. 356.

55.   Latouche, John & Jerome Moross, The Golden Apple
       (Random House, New York), Copyright, 1954, pp.
       3-133.

56.   Wallach, Ira, Phoenix'55, (Samuel French, Inc.,
       London, Toronto), Copyright 1957, pp. 7-39.

57.   Joudry, Patricia, Teach Me How to Cry, Dramatist's
       Play Service, Inc., Copyright, 1955, by Patricia
       Joudry Steele, pp. 15-76.

58.   "Annual Awards," Show Business Anniversary Issue,
       May, 1955, p. 3.

59.   Ardrey, Robert, Sing Me No Lullaby, Dramatist's
       Play Service, Inc., Copyright, 1955, by Robert
       Ardrey, pp. 5-67.

60.   Robinson, Earl and Waldo Salt, MSS, "Sandhog,"
       produced Nov. 23, 1954, Theater Collection, New
       York Public Library, Act 3, Sc. 5, p. 21.

61.   Cobin, Harold, MSS, "Annie's Son," copyright 1954,
       from author, 6/12/59.

62.   Steuer, Arthur, MSS, "The Terrible Swift Sword
       (4th version) Theater Collection, New York Public
       Library, produced Nov., 1955.

63.   Mayer, Edwin Justus, MSS, The Last Love of Don
       Juan, William Morris Agency.

64.   Tallmer, Jerry, "The Last Love of Don Juan,"
       The Village Voice, Vol. 1---No. 6, Nov 30, 1955,
       p. 8.

65.   Pergament, Lola, MSS., A Switch In Time, copy-
       right, 1955, from author Lola Pergament, 6/13/59.

66.   Program for "2 for Fun," "Changin World in Fun..."
       National Guardian, at Greenwich Mews Theater,
       1955.

67.   Playbook, Five Plays for a New Theater, A New
       Directions Books (Published at Norfolk, Conn. by
       James Laughlin), copyright 1956 by New Directions,
       p. 295.

68.   Ibid., Robert Hivnor, "The Ticklish Acrobat," pp.
       27-127.

69.   Machiz, Herbert, "The Challenge of a Poetic Thea-
       ter," Theater Arts, Vol. XL, No. 2, pp. 72-84.

70.   Playbook, Five Plays for a New Theater, op.cit.,
       Jacket quotation.

71.   Ibid., p. 296.

72.   Houghton, Norris "Why an Off-Broadway Theater,"
       Advance from Broadway, 19,000 Miles of American
       Theater, Harcourt, Brace and Company, New York;
       copyright, 1941, p. 383.

73.   "Scarcity of Good Dramas Stumping B'way Producers,"
       Show Business, Vol. XI--No. 11, Monday, March
       12, 1951, p. 1.

74.   Houghton, Norris, op.cit., p. 383.

Chapter V

Theater Prospectus and Analysis of Some
Interesting Plays Produced in the Fifties
Haven in the Dark by Paul Nord
Aegean Fable by Bill Long
A Double Bill
A Switch in Time by Lola Pergament
I Believe In Rubble by Deric Riegen
Sandhog by Earl Robinson and Waldo Salt
A Time of Storm by Sheldon Stark
Sign of Winter by Ettore Rella

We are always in search of new and exciting theater, a theater of ideas which will stimulate a thinking audience. Only through those playwrights who express and
create a new form of dramatic expression can Off-Broadway be established as the stage of modern thought.

Many of the plays discussed in the preceding chapters
have been published. Some of the unpublished works, however, are the most exciting as drama. Since these plays
are not easily obtainable, it is rewarding to study them
intensively as an insight into the theater of new directions.

Any theatrical organization which wished to present
a program of theater and to stimulate interest in a public
sensitive to new ideas, could present a season of the following unpublished plays. All of these plays which have been
presented Off-Broadway or in community theaters, would be
well worth the producer's and the audience's time and
effort. This Off-Broadway theater of the fifties is courageous and rewarding.

One of the most highly publicized and unusual of

76

these plays was <u>Haven in the Dark</u> by Paul Nord. It provoked full page articles in <u>Show Business.</u> Eddie Dowling
considered the play for Broadway and it was finally produced by the Originals Only group.

The style is both representational and surrealistic,
hovering between the reality of a situation and its illusion
in a manner indicative of the greatest master in this field--
Pirandello.

This is a psychological drama but not a burdensome
analysis. Presented in unusual style, it has a forceful
impact. Always the drama holds ones interest, perhaps in
the constant search for some comprehension of the reality
of the dramatic situation presented. One realizes
that which seems truth at one moment in the drama becomes only illusion, gone before it is fully realized.

The father and the son of the drama are writing a
play. This play within the drama evolves gradually in a
nightmarish fashion into the reality of their lives. Tragic
scenes are played as make believe, but which, abruptly,
are discovered by a technique of derealization to be actually
the enactment of the character's actual life. Which events
constitute the reality of the lives of the characters and
which events constitute the fabric of the play written by
Leo and his father, is the mystery which disturbs the
audience.

<u>Haven in the Dark,</u> a play in two parts by Paul
Nord, with incidental music by Bernard B. Bossick was
produced March 4, 1954, at the Originals Only playhouse.
The author in his prospectus stated:

> What I have tried to do in this play <u>Haven in the Dark</u>
> was to watch both the everyday habits of my characters
> and their moments of sharp, passionate crisis and
> expose them in such a manner as to have them culmi-

"Haven in the Dark" by Paul Nord. This is the 1954 production, l. to r.: Donald Stuart, Mary Stewart, Henry Hood, Eleanor Lee.

nate in a drama.[1]

The characters consist of a father with noticeable restraint in all his moods, whether harsh or tender; the mother who is self-effacing with the actions of a perfect lady, wife and mother; Leo, 25, foreign, who even in repose looks as though fires were smoldering within him; Judy, 20, pretty, childishly rapturous about things, sometimes, and at other times displaying a sophistication under which the very young hide their inability to cope with a situation; and Flo, a streetwalker.

The play begins with the author's voice off-stage in the dark. One of Leo's first lines is:

It so often is! Sometimes, I can't tell which are the real and which the imagined horrors that haunt me.[2]

What has appeared in the beginning to be a quite normal family is revealed to be unrelated as the father and son are a separate family from the second wife and daughter.

In another scene, which also begins with the mysterious voice in the dark, Judy inquires into the philosophy of truth.

Judy: But, mother, you must tell me the truth.
Mother: What truth?
Judy: Who my father was.
Mother: (Brightly) Oh, I'll think of somebody.[3]

Ultimately the mother and daughter are forced to leave. Leo timidly inquires:

Have they gone, Father? Are they out of here for good?
They will not bother us any more. Will they, Father?..
I'll be a fine son to you, Promise. And you will be
proud of me, too. We'll be so happy together. (Attitude of child asking forgiveness)
You'll be reliving your youth all over again with me.

And another thing: I'll try to fall in love with a nice
little girl.......................................
The Voice-Off-Stage interrupts: And this, ladies and
gentleman, was our play.

The spotlight reveals Leo:

Thank you, father, for taking me to the theater tonight.
Father: It's all right, Leo... Let us go home now.
(Father takes Leo by the arm and leads him away. It
is apparent now that Leo is blind. The lights gradually
dim out, fading into a small spot on Leo---and then
darkness). Curtain.[4]

Following the emotional impact of an author of
Nord's capabilities, it is interesting to turn to a light yet
far from negligible play such as Aegean Fable by Bill Long.
It has a delightful set of characters, who would provide an
enjoyable evening in a well staged production. Aegean
Fable is a delightful spoof of our intensely materialistic
world which tends to take itself too seriously. This play
was performed at Originals Only.

The first presentation was approved in that "every
once in a while, his (Long's) writing takes on a brisk and
sophisticated quality" in this drama intended "as a parable
with contemporary significance."[5]

The characters include Aesop, the writer of Fables;
Thales, first philosopher of Western culture; Anaximander,
second philosopher---pupil of Thales; Harmodius, wealthy
landowner of Miletus; delegates from the Ionian league;
Penelope, the ward of Thales; Croesus, emperor of Lydia;
Nautaldes, a pirate captain; and Solon, lawgiver and poet of
Athens.

The time is the first half of the 6th century B.C.
The first scene is delightful comedy and Thales' entrance
establishes him immediately. As he enters he falls into

a well. His comment is typical of his positive individual-
ism:

> I tell you it is far better to walk into an occasional well
> through looking at God's sky then to be forever concern-
> ed with every step you take on earth.[6]

Thales wisdom is sought by the great of the world,
but very seldom taken:

> Are the Oracles out of business?---Must my life be
> interrupted each time there is a crisis in the state?
> Why can I not be left in peace?[7]

Thales wearies of being railed at by his ward,
Penelope, and others as a failure because of his lack of
financial success. His intellectual success has been phenomenal, rivaling those of the soothsayers and oracles of
the time, but is is disregarded as inconsequential.

Deciding to beat the world which marks a path to
his door at their own game he plots to exceed the financial
exploits of Croesus and Cyrus through, as he expresses it-
"a new low." Thereupon Thales proceeds to rent all the
olive presses throughout the Mediterrean on the strength of
his astronomical knowledge, by which he predicts an early
crop. All the presses will be in his hands for the harvest.

His success brings about a redistribution of wealth,
thereby producing peace in Greece and bringing a myraid of
benefits to civilization. A philosopher gainfully employed,
says Mr. Long, could change the direction of our lives.
In an ironic twist, however, Thales as usual changes
everyone's life but his own, and comes off just a shade
worse than it had been at first---both Penelope and her
husband, the ambitious Harmodius, decide to live with
Thales and share his newly wrought fortune. Thales is dis-
mayed by this turn of events. He had wished to be rid of

them both.   He declares.

> Solon, I have proved that a philosopher can make a
> great fortune if he chooses to do so.   I leave it to a
> greater philosopher than I, to figure out why, in the
> name of reason, he should so choose.   (Curtain)[8]

After these two plays as an auspicious beginning, we
should comment on two masterful modern dramas which
whould win real approval from an eclectic audience.   A
Switch In Time by Lola Pergament, a brilliant satire,
coupled with an inspired verse drama by Deric Riegen, I
Believe In Rubble, both of which have won acclaim even
though they remain unpublished.

The author explains A Switch In Time as a "satire
on the international scene...today, particularly timely.   It
was also the first play to use a science fiction framework
for the fantasy."[9]

The New York Times said:

> ...A Switch In Time deals with what happens when two
> occupants of a space ship hovering over Earth decide to
> experiment with human nature...the funniest thing here
> is a series of dramatized letters to the editor of a
> tabloid newspaper.   The highly emotional letters are in
> the true vein of satire.[10]

The play, creates an hypothetical world crisis in-
curred from the relocations simultaneously of Canada and
the U.S.S.R.   It was called an evening of "healthy fun."[11]
Show Business called it the Best Off-Broadway play, playwright, acting and direction of the season.[12]

The play was done at the Greenwich Mews Theater
as part of a program entitled "2 for Fun" directed by Jack
Sydow.   This was a community project sponsored by the
Village Presbyterian Church and the Brotherhood Synagogue.

The opening scene reveals the adored Mona Sona, movie star, and Jack, her love, on a Canadian honeymoon while Zog and Abo, another couple, in a space ship, hover above earth discussing earthy love. Abo decides that:

> I shall offer to the Earthlies a spherical experience in great alternatives. Perhaps then they can come closer to our great Goz concept of simultaneously loving all and being loved by all...[13]

The fun really begins after the switch when comments on the phenomenon such as the following are expressed:

> London---Rumania Reports Canadian on Rumanian-Soviet Border.
> Niagara Falls---Mona's Whereabouts Unknown Police Tell Frantic Film Executives.
> ....
> New York Post---Where's the Soviet Union?[14]
> ....
> Seattle Journal---Where is Canada?[15]
> ....
> NATO is no longer necessary, they say, now that both the U.S. and the U.S.S.R. are west of the Atlantic Ocean and Europe is no longer caught between them.[16]
> ....
> All is well as Moscow plans to buy our citrus fruits and store the world-famous Moscow gold at Fort Knox---brothers under the skin.[17]

The play becomes almost broad farce in reductio ad absurdum style. Finally, hearkening back to the planentary visitors hovering above the turmoil on earth, Abo remarks that:

> The rejected Nation becomes loved---and the loved Nation is rejected.[18]

Finally, just as the nations have resolved the situation, all new alliances are dissolved in the final switch.

> And...Canada Returns to Her North American Sky. (Roll of bass drum) Curtain.[19]

From: "A Switch In Time" by Lola Pergament.

An unnamed source (James N. Clark wearing mask)
whispers Pentagon gossip as newspaper reporters played by
Ellen Holly, Charles Randall and Ruth Volner listen for
rumors in this topical satire which opened May 25, 1955,
at the Greenwich Mews Theater, under producer Lily Turner.

I Believe In Rubble is also concerned with the world situation. Although the characterizations are humorous in their bungling incongruities, the author describes the play as the depiction of "the post-war Western world under the menace of Fascism from one side and Communism from the other."[20]

The work was first performed at the International Student Center, 406 Prospect Street, New Haven, Connecticut, and copyrighted in 1953. It is in verse and the cast includes Zedekiah, the monarch; Jeremiah, the prophet; Baruch, the disciple; Zephaniah, the priest; Chanael, the patriot; and Samgar Nebu, the enemy. The costumes are modern. The setting reflects the light and the shadows of a metropolis at twilight when Jeremiah makes his first appearance.

It might be interesting to note that Jeremiah: 29: 13 says:

And ye shall seek me, and find me, when ye shall search for me with all your heart.

Jeremiah, who has been imprisoned and defiled by his own people, is then asked by the enemy to betray his government to them. Jeremiah speaks the truth of his situation when he states:

I could have been honored with the toasts of flattering mouths if I had stuck to the creamy m's of community. But since the Eternal has called me to utter sounds that tear the old tissues of society's civilization, now my words have become hated as the cough of a festering dog.[21]

The destruction of Egypt and Babylon brings an attitude of nihilism and dejection to the conclusion of the drama---an attitude which mirrors some segments of modern thought.   Jeremiah says:

> ...I have given you my hand.
> But we will be going here:
> In the rubble-corners, in the scorched maze.
> ● ○ ○ ● ● ○ ● ● ● ○ ● ● ● ○ ○ ○ ○ ● ● ● ○ ○ ● ○ ● ● ● ○ ● ● ○ ○ ● ● ● ○ ○ ● ● ○
> Amidst the fragments of our power.
> ●
> We shall go around in poverty,
> in the perfect freedom of the non-possessors, the holy
> service of the rubble-clearers.
> I believe in rubble.
> I believe in chaos.[22]
> ●
> I believe that the God of Israel wants us as chips
> and fragments
> And not as a glossy statue---
> Have you faith?
> Zephaniah!
> I have nothing, I have fear![23]

Only in the midst of chaos, as is admitted even by
the conqueror who is impotent in time of crises and national need, can the man of truth find his place as a leader.
Most men, whichever philosophy they may claim, need,
like the potter in Jeremiah, the dictates of an organized
order, even if it be an alien one in which they lose their
identity.

The play, written in verse and in an allegorical
style, is translated from its biblical context into a modern
philosophical study.   It gives the audience a discomforting
awareness of life.

Since America is composed of many cultural groups,
a play such as Sandhog by Earl Robinson and Waldo Salt,
besides its lyric power, brings better understanding of one
segment of America's population.   This play with its charming love story would be an appropriate fourth entry to a
season of significant plays.

Sandhog was produced at the Phoenix Theater on

Phoenix Theater's Production of Sandhog, 1954

November 23, 1954. The time is the late 1880's during
the excavation of the first Hudson River tunnel. The play
is written in a poetic form. A chorus opens the play:

> Some said they were crazy
> Some said they were brave
> Some said they were digging
> A muddy grave
> A muddy grave
> A muddy grave
> Under the old North River...
> (In the blackout, the sounds of the harbor build into a
> rhythm)[24]

There are some powerful scenes in the drama;
particularly the one in which Johnny, the hero of the story,
saves a boy's life during an emergency in an air lock of
the tunnel. The love story of Katie and Johnny is an
idyllic one. One effective and powerful scene takes place
in the Cavanaugh flat when Katie is expecting her first
child. At this crucial period in Johnny's life, he has been
offered a job as a foreman. Tim, his friend, who is also
offered the job at first, decides to turn it down:

> I'm sore at myself because I want the job and I haven't
> enough lack of character to take it.

Johnny takes the job. He states---I'll make a
damn good foreman, too!"---to which Tim replies, "That's
what I'm afraid of."[25] Tim had fought the landlords in
Mayo. His love for freedom keeps him from imposing his
will upon his fellow men. One of the major themes of the
play is introduced as management pits labor against itself
by choosing foreman from among the workers.

The climax occurs when Johnny risks his own life
preventing Tim's son from being killed. He is accepted
back by his group which had resented his position as a

foreman.

In the ending salute to the Irish brought to America
for the dangerous task of building the Holland tunnel, the
chorus chants:

> The old North River, one mile wide.
> Where the Hudson meets the Atlantic tide
> Over the tunnel the sandhog built
> Through rock and gravel, sand and silt
> Under the old North River...(Slow curtain through
> Chorus)[26]

Another fine production in a season of community
theater would be Sheldon Stark's A Time of Storm with its
insight into the consequences of the loss of love. It was
reviewed as "a new play at Greenwich Mews...an honest
effort at explaining an early American experience with
emotional and unsupported accusation: the seventeenth
century Massachusetts Bay Colony witch trials."[27]

Brooks Atkinson called it "a stern, well-written
play about the witch hunt in Massachusetts in 1693."

> Mr. Stark does not climb up on any soapbox. Even in
> a normal period of American life it could stand on its
> own feet as a work for the stage. But, presumably
> Mr. Stark has been drawn to the theme, as Mr. Miller
> was, by the similarities between the Massachusetts
> witch delirum and the fear, hatred, suspicion and reck-
> less defamation of character common to American life
> today...
> Mr. Stark's general account of the irresponsibility of
> accusations, brought by excitable children, the solemn
> acceptance of guilt as synonymous with the charge and
> the relentless and almost automatic piling of one un-
> founded charge on another, is well done in dramatic
> terms, chiefly because Mr. Stark has portrayed his chief
> characters, both good and bad, with understanding.[28]

In the dramatically powerful third act, Mercy con-
fronts her husband Nathaniel, and asks him to confess to
being a wizard as his stepdaughter Sarah, had accused.

This confession would prevent his being pressed to death by stones and would allow Mercy to retain the property she married him for. Brutally unmerciful, the wife exclaims:

> What is the fact but the truth? Fact is what happened here an hour gone by...fact is what's been said since. You've been cried out for a wizard, that is a fact!
> Nathaniel: And the truth?
> Mercy: The truth is what people make it. If all people believe one way and you another, truth is on their side![29]

Nathaniel will not confess but before meeting his fate he makes his will in favor of his two friends, Cadmus and Melinda, who have stood by him and who love each other. Thereafter, through hatred, the total disintegration of character of the mother and daughter is revealed when Mercy left alone is confronted by Sarah:

> Sarah: I never liked this house. Never!
> Mercy: Be Still. It was a roof. It was ---It was--- all there is or was---I am left with nothing...Be Still! Oh, you imp of Satan, be still! See now what you've done to us. What you---........................
> Sarah: I be not an imp of Satan...I be...(In the taut silence Mercy's head comes partly up, then around. As her eyes meet Sarah's she stiffens in her chair. Then slowly, in horror and fear, she starts to rise in dreadful anticipation.) Curtain[30]

A Time of Storm is a hard hitting dramatic work. Its last act is powerful and the final scene holds the audience in the grip of the horrifying realization of terrors provoked when love is lost among people.

This prospectus for a season of original plays taken from those produced Off-Broadway, is dedicated to furthering a drama which would create a pioneering theater. A devoted audience, willing and eager for extended dramatic horizons, could stimulate an awareness and evoke an interest in the potential of new American drama.

A gripping verse drama to produce would be Sign
of Winter by Ettore Rella with its presentation of problems
in our modern world, including an outspoken statement on
integration. This play is a bold new venture in theater.

It was presented on May 7, 1958, at Theater 74,
with music by David Amram. The setting is in the present,
early in November, in an old, three-story house in Manhattan.

The characters include:

Henrietta Taylor, owner of the house;

Henry Stone, the little old man, who earns his living
by selling "A Look at the Truth of the Stars: Ten Cents--¹'
through his telescope which he sets up on 42nd Street;

Jackson Thorpe, 48, a leading political figure in
the District Club;

Homer Jones, a Negro veteran of the Army, 27,
who is going to college in Manhattan and who supervises
the house in return for a low rental;

Jimmy Taylor, Henrietta's son, who, following his
discharge from the army, has settled into vague but occa-
sionally lucrative political service at Jackson's District
Club;

Flora Taylor, Henrietta's daughter, 25, who works
as a waitress in a small cafe on Columbus Circle, but
has a clear-headed drive toward what she wants;

Wycherly, Jimmie's companion.

The setting includes these areas: Homer Jones's
room, Henrietta Taylor's dining room, Jimmie Taylor's
sitting room, Henry Stone's room, Jackson Thorpe's
sitting-room and also a portion of the entrance hall with
the double door leading to the street.

In this drama the speech and conversation of every-
day life is translated into poetic expression. It is easier
to accept verse in an historic setting than in a modern one.
The introduction brings into focus an unusual subject per-
tinent to the plot---stars and the horoscope.

The life of the major character, the landlady, is
related symbolically to the house which is represented as
a living force. Henrietta states in the first act in speaking
to Jackson:

> I'd die for this house---do you hear? I am this house.
> I could bring in these walls like the feathers of a bird,
> a big, black bird,
> and smother you in your sleep!
> Why don't I do it? I should do it.[31]

The poetic form of drama projects the universal
thoughts of mankind which allows the playwright to commu-
icate to his audience a greater dramatic experience than
with the prose form of realistic drama.

In Sign of Winter, Jackson, Henrietta's former lover,
took her money, her youth and her hope and is now intent
upon taking her daughter, Flora. He has managed to get
his grip on Jimmy, Henrietta's son, supposedly to teach
him politics but instead teaching him how to cheat, the
rackets, and how to outwit the police.

Henrietta, knowing that the events of her life have
led her to an inescapable fate, tries to prevent her life
from touching her daughter.

Jackson is the more insidiously characterized in
that he as a printer is capable of being independent, but
rather chooses deceit and subterfuge, the preying on the
lifeblood of the Taylor family, for his existence in the
world.

The Negro, Homer Jones', conception of life is well defined in his incertitude as to his independence and rightful claim to live in a world of white supremacy. Homer states:

> Everybody with black skin is looking for himself.
> ●
> walking through the college library,
> heading for a reference book,
> I'll bet he looks like a fugitive!
> the escape, the search, they're inseparable---
> his eye on his new self,
> his ear on the sound of the dogs---
> maybe, just maybe,
> he will escape and find himself safe.[32]

Homer Jones becomes the vengeful figure of John Troy, the son of Oliver Troy, who was hanged in the South because Jackson opened his prison and let the mob enter to lynch him. John Troy finds his prey in the haunted skeleton of Henrietta's house.

Complications develop when Jimmie, the son, becomes involved in the murder of a man while carrying out Jackson's orders. Jackson tries to involve the others in the murder in order to escape. Henry, the star-gazing boarder with amnesia, warns Henrietta against the impending disaster to her children:

> You're a mother, Mrs. Taylor---first of all you're a mother---look for your children---always look for your children---they keep the noise going, generation to generation---otherwise it's god-awful quiet![33]

Flora is in love with John Troy; a love with a purpose which she chooses in preference to a love for acquisition as advised by her mother and as offered to her by Jackson and another suitor.

Henrietta, in order to save Flora and to save the

house which is the concrete symbol of her life, kills Jackson and then herself.   Flora upon seeing the tragic death of her mother states:

> This is her dream---this house---
> Thank you, mother---thank you, ---for the house.
> ○○○●●●
> She's watching everything we do---
> She wants us to hurry and be happy---
> and I think it will take some time.[34]

Brooks Atkinson stated that Sign of Winter was..."a strange, hypnotic drama..."

..."it is not the story of "Sign of Winter that makes it engrossing. It is the style and the mood."

> But Mr. Rella sees them (the characters) as figures of fate, under the control of the planetary configurations in the nights of November and marked down for destruction...the inscrutable mind of the universe orders their fate according to its own inscrutable methods.
> "Sign of Winter" is a little remote like something seen from a distance.[35]

Sign of Winter dramatizes some universal human exigencies in this critical period of mankind's history.

Haven in the Dark, Aegean Fable, A Switch in Time, I Believe in Rubble, Sandhog, A Time of Storm and Sign of Winter comprise a vital program of drama which offers an audience a highly provocative theater. These dramas would provide a season of playgoing which would not be easily forgotten.

Notes

1.   Nord, Paul, MSS. "Haven in the Dark," in Theater Collection, New York Public Library.

2.   Nord, Paul, op. cit., Part 1, p. 7.

3.   Ibid., Part II, p. 26.

4.   Ibid., Part II, p. 30.

5.   Stern, Harold, "Reviews," May 28, 1951, (Vol. XI---
     No. 22), p. 7.

6.   Long, Bill, MSS. "Aegean Fable," Copyright 1949,
     in Theater Collection, New York Public Library,
     1-1-4.

7.   Ibid., 1-1-7.

8.   Ibid., 3-2-12.

9.   Pergament, Lola, in letter to Julia Price, 6/13/59.

10. Program, N.Y. Times, sent by Lola Pergament,
     6/13/59.

11. National Guardian, op. cit.

12. Ibid.,

13. Pergament, Lola, MSS. "A Switch In Time, from
     author, 45 Perry St., N. Y. 14, N. Y. p. 3.

14. Ibid., p. 7.

15. Ibid., p. 8.

16. Ibid., p. 9.

17. Ibid., p. 18.

18. Ibid., p. 26.

19. Ibid., p. 27.

20. Riegen, Deric, letter from; Pleasant Valley, New
     York, 6/12/59.

21. Riegen, Deric, MSS. I Believe In Rubble, from
     author, RD 2, Pine Bush; New York, p. 26.

22. Ibid., p. 39.

23. Ibid., p. 40.

24.   Robinson, Earl and Waldo Salt, MSS, Sandhog, in
       Theater Collection, New York Public Library, Act I,
       Sc. 1, p. 1.

25.   Ibid., Act II, Sc. 2, p. 10.

26.   Ibid., Act III, Sc. 6, p. 24.

27.   Show Business, Monday, March 1, 1954, (Vol. XIV--
       No. 9), p. 8.

28.   Atkinson, Brooks, "At the Theater, The New York
       Times, Fri., February 26, 1954; from Daniel Holly-
       wood Associates, 101 W. 55th St., NYC, 6/13/59.

29.   Stark, Sheldon, MSS. "A Time of Storm," from
       Daniel Hollywood Associates, 101 West 55th St.,
       NYC, 6/13/59, Act III, p. 7.

30.   Ibid., Act III, p. 24.

31.   Rella, Ettore, Sign of Winter, MSS, p. 16.

32.   Ibid., p. 54.

33.   Ibid., p. 86.

34.   Ibid., pp. 98 & 99.

35.   Atkinson, Brooks, "Theater: Drama in Verse," The
       New York Times, Thursday, May 8, 1958.

Chapter VI

Production Trends, 1950-1960
The Phoenix Operation
Circle-in-the-Square
Cherry Lane Theater

Impetus for the new play Off-Broadway
Producing units formed to produce the new
play
Abbey Theater
Dramatist Workshop
New Playwrights
Originals Only
The Cricket Theater
Living Theater
Drama Desk
New Dramatist's Committee

The Present Repertory Stage Off-Broadway

Off-Broadway since 1950 has been mainly revival
theater, which introduced important foreign playwrights such
as O'Casey or Anouilh and previously successful Broadway
productions. Off-Broadway scripts are usually less slick
and more experimental than those successful on Broadway.
Broadway playwrights will do scripts Off-Broadway only if
they feel they are compelled to do so.[1] The reason may
be a financial or an artistic one.

It is startling to note that 40% of the plays being
done Off-Broadway in 1950 were tryouts of new scripts
(2 out of every 5) and there were 300 groups of various
categories on record. There would be occasions when as
many as 60 to 75 Off-Broadway shows would open in a
single week[2] of which 24 could be estimated to be new plays.

97

Twenty-four new plays in a week seems a fantastic ratio and hearkens back to the days of the Broadway shoestring producers.

Among the Off-Broadway major producing organizations since 1950 is the well-known Phoenix theater. It was founded by the producing team of Norris Houghton and T. Edward Hambleton who were "weary of the economic stalemate of Broadway." They founded a "popular priced theater" Off-Broadway where "unusual plays can be done out of enthusiasm for the theater as an art and where professional actors can adventure off the beaten track."[3] There was to be a different director for each of five plays given each season. The theater was modeled after the London suburban house, the Lyric Hammersmith.[4] This arrangement has been altered somewhat since.

The Phoenix opened in the 1953-1954 season and used the "Broadway practice of financing shows via limited partnership." The first year of the organization's operations involved a $125,000. investment and with the stake raised in 1955, the figure was brought to $184,375.[5]

The first production was Madame, Will You Walk? by Sidney Howard. Sing Me No Lullaby, Sandhog, The Golden Apple and Coriolanus were also given the first year. Three new plays were presented in this perhaps most successful of Off-Broadway houses which vies with the Broadway theater by employing the talents of well-known theatrical personalities in its casts. Being Off the geographical limits of Broadway makes possible productions on a smaller budget.[6] Other Off-Broadway producers have adopted the same methods.

The producing unit which best exemplifies the Off-Broadway scene today is the now famous Circle-in-the-

9629

Square. It was begun as the Loft Players, and the first
production was Dark of the Moon, which won critical
praise and four Off-Broadway awards in 1950.[7] It was presented by the "fortuitious"[8] director of the group, José
Quintero. The second production, Amata, an original light
fantasy, lost heavily.

At this time everyone working at Circle-in-the-
Square was getting $15.00 a week. The group continued,
however, and did Antigone by Anouilh and The Heiress by
Goetz under Quintero's direction.[9] Two plays which had
been unsuccessful on Broadway were given next, The Enchanted by Jean Giradoux[10] and John Steinbeck's Burning
Bright.[11]

Circle-in-the-Square maintained its financial stabil-
ity by such expedients as a weekend children's theater,
concerts on Sunday and Monday nights, and a midnight
chamber of horrors on Friday and Saturday.

The theater hit its stride with Summer and Smoke
by Tennessee Williams, a Broadway mistake. The comments on the show mentioned that "there are facets of the
play revealed in this run which no one would have guessed
from the original production..."[12] and it created a new
star---Geraldine Page. It ran for 357 performances.[13]

Another play in 1953 staged more "appealingly than
when it was done on Broadway..." was Truman Capote's
The Grass Harp.[14] Other productions have included La
Ronde,[15] adapted from Schnitzler; Cradle Song[16] by the
Sierras and the very successful The Iceman Cometh by
O'Neill which introduced Jason Robard, Jr. to an enthusi-
astic public.[17]

For the first time in November, 1951, Theater Arts
accepted Off-Broadway theater, acknowledging it in a

separate section.

In 1953, Off-Broadway theaters began paying off as critics gave their approval. Some of the 125 Off-Broadway theater groups were getting better reviews than many Broadway shows of the same season. An original show, The World put on by Rachel Productions with a cast of 12 at union scale salaries, played to full houses and returned to its backers their full $19,500. investment.[18]

The Off-Broadway Proscenium Productions, housed in the revered old Cherry Lane Theater, were exceptionally successful in 1954-1955. This was the first Off-Broadway group to win the Antoinette Perry Award. Among their successful productions was Congreve's The Way of the World, Thieve's Carnival by Anouilh, and Morning's at Seven by Paul Osborn.[19] Such bill, consisting of foreign and American revivals, is typical of Off-Broadway.

The audience, too, grew larger in 1954 as "ordinary theater-goers began to attend these shows that have in the past appealed primarily to college students and show people."[20]

Some producing organizations of this time advocated the use of original plays by American playwrights. Miss Helburn in a speech at the Hotel Statler in January, 1954, felt "young writers should get Off-Broadway tryouts as well as college experiments with untried writers. Citing A Trip to Bountiful, she thought future top dramatists might come from TV."[21] Several Off-Broadway writers like Tad Mosel and Ken Parker have been successful in TV. Television has proved a welcome field of opportunity for the writer.

As of 1947, many Off-Broadway groups were established primarily to encourage the playwright. The Abbe Workshop, an experimental stage at the Master Institute,

listed among its objectives "the presentation of efforts by
playwrights for whom professional outlets are not available."
Offering The Edge of the Sword by George Bellak in 1949,
the Workshop won the Dubose Heyward Award of the Carolina Art Association and "did a service for experimental
theater-goers as well as for Mr. Bellak."[22]

Since 1950 Erwin Piscator's Dramatic Workshop has
proved a noteworthy theatrical venture.   Dramatic Workshop
held a seminar for new playwrights with presentations given
on Saturday evenings.   It might be argued that workshops
are not truly Off-Broadway.   Nevertheless, the workshop
presentation of Wedding in Japan by Ted Pollack on November 15, 1949, and considered by a reviewer to have "the
potential for sizeable popular and commercial success."[23]

On February 16, 1950, Anthony Palma's new play,
There Is No End, was presented at the President Theater
by Piscator's Workshop.   It was described as "skillfully
interpreting a drama of American soldiers interned in a
German prisoner-of-war camp that proves at once touching,
sensitive and horrifying."[24]

"New Playwrights," formed in 1950, was established
in order to present new ideas.   The group produced Herb
Tank's Longitude 49 in August of 1950.   It was controlled
by authors rather than actors and designed to "concentrate
on producing a series of new plays instead of finding vehi-
cles for an assemblage of acting talent."   The aim was for
"social content "[25] in scripts.

The Playwright's Educational Theater operating in
1950 was also intended to develop and encourage new playwrights.   One of their plays, presented on November 6,
1950, was Hope Deferred by Abraham Mandelstran, which
"concerned the efforts of a country nurse to establish a

community health center in her home town but who in so
doing was also forced to face the issue whether good inten-
tions justify the means used to obtain the desired re-
sults."[26]

A very interesting article in the July 13, 1953,
Show Business stated that Off-Broadway producers were
beginning to realize that only new plays will bring reviewers and agents to their productions.

This did not seem to effect the Off-Broadway production picture. Only a half dozen new plays were being
readied for fall production in 1953 and there were fewer
new plays Off-Broadway every year.[27] Of course, as there
is a scarcity of good scripts even for the Broadway producers,[28] so it is not surprising under present production
standards that new scripts are scarce Off-Broadway.

In 1955, a writer's group presented a program
called Three by Two at the Malin Studios, one of the most
economical houses in New York. Two plays by an Augusto
Boal, The Horse and the Saint and The House Across the
Street showed promise. His ideas were unusual but lack
proper development. Howard Abramowitz's Old Man, another play on the bill, was considered better written.[29]

The groups which were established for the writer
presented a variety of interesting and stimulating plays.
However, of the many producing units, one group was founded exclusively with the playwright in mind, existing solely
to encourage and to test new dramas---Originals Only. New
plays were to be read in front of members (50) and if the
consensus was favorable, a "workshop" production was
arranged. One of the plays presented by Originals Only,
Haven in the Dark by Paul Nord (see p.   ), was on
Eddie Dowling's schedule for Broadway production in 1950.

A group patterned after Originals Only was being formed at Black Mountain College and two more were being formed in other parts of the country.[30]

The initial entry of Originals Only was Dream House, a psychological study of a paralyzed war veteran and his immediate family, but it lacked the emotional impact "to give it a fighting chance on Broadway..."[31]

The Warrior's Return by Jules Koslow, presented in November of 1950, enjoyed some success. It dealt with an emasculated G.I. who attempts to satisfy his wife's natural physical desires by arranging an affair between her and his best friend.[32]

Other productions included Aegean Fable by Bill Long and Bed of Neuroses by Gordon White. The latter was below par. Bundle from Heaven by Deborah Frankel, and Gordon Reilley by Charles Best. Gordon Reilley concerned the growth of juvenile delinquency. Voluntary contributions from patrons support Originals Only.[33]

Another of the theaters dedicated to the discovery and nurturing of new playwrights opened in 1957. It was in a converted gymnasium in New York's lower Second Avenue and called The Cricket Theater. Its intention was to revitalize the Off-Broadway scene. The crusaders were Rhett Cone and Joe O'Brien, and their motto appears to be "the playwright's the thing."

Among Rhett Cone's discoveries was Meade Roberts who has written for TV and the films since his debut at The Cricket with Palm Tree in a Rose Garden.

Miss Cone also has a series on Monday nights called "Theater for the Connoisseur" which presents one playwright a month in productions managed by new actors and directors.

When asked how far she nurtures the new playwright, Miss Cone smiled broadly and said, "We do as
much as we can...We pay them."[34]

One of the oldest of the Off-Broadway companies in
New York City, The Living Theater, is considered one of
the pioneers of the Off-Broadway movement. It was con-
ceived by Judith Malina and Julian Beck in 1946 and first
incorporated in 1947. Miss Malina does not think the
Living Theater should be classified as Off-Broadway but
rather as poetic theater.

The Living Theater wants "a theater free enough so
that one can at least search for truth; we want the playwrights who make the theater a mirror of the world."[35]

Paul Goodman, who leads the vanguard of American
playwrights, examined the problems which beset youth in
its search for ultimate wisdom in The Young Disciple, a
Living Theater production. The Young Disciple was a re-
telling of the Gospel of St. Mark.[36] His Faustina was also
presented in 1952.[37] Living Theater has produced many
new works by leading avant-garde playwrights.

Drama Desk, the New York theater editor's and
reporter's organization, voted at its December meeting in
1955 to sponsor a Vernon Rice Memorial Award, in memory
of the critic who did so much to further Off-Broadway.
The award was for outstanding talent among producers,
writers, directors and actors in Off-Broadway theater.[38]

Some of the Off-Broadway playwrights are members
of an organization to provide the young playwright with a
forum and the opportunity to practice his art. This organization is the New Dramatist's Committee formed in 1948.

Michaela O'Harra instituted the idea to present such

an opportunity to a few select fledgling or already known
young playwrights. She, herself, had experienced the trials
of the young playwright. She knew the humiliation of re-
jection of script and author by the very world which ironi-
cally enough needs above all drama with a fresh approach.

The New Dramatist's Committee was formulated upon
a Five-Point Plan established by Miss O'Harra. The points
were:

Free tickets to Broadway productions, run-throughs,
dress rehearsals; craft discussions; productions observance;
sounding panels and rehearsed readings by Equity actors
working under a professional director. To this program
has been added lectures by prominent theater people.

The organization began functioning atop the Hudson
Theater, quarters obtained by Mr. Howard Lindsay, well
known Broadway playwright. The New Dramatist's Committee may now be found at the City Center Building on
West 56th Street.

Some of the New Dramatist's who have been presented Off-Broadway are Theodore Apstein, Robert Guy Barrows,
Walt Anderson and Charles Best. The organization began
with no more than 20 talented playwrights all under forty
but now has a nucleus of 30 to 35.[39]

New plays are lacking in our theaters compared with
earlier American theater. Mr. Harold Clurman, who was
one of the guiding lights of the Group theater,[40] felt there
was more theater in 1923 outside as well as in New York.
Almost "every producer, actor, designer, writer of whom
we have a right to be proud began his career or came into
his own in the earlier period...experimental theater flourished."[41]

As far back as 1950 Nicholas Biel, a playwright,

stated that "we in show business have reached our economic
nadir and we are searching desperately for a means whereby
we can survive...We must build a theater tradition in A-
merica whose roots go way below the carriage-trade level
down to the great mass of our people."[42]

Off-Broadway presents many classics of which we
would be deprived if we depended on Broadway for their
production. Broadway theater cannot afford a revival type
theater within its exorbitant economic framework. Off-
Broadway is an interesting theater for revivals but it has
not developed, unfortunately, into a theater dedicated to
original dramatists.

The American audience may see live dramatic presentations of Strindberg, Pirandello, Lorca and Genet Off-
Broadway. Otherwise this drama, with the exception of
college theater productions would be seen rarely if at all by
the American public. Dramas of established merit such as
Congreve's The Way of the World and Chekhov's Uncle
Vanya receive unique productions Off-Broadway.

Today, Off-Broadway is indispensable to our theater
in its development of talent. It may not be as significantly
expressive of our national culture and artistic ideas as the
Off-Broadway theater of the 1920's and the 1930's was.

In its evolution Off-Broadway theater has gone
through distinct phases of development. The beginnings can
be attributed to the idealism and experimental freedom of
the Provincetown group in its pre-Broadway days.

The next Off-Broadway movement of the 1930's drew
vitality from its strong social emphasis. The Group theater at the height of its activities channeled its creative
fervor into Off-Broadway through the work of many of its
members. Some groups presented works of social protest,

directed many times by people who had never before engaged in a dramatic production.

The second World War disrupted the Off-Broadway
scene and there is little record of activity until the "renaissance" of 1947.   Then there was great activity with
many original plays being presented.   A formula was being
established, also: a formula which depended heavily upon the
box office.

The present Off-Broadway stage, which has developed from the renaissance after the second World War, may
arbitrarily be set as beginning in 1952.   It was signalized
by the cycle of revivals of famous dramatists by some
groups, such as the Circle-in-the-Square and the Fourth
St. Theater.   Off-Broadway was envisioned as the place to
present European playwrights, who, otherwise, would never
be seen on the American stage.   The revival of plays
commercially unsuccessful on Broadway was added to the
Off-Broadway program.

These are the developments which ushered in the
present Off-Broadway "Library stage."[43]   In the future we
may hope for the needed continuing development of a strong
dramatist's stage.

Notes

1.   Hutto, Ted, Interview 6/7/59, William Morris Agen-
        cy, 1740 Broadway, New York City.

2.   "Off-B'wy Groups Thriving, Training 1000's of
        Actors, Directors, Technicians Yearly," Actors Cues
        Show Business, Monday, March 6, 1950, (Vol. X---
        No. 10), p. 1.

3.   Atkinson, Brooks J., "Phoenix Rises," N.Y. Times,
        Dec. 20, 1953, Stage: U.S.: N.Y.: Off-Broadway
        Clippings, through 1954; in Theater Collection, New
        York Public Library.

4.   Jacobson, Sol---Press Representative, Theater
      Press Release, in Stage: U.S.: N.Y.: Off-Broad-
      way Clippings, through 1954; op.cit.

5.   "Off-Broadway Production's New Big---Coin Status
      10G to 184G in Stakes, Variety, 1955, Off-Broadway
      Clippings, through 1954, op. cit.

6.   Hambleton, Edward T., and Norris Houghton,
      "Phoenix on the Wing," Theater Arts, November
      1954, p. 94.

7.   Atkinson, Brooks, N.Y. Times, 1955, Off-Broadway
      Clippings, through 1956, Personal file of theater
      clippings.

8.   Morton, Frederick, "Quintero the Fortuitous,"
      Drama Section, Sunday N.Y. Times, 1955, Personal
      collection of theater clippings.

9.   Shaeffer, Louis, "Curtain Times," Brooklyn Eagle,
      Tuesday, November 6, 1951, Off-Broadway Clippings,
      through 1954; op. cit., New York Public Library.

10.   Rice, Vernon, "Loft Players 'Enchanted' at the
      Circle in the Square," N.Y. Post, June 11, 1951,
      Off-Broadway Clippings, through 1954; op. cit.

11.   Shaeffer, Louis, "Curtain Times,"' "Burning Bright"
      Helps Make Things Hum at Circle in Square,' Brook-
      lyn Eagle, Tuesday, November 6, 1951; in Off-Broad-
      way Clippings, through 1954; op. cit.

12.   Hawkins, William "Tennessee's Play a Hit in Village,"
      N.Y. World-Telegram & Sun, Wednesday, May 7,
      1952; in Off-Broadway Clippings, through 1954;
      op. cit.

13.   Kronenberger, Louis, editor; "Off-Broadway," The
      Burns Mantle Yearbook, The Best Plays of 1953-
      1954; (Published by Dodd, Mead and Company, New
      York, 1957), p. 356.

14.   "Truman Capote's 'Grass Harp,' Presented by Circle-
      in-the-Square---Quintero Directs," N.Y. Times,
      April 28, 1953; in "Off-Broadway Clippings, through
      1954;" op. cit.

15. "Off-Broadway," Cue, July 14-July 23, 1955; Per-
     sonal collection of theater clippings.

16. "Art (And Profits?) Off-Broadway," The New York
     Times Magazine, February 12, 1953, p. 29.

17. Atkinson, Brooks, "Theater: O'Neill Tragedy Re-
     vived," The New York Times, Thursday, May 10,
     1953, in Personal collection of theater clippings.

18. "Off-B'way Theater Paying Off As Critics Give Their
     Approval," Show Business, Monday, November 2,
     1953, (Vol. XIII---No. 44), p. 1.

19. "Young in the Theater," Vogue, August 1, 1955; in
     Personal collection of theater clippings.

20. "Off-Broadway Finally Recognized by Critics; Draw-
     ing Lge New Audiences," Show Business, Monday,
     February 8, 1954, (Vol. XIV---No. 6), p. 1.

21. Stewart, Robert J. "Arthur Miller Urges College
     Theaters To Take Risks; Use Untried Scripts," Show
     Business, Monday, Jan. 4, 1954; (Vol. XIV---No. 1),
     p. 1.

22. "The Theater, 'The Edge of the Sword'," N.Y.
     Times, November 10, 1949; in "Off-Broadway Clip-
     pings, through 1954; op. cit.

23. Hawkins, William, "Wedding in July," New York
     World Telegram, Nov. 16, 1949; in "Off-Broadway
     Clippings, through 1954; op. cit.

24. Rice, Vernon, "Curtain Cues," Feb. 17, 1950; "Off-
     Broadway Clippings, through 1954; op. cit.

25. Actors Cues Show Business, Monday, August 28,
     1950, (Vol. X---No. 34), p. 2.

26. Stern, Harold, "Reviews," Actors Cues Show Busi-
     ness, Monday, Nov. 6, 1950, (Vol. X---No. 45),
     p. 5.

27. Show Business, July 13, 1953; (Vol. XIII---No. 28),
     p. 1.

28.   "Scarcity of Good Dramas Stumping B'way Produc-
      ers," Show Business, Monday, March 12, 1951,
      (Vol. XI---No. 11), p. 1.

29.   "Writer's Group (P.P.)," Off and On Broadway,
      (publ. New York City, June 25-July 9, 1955), p. 5.

30.   Shipley, Joseph T., "On Stage," The New Leader,
      Sept. 30, 1950; "Off-Broadway Clippings, through
      1954;" op. cit.

31.   "Dream House," Variety, November 23, 1949; "Off-
      Broadway Clippings, through 1954;" op. cit.

32.   Pihodna, Joe, N.Y. Herald Tribune, November 21,
      1950; "Off-Broadway Clippings, through 1954; op.cit.

33.   "Gordon Reilley' Opens at Originals Only Playhouse
      Under the Direction of Tom Hill," N.Y. Times,
      Nov. 26, 1952; in "Off-Broadway Clippings, through
      1954;" op. cit.

34.   "On Off-Broadway, The Playwright's the Thing at the
      Cricket Theater," The Theater, March, 1959,
      p. 20-40.

35.   "A History of the Living Theater," MS. from James
      Spicer, Living Theater Public Relations representa-
      tive, 6/18/59, 530 Sixth Ave., New York City.

36.   Ibid., p. 6.

37.   Ibid., p. 3.

38.   Magazine 8:40, May 24, 1955; in personal collection
      of theater clippings.

39.   Keating, John, "A Bridge for Young Playwrights,"
      Theater Arts, Vol. XLIV, No. 7; July, 1960; p.17.

40.   Clurman, Harold, The Fervent Years, Alfred A.
      Knopf, New York, 1945.

41.   Clurman, Harold, "Forward and Backward in the
      Theater," 1954, "Off-Broadway Clippings, through
      1954;" op. cit.

42.   Biel, Nicholas, "A Playwright's Solution to the Ills
      of Our Theater," Actors Cues Show Business, Tues-
      day, Jan. 31, 1950, p. 37.

43.   Sylvester, Robert "Dream Street, The Living Thea-
      ter...," Daily News, Tuesday, February 10, 1959,
      p. 48.

Chapter VII

Financial Aspects of the Off-Broadway Theater
    The Actor
    The Scene Designer
    The Stage Hands Union
    The House
    Off-Broadway's Approach to the Producing Problem
        Theater League---1949
        Theater League---1955
    The Financial Situation and the American Play-
        wright in the Off-Broadway Scene
    Off-Broadway and the Producer
    Financial Outline for 1960

Off-Broadway scene is confronted by unpromising

financial considerations. The years 1950-1960 have evoked

a tremendous change in its financial aspects. It has

brought a drastic change in the type of people who partici-

pate and in the type of drama which can be produced. When

a play can be produced for $150.00, there is little hesita-

tion about putting on a new, aspiring writer's work. How-

ever, when the cost is $8,000. to $12,000. the producer

is inclined to be more cautious---that is, cautious in re-

gard to known audience appeal. If an author has received

a large and enthusiastic audience in Europe, the producer

is more apt to feel that the work will stand up under criti-

cism.

For the same reason a producer will choose a re-

vival which he knows will be popular with American audi-

ences or even an uncussessful Broadway show which may

succeed with different production. Summer and Smoke,

although it received an elaborate production on Broadway,

112

failed because it needed exactly the type of setting ultimately given it by Circle-in-the-Square.

Harold Clurman stated in The New York Times
that "the economics of Broadway, and the audience psy-
chology that goes with it, imposes severe limitations on the
channels of expression open to the Broadway producer."[1]
One of the great difficulties confronting the unusual production Off-Broadway and a major reason for the lack of
experimental theater, is economic; the problem of rising
costs.

To gain a perspective of the economic situation
one needs first to take a look at Equity. At first, Equity
would not allow its members to work Off-Broadway. Since
1949 Equity has allowed its members to do so, a policy
that has caused a professional level of production which Off-
Broadway rarely attained before the ruling. Many amateurs
have lost valuable experience as a result, but Equity has
been very considerate in its demands upon the producers.

An agreement with Off-Broadway was worked out in
September, 1949, which was an adaptation of the "contract
which has been used successfully in the Los Angeles area
for the past ten years."

> This contract permits professional members of any
> branch of the Four A's (Actor's Equity Association
> divisions) up to and including 49% of the cast, to work
> with non-members. Non-members must, however,
> obtain Work Permits from Actor's Equity Association.[3]

No actual pay scale had been determined at that
time, but on December 6, 1950, a meeting of the Council
of Actors' Equity Association extended the contract until
March 31, 1950.[4]

The usual Off-Broadway Equity rate as of January 4,
was $25.00 a week. However, under this contract the

producer is confronted with other considerations. Under the
Equity contract, concessions are made according to the
gross house. For example, if it is under $1,000., 3
Equity actors are required; $1,000-$2,500., 5 Equity people are required and between $2,500-$4,500., 7 Equity
members are required.[5]

As of September 1, 1954, the minimum salary on
Off-Broadway contracts under Equity negotiation was $30.00
per week, with rehearsal expense money at $5.00 per
week.[6]

Equity progressively raised its scale, so that by
1957 the following had been adopted;

> Dramatic Companies: For any week the weekly Box
> Office gross, less taxes, is:
> Under $3,000., the weekly compensation shall be no
> less than: $40.00
> Over $4,500., the weekly compensation shall be no
> less than: $75.00
> The rehearsal pay will be at the rate of $15.00 per
> week.

The contract proved to be a little more liberal for
musicals. "Over $6,500. the weekly compensation shall be
no less than: $75.00."[7]

Even the Phoenix Theater, which is unusual in that
it is subsidized by a regular membership, paid Robert
Ryan $100.00 a week in 1954 when he played the lead in
Coriolanus. When the production moved to Broadway Ryan
received $15,000.[8]

Most actors could barely get by on $40.00 a week.
Alfred Drake, acting in Tis Pity She's A Whore, by John
Ford, Off-Broadway in 1959, was threatened with eviction
from his apartment for not paying the rent. His $40.00
earnings were not adequate to cover his most meager

needs.[9]

Rising costs Off-Broadway certainly brought surprising innovations, one of which occurred in 1954 when Claude Dauphin was paid up to $700. a week for performing in Clerambard, by Aymé. His salary was the highest ever paid an actor appearing Off-Broadway.[10]

Actor's Equity changed its salary rulings again September 1, 1959. The weekly compensation for dramatic companies was as follows for any week the weekly box office gross, less taxes was:

> Under $3,000, weekly compensation shall be no less than: $45.00
> Between $4,500-$5,500, weekly compensation shall be no less than: $75.00
> Between $5,500-$8,000, weekly compensation shall be no less than: $30.00
> Over $8,000, the standard production minimum salaries shall apply.

For Musical companies the salary scale was:

> Under $4,000, weekly compensation shall be no less than: $45.00
> Between $7,000-$9,000, weekly compensation shall be no less than: $80.00
> Over $9,000, the standard production minimum salaries shall apply.
> Rehearsal pay shall be at the rate of $20.00 per week.[11]

The rates are slowly rising but still hardly a living wage for the devoted actors who appear Off-Broadway.

As of 1953, the director under the usual budget received about 5% of the profits. This is a purely nominal amount if the gross is meager.[12]

Noel Behn, producer of the Cherry Lane Theater, stated that as of 1961, there is no standard method of paying a director.

Most usually a director is given a flat fee of from
$150.00 to $500.00, with $250.00 being the average.
This covers all of his work which included re-writes,
casting and rehearsal period.

Once the show is opened he is given a flat fee of
$25.00 to $50.00, or 1% of the gross, which would
still come out to $25.00 or $50.00. For the director,
more than any one else with the exception of the playwright, Off-Broadway is his best possible showcase;
therefore, he is willing to work for a minimal amount.

As Behn emphasized, the producer is not trying to
get a "deal" on a director. The economics of production
simply work out this way.

In a study of the growing costs, we must consider
the ever increased demands of production as significant
factors in the changing trend toward a more commercialized
theater Off-Broadway.

A paradoxical aspect of this scene is that without the
recognition of Equity and the other unions, as Fred Cotton
of Actor's Equity noted, the reviewers will not attend.[13]
If Off-Broadway shows are not publicized in newspaper
reviews, they cannot hope to break even at the box office.
Conversely, to get experienced Equity people to participate,
an assured vehicle is necessary.

Contracts must be negotiated with the United Scenic
Artists and the Costume Designers. Their scale in 1959,
was a progressive one which, for the scenic artist, ranged
from a minimum bond of $157.43 for a house seating 200
or less, the minimum rate for three days at $40.81 per
day, to a $239.00 bond for a house seating 299 or more
than 250 with the minimum rate for 5 days at $40.81 a day.
In addition the contract required that a costume designer
had to be employed for not less than one day at the rate of

$35.00 per day.[14]

Arthur Romano of the scenic artists' league stated
said scenic artists were only paid once-or sometimes not
at all-no matter how long the extended run of a show.[15]

The scenic artists' contract was subsequently changed.
Since 1960, the United Scenic Artists' Off-Broadway contract requires a minimum of 5 days employment at $40.81
per day with a rider attached to the agreement in that for
a house seating 299 or more than 250, the manager shall
pay the designer after the fifth week and beginning with the
sixth week of the run of the production, $40.81 per week
thereafter. The minimum bond to be posted with the union
was $204.05.

For a house seating 250 or more than 200, the
minimum rate is four days at $40.81 per day and beginning
with the sixth week of the run of the production, the manager shall pay the designer $32.64 per week thereafter. The
minimum bond is $163.24.

For a house seating 200 or less, the minimum rate
is three days at $40.81 per day and beginning with the
sixth week of the run, the manager shall pay the Designer
$24.48 per week thereafter. In this case the minimum
bond is $122.43.

The costume designer still receives $35.00 per day.
A bond of at least $35.00 must be deposited for him.[16]

Today, Off-Broadway employs commercial methods.
In 1950 one could see the beginning of the trend toward
higher production costs and the change as box office profits
began to matter.

ATPAM the press agent's union first changed its
work rule for Off-Broadway in July of 1950. It was then
announced that apprentices could handle Off-Broadway

productions only if a union member supervised the apprentice.
Off-Broadway groups formerly unable to pay union members'
fees could now hire an apprentice at $25.00 a week minimum.[17]

Off-Broadway now depends on advertising to attract its
audience. Milton Weintraub of ATPAM has explained its
relationship to the Off-Broadway show. ATPAM has a standard rate. If the audience ranges from 150-200, the ATPAM
manager gets $125.00 per week while the press agent receives
$144.40. If the seating is over 200 the manager will
receive $165.40 per week and the press agent $137.80.
The press agent must be hired one week prior to the Monday of the week of the first public performance, not including preview performances.

A treasurer must be hired who will work eight hours a
day on a six day basis at $130.00 a week, one week prior to
Monday of the week of the first public performance, not including preview performances. This ruling applies to the house
manager, too.[18]

Stage hands must be paid $16.06 a day or $156.77 in
a week.[19] The number of stage hands is scaled according
to the house and also according to individual contracts
negotiated with the producer. Usually, for a house of 125
seats or less, union labor is not required; with a seating
capacity from 125 to 200 the union scale calls for one stage
hand; while anything over 200 seating capacity calls for a
minimum of 2 stage hands. In a case of unusual house
construction, such as the York Theater and the Orpheum
Theater on Second Avenue, three stage hands are required
because of such features as a lighting board at the back of
the house. If the house has less than 200 seats the contract is prorated.[20]

The number of ushers and ticket takers employed
depends upon the size of the house. The usual rate is
$30.00 a week for ushers and $51.00 for doormen.[21]
Off-Broadway has always had trouble with the quality of the
house. The first shows were given in abandoned cellars,
dark walkups, or converted barns. Nobody except the reviewers seemed to mind, as the audience was devoted to
patronizing a certain type of drama and the physical dis-
comfort occasioned counted for very little. Today, too, the
audience is on the whole drawn by plays with intellectual
appeal.[22] Off-Broadway, though, is attracting more and
more out-of-towners, people who want to be intellectually
stimulated, but who nonetheless prefer a comfortable house.

Previous Off-Broadway groups who gradually renovated the houses out of their meager earnings and who
hardly drew the attention of the landlord, suddenly came
into the limelight as they proved to be successful. Consequently, property which had had little value suddenly was
viewed by the landlord as a means for profit. Some Off-
Broadway groups renovated their houses and then lost them
as they were torn down to make way for modern buildings.

With rising costs in real estate, some ventures Off-
Broadway proving to be profitable, long runs leaving fewer
theaters available, and new construction eliminating some
of the old theaters, the rents of Off-Broadway houses have
skyrocketed. Payment must usually be made well in advance to get a suitable house on time.

The following list is indicative of Off-Broadway
rents. Usually payment is required six weeks in advance.

Cort Theater, 3rd Avenue, Lexington on 27th, 199 seats,
$450. per week.
Sullivan St. Playhouse, 181 Sullivan St., seats approx.
140, $400. per week.

Orpheum Theater, 2nd Ave. at 8th St., 299 seats,
$800. per week.
Sullivan St. Playhouse $6,000. to $6,500. for 6-6 1/2
years.[23]
Avlon Studio Theater, 220 West 43rd St., 75 seats,
$35. a night.
Barbizon-Plaza Theater, 106 Central Park So., 505
seats, $225. a performance.
Carnegie Hall Playhouse, 7th Avenue at 57th St., 209
seats, $850 a week.
Royal Theater, 62 East 4th St., 110 seats, $125. a
week.
Greenwich House, 27 Barrow St., 225 seats, $35. a
night.
Master Institute Theater, 310 Riverside Drive, 286
seats, $200. a week.
Provincetown Playhouse, 133 MacDougall St., $250.
a week.[24]

Off-Broadway must consider in its budget such items
as legal expenses and fees, scripts, tickets, programs,
photographs and signs, insurance and compensation, phone,
taxes; all of which in an average amounts figures today to
about $1,525.[25]

Where do all these costs leave the struggling playwright? Many of them are glad to give their scripts to
anyone who will produce them. If they are lucky, they will
get a percentage of the weekly income, but the satisfaction
of getting the script produced is usually compensation
enough. This altruism does not guarantee the playwright's
work being produced. Those who have had works produced
or who are at all known prefer to offer their plays to
Broadway. If established playwrights such as Williams
and Miller have any of their works produced Off-Broadway
there are high royalty fees. This gives an opportunity to
the outstanding new playwright if he can bring his script to
proper attention.

Broadway usually pays the playwright $2,000 and

royalties during the run.[26] This precludes many Off-
Broadway groups from the competition for new scripts of
known writers, for Broadway, too, searches for the script
that will sell and which offers something unusual. Broadway as well as Off-Broadway has competition for available
scripts from television, where the writer receives $1,500.
to $3,000. for a script and payment has been known to go
as high as $10,000. Of course, all writers--TV, Broad-
way or Off-Broadway, enjoy their best returns when a show
is filmed. This brings in a substantial down payment plus
bonuses on the legitimate production's profitable weeks.[27]

In 1948 and 1949 during the first resurgence of Off-
Broadway theater little attention was paid to it as a money
maker. It was not until 1950 that Show Business announced
that "Off-Broadway Grows; Becomes Big Biz:"

> The groups instead of being collections of actors
> chipping in a few dollars each to put on a play so that
> they might be seen, have been adopting big business
> methods of operation...the more intelligently managed
> are resorting to professional methods of financing, ac-
> quiring angels, and functioning under the guidance of
> theatrical lawyers.[28]

Writers' and actors' interest in Off-Broadway began
to wane with the emergence of television as the shortest
route to fame. Immediately after the optimistic reports in
1950 on the Off-Broadway theater, a very gloomy picture
followed in October of the same year. "Actors passed up
offers to work for $25.00 a week or a share in the profits
to try their luck on TV. One good part paid more than 5
weeks of Off-Broadway and even a walk-on got better pay."
The irony of the situation was that experience was also
needed for TV. Consequently, the Off-Broadway scene,
which provided valuable training, took a new swing upward

in 1952.[29]   Still, only 35 groups were left in operation as of July 13, 1953.[30]

But by November of that year 150 Off-Broadway groups were thriving, verifying the predictions that there would be a comeback.   At any one time 50 active groups could be found running, as compared to 25 on Broadway, playing to people who otherwise could not afford legitimate theater.[31]   Off-Broadway theaters still outnumber Broadway theaters.

In July, 1949, Off-Broadway theaters made the first effort to get together to meet the encroaching financial problems.   The new League asked Equity and other unions to allow their members to appear Off-Broadway.

The Off-Broadway Theater League tried to deal with other questions, including real estate, admission of new members, organization, and joint ticket distribution.   It might be interesting to note that tickets of the five groups composing the first Off-Broadway League (including Lee Nemetz, representing People's Drama; Mel Goldblatt representing the Interplayers; Bob Fuller for We Present; Gene Welsh for Studio 7; and Max Leavitt for Leomonde Opera, and Off-Broadway, Inc.) were scaled from $1.85 to $2.40.[32]   Some groups offered their tickets free.

Because of growing commercial considerations and evolving high voltage financing problems, the Off-Broadway producers formed a second major league in October of 1955. It was called the Off-Broadway Theater Association, Inc. Among its first goals, later abandoned, was mutual financial support.[33]   It also planned a central box office to promote ticket sales and took on the styling of an appropriate playbill as a joint project.[34]

Today, the Off-Broadway League still exists.   Mann

of Circle-in-the-Square, who is also on the Board of Directors of the present Off-Broadway Theater League, stated
that the association has been beneficial in that it has drawn
the Off-Broadway theater together in its negotiations with
the unions. Another benefit came during the newspaper
strike of 1953, when the long-sought goal of mutual advertising[35] proved successful in keeping the theaters going.
Anyone producing a play Off-Broadway is eligible for membership.

  With rising commercial costs has come a rise in
commercial interests. With top ticket prices now ranging
from $4.90 to $3.45[36] in many Off-Broadway theaters, it
would seem that many of those who can afford Off-Broadway today can afford Broadway as well. Eugene Lion, producer of Burnt Flower Bed, a hit, stated in 1959:

> A few years ago, Off-B'way was a place young actors
> could learn their trade, where playwrights tested their
> ideas, where producers and directors experimented.
> Today, it's become business and everyone is trying to
> make a living from Off-Broadway, but they can't. Only
> two or three Off-B'way plays a season ever show any
> profit.

  Lucille Lortel in confirming this estimated that
she could stage a show for $3,000. in 1952, but that she
would not even think of trying to do so for less than
$10,000. today.[37]

  Prior to the opening of the Circle-in-the-Square, the
theater held by many people Off-Broadway to be responsible
for the change, production would have cost about $2,000.[38]
Even at the Circle in 1951, a production such as Alfred
Haye's Girl on the Via Flamina would play at an initial
cost of $3,500. and gross $2,700. a week. But this play
went to Broadway,[39] which may have started this particular

trend.

Leslie Stevens', <u>Bullfight</u>, done at the Theater de Lys
on January 12, 1954, was a $10,000. hit production with a
three-man stage crew and $25.00 a week actors.[40]

A musical produced by the Phoenix theater in the
1954-1955 season, <u>The Golden Apple</u>, cost $75,000, quite a
budget for a production Off-Broadway, but it would have
cost $250,000. on Broadway. It should be considered also
that only a 7-man stage crew was used, as compared to
the 33-man stage crew for <u>Wonderful Town</u>, a production
running at the same time on Broadway, which cost $225,000.
The top ticket price at the Phoenix was $4.80, while the
top for <u>Wonderful Town</u> was $6.20.[41]

In 1955, theaters such as the Phoenix, the Theater
de Lys, and even the 293 seat President Theater had to
have budgets over $5,000. to open, while small theaters
such as the Circle-in-the-Square, Originals Only, Provincetown Playhouse, the Actor's Playhouse and the Cherry
Lane had budgets ranging from $800. to two or three
thousand dollars.

There were groups which still put on shows for a
$100. in 1955,[42] renting such halls as Malin's Prevue Thea-
ter for $35.00 a night, but without Equity casts, and un-
seen by the critics.[43] Plays cannot last without an audience and only publicity can get one.

In 1957-1958, the total investment Off-Broadway was
estimated at $600,000, spread over 59 shows. The average
investment was just over $10,000.[44] At this rate the
financial risk was not as yet excessively hazardous, but it
certainly did not allow the theater groups the freedom they
had previously enjoyed.

Tennessee Williams recognized Off-Broadway when

he presented his Garden District there rather than on
Broadway. He stated, "I couldn't cope at this time with doing
another controversial play on Broadway. The financial
risk Off-Broadway is not so great and the conditions, therefore, are less of a life and death matter."[45]

With productions such as Volpone at $16,000. and
An Enemy of the People at $14,000. in 1959[46] more people
who invest are interested in getting their money back. Today, the safe revival is the best guarantee of financial profit Off-Broadway and the success of new playwrights "is
practically nil" according to Gene Frankel, director of An
Enemy of the People.[47]

New authors were presented by 20% of Off-Broadway
shows in 1959.[48] In 1950, 40% of the shows had been tryouts
of new scripts: that is, 2 out of every 5 Off-Broadway productions in 1950 were originals.[49] New plays by unknown playwrights are increasingly becoming a greater risk. Established playwrights still tend to offer their plays to Broadway.

By the spring of 1959 production costs had risen to between $5,000. and $20,000. In 1962, one legitimate Off-
Broadway show was budgeted at $70,000. According to statis-
tics in 1959, only 7 out of 200 Off-Broadway shows broke even
and the few that did so needed very long runs.

Even with the "success formula" of revivals and an extended Broadway circuit, it seems that producers are always
searching for the plays that will assure the theater's continu-
ance. Off-Broadway even made plans to establish a road circuit.[50] The Fantasticks by Harvey Schmidt and Tom Jones
and The Zoo Story by Edward Albee were both well received
on tour in Chicago. Off-Broadway is now making plans to
tour abroad.

Today, the playwright who does go over to Off-Broadway
can expect bigger rewards financially. Often a

production is "considered not as an end in itself but as a
step to something else." Wayside by John Duff Stradely
was bought by Columbia Pictures for $35,000. which
hired Mr. Stradley for $12,500. to write the screenplay.[51]

"With Off-Broadway theaters charging as high as
$4.90 for tickets...the theaters are beginning to force
much of their old audience away by the growing steepness
of their prices."[52] According to Variety, the trade journal
of Show Business, Off-Broadway has developed into a mil-
lion-dollar-a-year business. Variety reported that between
$900,000. and $1,000,000. was spent in the 1959-1960
season on 76 productions. That means an average of
$12,500. was spent for each show in 1959-1960. Angels
are now sought as assidiously Off-Broadway as on. An
Off-Broadway producer can still be offered as little as
$10.00, although the usual amount invested by little angels
is $300.00.

However, the angel must be quite altruistic, as of
all the shows produced in the 1959-1960 season only 20,
or less than 30% ran more than 100 performances. Seven
out of ten shows never had a chance to make back the
initial investment.[53]

Theater-wise managements Off-Broadway try to
make their theaters as much a business proposition as
possible. Like Broadway they use a limited partnership
form of agreement. The producer forms one-half the partnership and is entitled to a 50% share of the profits. The
investors individually form the other half and share in the
other 50% in the proportion that their individual stakes
bear to the total. Some Off-Broadway producers vary the
split 40-60, reducing their own share.

One theater is self-financing, Circle-in-the-Square,

which began on an original investment of $7,000. It has
produced 20 plays and once during the rehearsals of one of
its greatest artistic successes, O'Neill's The Iceman Cometh,
the co-producers, Theodore Mann, José Quintero and Leigh
Connell, had to turn to a friend, Roger L. Stevens, a real
estate man and a major Broadway producer, for $2,000. to
continue. Circle-in-the-Square, today, is a continuing
artistic and financial success. [54]

Some shows such as Little Mary Sunshine by Rick
Besoyan still hit it in a big way. The preopening sale was
$8.70; the take since its opening in 1959 has been almost
$50,000.

> Broadway theater owners have urged Little Mary to
> move uptown. At least four British impresarios are
> currently dickering to take the show to London.

But it maintains its allegiance to Off-Broadway.
Eileen Brennan, hit of the show said: "Besides, with the
addition of 100 seats to the theater my salary went up from
$45.00 a week to almost double that. That means I can
move out of my very cold water flat." [55]

> Whatever, the impetus, the earlier version of Off-Broad-
> way activity involved the bringing together of a group of
> people, drawn by a shared idea or need and their in-
> evitable splintering through failure or success. By con-
> trast, today's Off-Broadway plays are presented by pro-
> ducers, many of whom also operate uptown or want to,
> in rented theaters, under union rules, with a respectable
> amount of capital to operate, often with safe playwrights
> and with actors who know that a good Off-Broadway
> notice is better than a tepid uptown mention. [56]

Gelb of the New York Times in reference to the
1959-1960 season, said that never have "so many shows
closed so quickly and so much money has been lost."
There are thirty theaters competing now in contrast to six

in 1950.

"One million two hundred thousand dollars was lost
Off-Broadway" in 1959-1960.[57] Gelb blames the art of the
press agent and rich, impressive stage settings for often
misleading the public about an inferior drama. This brings
about the rapid demise of well-received productions which
do not draw enough people in the competition among too
many theaters.

Craft union requirements for technicians, box office
people, lawyers fees, theater rentals and higher priced
talent have all contributed to the steady rise of costs which
is pricing many worthwhile productions out of the market.

Off-Broadway is still the only theater today where
experimental dramas can be produced, where the classics
can be revived and new playwrights given a showing. Then,
too, Off-Broadway is especially needed since Broadway's
recent offerings have been accused of being "tinny and
tasteless productions---a kind of sub-Broadway."[58]

On Broadway where production costs run as high as
$400,000, the classics are seldom presented. Intelligent
theatergoers owe a great debt to the courage of producers
who give the Off-Broadway audience stimulating plays by new
authors and the forms of an advanced theater which would
otherwise be unknown in America.

A Sample of an Off-Broadway Budget

The following is a theatrical limited partnership plan
for Alfred de Musset's No Trifling With Love as produced at
the St. Marks Playhouse, 133 Second Avenue, in November,
1959. This production had a very short run.

The following estimated Pre-Production Budget and Weekly Operating Costs show how the capitalization will be

spent...The St. Marks Playhouse is scaled to produce
approximately $3,500. weekly gross, after taxes. Since
the show can operate at a modest $2,200. per week, it
is possible to realize a profit of approximately $1,300.
per week at capacity. With actual pre-production costs
at only $6,700, it is possible to repay this cost in less
than six weeks.

Estimated Pre-Production Costs

Cast salaries (Rehearsal)	$660
Stage Manager	180
Rehearsal space	250
Scripts	50
Director's expenses	150
Casting expenses	100
Advertising	1200
Press Agent (2 weeks)	290
Photos and signs	150
Mailing	100
Sets, Costumes, Lighting, Designers' Fees	1500
Music	100
Tickets	50
Programs	60
Company Manager	180
Insurance and Compensation	375
Taxes	150
Legal Expenses and Fees	650
Box Office	100
Stage crew	100
Phone	40
Royalties	250
Pre-production costs	$6685

Returnable Bonds and Advance Deposits

Equity Bond	$810
Press Agt. Bond	290
Theater Rental (6 weeks)	2400
Breakage and Phone Deposit	300
	$3800
Contingency Reserve	4515
Pre-Production Costs	6685

Total Capitalization $15,000

Estimated Weekly Operating Costs

Scenic and Lighting	$ 25
Costumes cleaning, repair	25
Actors' salaries	530
Stage Manager	50
Crew	100
Company Manager	45
Press Agent	145
Tickets	20
Programs	20
Advertising	500
Theater (at capacity)	475
House Managers	75
Box Office	50
Phone	15
Insurance & Compensation	80
Attorney	20
Accountant	20

Total Weekly Operating Cost $2195

Notes

1.   Clurman, Harold, "Is Off-Broadway On or Really Off?" The New York Times Magazine, March 22, 1959, p. 61.

2.   "Elia Kazan Calls For More Experimental Theaters In the U.S.," Show Business, (Vol. XIX---No. 8), p. 1.

3.   "Agreement for Off-Broadway Group," Equity, Official Organ of the Actor's Equity Association, September, 1949, (Volume XXXIV---No. 9), p. 18.

4.   "Off-Broadway Contract Extended," Equity, Official Organ of the Actor's Equity Association, (Volume XXXV---No. 1), p. 19.

5.   "Shakespeare Festival and Off-Broadway Groups Discussed at AETA Meeting," Show Business, (Vol. XIV---No. 1), Monday, Jan. 4, 1954, p. 3.

6.   "Amendment to Equity Rules Governing Employment
      as Applied to Off-Broadway Productions as of Sep-
      tember 1, 1954," 11/24/54, Actor's Equity Associ-
      ation.

7.   "Amendments to Equity Rules Governing Employ-
      ment As Applied to Off-Broadway Productions,
      Effective September 1, 1957," 10/31/57, Actor's
      Equity Association.

8.   "Boom Off-Broadway," New York Times Magazine,
      November 29, 1954; Stage: U.S.; N.Y.: Off-Broad-
      way Clipping, through 1954; Theater Collection, New
      York Public Library, New York City.

9.   Herridge, Frances, "Across the Footlights," New
      York Post, Monday, February 23, 1959, p. 22.

10.   "Exciting Commotion Off-Broadway" il Life, March
      24, 1958, 44: p. 115.

11.   "Amendments to Equity Rules Governing Employ-
      ment as Applied to Off-Broadway Productions,
      Effective September 1, 1959."

12.   Show Business, Monday, January 12, 1953; (Vol.
      XIII---No. 2), p. 1.

13.   Telephone conversation with Fred Cotton, 4/27/59,
      Actor's Equity Association Off-Broadway representa-
      tive.

14.   "United Scenic Artists Off-Broadway Scenic Design-
      ing Artist's Contract," from Arthur Romano, Local
      829B of P.D. & P. of America, 319 West 48th St.,
      New York 36, 5/9/59.

15.   Conversation with Mr. Arthur Romano, 6/9/59,
      Local 829B of P.D. & P., of America, 319 West
      48th St., New York 36.

16.   "Official Artists Agreement, United Scenic Artists,
      Off-Broadway Scenic Designing Artists Contract,
      "Form 1-4' 60.

17.   "ATPAM Changes Work Rule for Off-Broadway," Show
      Business, Monday, July 24, 1950, (Vol.X---No.30) p.3.

18.   Interview with Milton Weintraub, 6/14/59, Corre-
       spondence, March 1, 1961, Association of Theatrical
       Agents and Managers, ATPAM; Mr. Weintraub,
       secty-treasurer, 25 W. 45 St., NYC.

19.   Interview with Mrs. Greene, New York League of
       Theaters, Mr. Reilley's assistant, 6/21/59, 234 W.
       44th St., NYC.

20.   Interview with Milton Weintraub, 6/14/59, op. cit.

21.   Interview with Mrs. Greene, 6/21/59, op. cit.

22.   Interview with Kip Hastings, 6/22/59, Berghof
       Studios, 120 Bank St., New York City.

23.   Interview with Marvin Berk, Berk and Krumgold
       Real Estate, 6/11/59, Paramount Building, 1501
       Broadway, New York 36, N. Y.

24.   "Off-Broadway Theaters," Leo Shull's Production
       Directory, 1959, Edition, pp. 13-24.

25.   Gerald S. Krone, "Theatrical Limited Partnership
       Prospectus," No Trifling With Love, opening date
       November 9, 1959.

26.   Interview with Elsie, secretary to Daniel Hollywood
       Associates, 6/19/59, 101 W. 55th St., NYC.

27.   Ibid.

28.   "Off-Broadway Grows; Becomes Big Biz," Actor's
       Cues Show Business, (Vol. X---No. 6), Monday,
       Feb. 6, 1950, p. 1.

29.   "Off-Broadway Begins to Perk Up; 1951-1952 Increase
       Forecast," Show Business, Monday, October 15,
       1951, (Vol. XI---No. 42), p. 1.

30.   "Off-Broadway Groups Will Begin Expansion Next
       Season," Show Business, Monday, July 13, 1953,
       (Vol. XIII---No. 28), p. 1.

31.   "150 Off-B'way Groups Thriving; Training Thousands
       of Actors, Directors and Technicians Yearly," Mon-
       day, November 9, 1953, (Vol. XIII---No. 45), p. 1.

32.   "Off-Broadway Theater League Sets Up Working
       Committees to Expand Scope," Actor's Cues Show
       Business, Tuesday, August 2, 1949, p. 1.

33.   "Another Big Year for Little Theaters," New York
       Herald Tribune, Sunday, October, 1955, personal
       clipping file on 1955 & 1956.

34.   "Theater Groups Get Together to Set Standards,"
       the Village Voice, Oct. 26, 1955, p. 7.

35.   "Off-Broadway Theater Assn. to Press for Central
       Box Office and Casting File, Show Business, Oct.
       19, 1955, p. 1.

36.   Leave It to Jane, mail order, Sheridan Square Play-
       house, 1959.

37.   "Quality Productions, 'Name Authors, Stars, Boom-
       ing Off-Broadway Shows,' " Show Business, June
       15, 1959, (Vol. XIX---No. 24), p. 4.

38.   Interview with Mr. Gene Frankel, Gene Frankel's
       Dramatic Workshop, 6/22/59, 115 MacDougal St.,
       NYC.

39.   "Boom Off-Broadway," New York Times Magazine,
       N.Y.: Off-Broadway Clippings, November 29, 1954;
       Theater Collection, New York Public Library, New
       York City.

40.   "Boom Off-Broadway," op. cit.

41.   Ibid.

42.   "Upsurge in Off-Broadway Productions, 30 Little
       Groups Now Preparing Shows," '15 Openings in Two
       Months,' Show Business, Monday, Sept. 19, 1955;
       (Vol. XVI---No. 38), p. 1.

43.   Interview with Fred Cotton, 4/27/59, op. cit.

44.   "Want to be a Little Angel?", Today's Living, Decem-
       ber 11, 1960., p. 4.

45.   Gelb, Arthur, "News and Gossip of the Rialto," The
       New York Times, Sunday, Dec. 15, 1957, Drama, p.3.

46.   Interview with Gene Frankel, 6/22/59, op. cit.

47.   Ibid.

48.   "New Authors Represented In 20% of Off-Broadway
      Shows," Show Business, March 16, 1959, (Vol.
      XIX---No. 11), p. 1.

49.   "Off-B'wy Groups Thriving, Training 1000's of Ac-
      tors, Directors, Technicians Yearly," Actors Cues
      Show Business, Monday, March 6, 1950, (Vol. X---
      No. 10), p. 1.

50.   "Off-Broadway Shows to Establish a Road Circuit to
      Tour Productions," February 16, 1959, (Vol. XIX---
      No. 7), p. 1.

51.   "Little Theaters Become Big Business," il Reporter,
      June 13, 1957, 16: p. 39.

52.   Ibid., p. 40.

53.   "Want to be a Little Angel?", op. cit.

54.   Ibid., p. 5.

55.   "Bright-eyed with Hope; Off-Broadway," Newsweek,
      February 22, 1960, 55:95.

56.   Weales, Gerald, "Box Office and the Muse: Off-
      Broadway Theater," Commonweal, September 25,
      1959, 70: p. 540.

57.   Gelb, Arthur, "Off-Broadway Second Act Crises,"
      il N.Y. Times Mag., March 13, 1960, pp. 26-7.

58.   Kronenberger, Louis, "Why Broadway Is Way-Off-
      Broadway," The New York Times Magazine,
      February 5, 1960, p. 46.

Chapter VIII

Original Drama Off-Broadway, 1955-1960

The outstanding new dramas of 1956 through 1960 cover topics meaningful to the modern world. Some subjects are considered too sensitive to be discussed on Broadway. Many of these problems must be resolved before some happiness may be attained in the lives of men in the twentieth century. The plays of the latter 1950's cover themes which range from racial and social problems to the abstract. There are not enough of these plays available. Some of these plays are written in verse and other highly experimental forms.

One of the needs of the young struggling playwright which is vital to the development of his art, is sympathetic encouragement and the opportunity to see and participate in dramatic productions through which he may learn the techniques of his craft. Off-Broadway has offered this opportunity, but to a lesser degree than in its early history.

Since 1955 only about twenty per cent of the Off-Broadway plays produced are original. It is constantly reiterated that not enough opportunity is given to the new playwright to get his work on the stage. Most producers, not claiming wizardry, even Off-Broadway, would rather rely upon an American revival or a play which has been tried successfully in Europe in the face of a precarious financial situation.

In 1956, Off-Broadway had more professional and

permanent organizations. The actual total of companies in
operation hovered "steadily around the forty mark and
casualties...(were)...few and far between."[1] Such an Off-
Broadway stage gave the playwright a better chance to be
seen by a larger audience and by professional people interested in their productions. Some playwrights want to be
seen Off-Broadway and even prefer Off-Broadway production.

To begin the list of new plays of the 1955-1956
season we will consider Third Person by Andrew Rosenthal.
The play deals with homosexuality. This is another play
which breaks down the wall surrounding its subject, which
is not usually discussed in public. Its dialogue subtly revealed psychotic manifestations in the characters with the
finesse of drawing room comedy.

The plot concerns a couple, Hank and Jean More-
land, who live in an East Sixties duplex. Their marriage
has been slowly drifting apart for a year when a war
buddy of Hank's comes to visit them for a weekend. The
weekend extends into a year, and Jean confides to one of
her friends, wife of a wealthy globe-trotter, that she has
not slept with her husband for six months. Felix, the
globe-trotter, who is visiting, makes known that the war-
time buddy, Kip, once lived with a notoriously homosexual painter for two years. The problem now is how to
get Kip out.[2] During accusations made in the following
scenes, it is disclosed that Felix, the globe-trotter, has
himself been hiding his latent homosexual tendencies toward
Hank, pretending his favors to him were motivated by
generosity toward an old college friend.

Kip, ultimately, reveals his depth of character as he
decides to leave and live his own life despite Hank's attempts to stop him. Hank and Jean, left together, show

that their frustrations with each other are deeply rooted
and that Kip's presence only acted as the catalytic agent.
They now have a realistic understanding of their problem.
As the curtain falls the two have agreed to try "desperately"[3] to find a life together.

The Thorntons, presented in February 1956, was a
study of a decaying American dynastic family. Its members,
even in decay, receive $100,000. annually (tax-free), and
"we learn in the third act that Cleveland Amory has devoted a full chapter to them in his The Last Resorts."
Some lines gave one a haunting feeling that "Noel Coward
alone would have written in this manner."[4]

The 1956-1957 season brought a play about integration, concerned with the problems of Puerto Ricans in New
York City. Me, Candido! was first produced in New York
City at the Greenwich Mews Theater on October 15, 1956.
The play has been presented practically without scenery in
schools and settlement houses all over the country. Greenwich Mews Theater used a full set in a style of simple,
selective realism.

The action takes place in a part of New York City
into which the Puerto Ricans are moving. This has led
to racial conflict within the affected neighborhood. The
family of Jesus Gomez has been in America for only six
months. There is a poetry in these people which reaches
beyond the mundane realities of their lives. Their imag-
inations and warm humanity open for them wide vistas
which allow them to enjoy a happier existence than is
theirs in reality.

Candido, befriended by the Gomez family, is an
orphan. The amusing and satirical play shows the plight of
Candido and the Gomez family when confronted by the laws

and social agencies of New York City. These agencies require that Candido not only go to school but that he be
legally adopted. The very laws made supposedly to pro-
tect these people disregard their individual needs and wants.
Through politics and a natural cleverness the Gomez family,
now wiser in the ways of the world, gets permission to
adopt Candido. Jesus Gomez works the ultimate victory.
A lawyer at the adoption trial exclaims that since he "met
up with these people law books have been collapsing on my
head."[5] Me, Candido! gives a truly inspirational message
in human understanding which is an ideal subject for community theater.

    Also presented in 1956-1957, Land Beyond the Riv-
er by Loften Mitchell is another story about integration,
but this time in the schools. The play was a "rare combination of comic entertainment and serious timeliness in
which the comedy grows right out of the material." It was
certainly timely. The characters were interesting, Grand-
ma Sims, older and sharper-tongued than the others
through her long identification with life and her wisdom
gained from it, was particularly memorable.

    The material was drawn from incidents in Clarendon
County, South Carolina, which led to a test case of the
"separate but equal" formula and resulted in the Supreme
Court decision. The central character is the Reverend
Mr. Layne, who in humanity is led into a fight for the
modest goals of his people, "but whose growing sense of
justice leads him to realize that gradualism as a principle,
is self-defeating." He matures and gains new perspectives
with his victories, but nonetheless he pays heavily for his
gains. His greatest struggle is in his "remaking of" himself. The Reverend Mr. Layne is transformed as he

"deals with the concrete problems which he and his neigh-
bors face."[6]

An Off-Broadway play in the early tradition was an
original teen-age musical revue, Delinquent Line-up, given
for an audience of 75, sans admission fee, at the home of
Mrs. Robert F. Wagner. It was presented again in February, 1957 at the Presbyterian Labor Temple.

The story details the adventures of a group of
teenagers who in planning a musical show are forced to re-
port to the police station because an irate neighbor com-
plains that they are creating a disturbance.

Among the adults in the cast were Virginia Payne,
of radio's "Ma Perkins," and actress Ann Seymour. Certainly such activities should arouse the creative spark in
potential young talent.[7]

Bivouac at Lucca, an unpublished play, opened at
the Royal Playhouse on October 29, 1957. It was presented
by James Bruce Productions and staged by its author,
Robert Guy Barrows, a member of the New Dramatist's
Committee.

The setting is the ancestral home of Don Carlo
Ruffoli in Italy in 1945. The home contains the bric-a-brac
of over four hundred years and an atmosphere of timelessness. It is a warm and comfortable place to live---"a
civilized haven in the midst of modern warfare."

The play opens with the meeting of two American
soldiers and the Ruffoli family: Francesca, the beautiful
daughter; Egli, the servant girl; Don Carlo and his Signora.
Dirk, one of the soldiers, is represented as a boor and the
typification of the brassy sergeant. He has never heard of
Machiavelli and is little impressed that the Ruffoli family
home dates from that period. Paul, the platoon leader, is

educated, sensitive, and wealthy.

Paul succumbs to Francesca's charms. Ruffoli, the head of the family, who yearns to be a general, tells Paul frankly when he asks for her hand in marriage:

> Without money, her fine education, her excellent back-
> ground, her ancient and honorable blood, the heredity
> of a Renaissance civilization...I wonder...Will they be
> worth even two eggs?[8]

Florio, the youngest Ruffoli, who is an American partisan comes through enemy lines to guide the American unit into the fighting. A German soldier is found who, left behind hidden in the cellar, is dying of pneumonia. Florio is enraged at the discovery and tries to kill the German officer but he is dragged off with the American army at the close of the second act.

To the rest of the family, Francesca seems too concerned about the German soldier with whom she is suspected of having had an affair. Francesca seems the antithesis of another Italian heroine in a rather similar situation---the girl on the Via Flamina who, haunted by her conscience, committed suicide.[9]

In the third act, the fully recovered German soldier is shown being entertained by the Signora and Francesca. He is hurriedly hidden when the love-haunted Paul, who has deserted, enters. Francesca does not offer him assistance until she realizes that no one saw him run away. She then offers her help, still hoping to gain his fortune.

Dirk, the complement to Paul's personality, the balance which both seem to need for their mutual strength, appears. Francesca in her frustration outwits herself by urging Paul to kill Dirk. Paul, now realizing the truth about Francesca, returns with Dirk to the battle. Ruffoli calls after them:

> You two? Conquerors? You Americans will never have
> the courage to rule the world...One of you ignorant and
> stupid---the other weak and indecisive. You hold the
> world's destiny in your hands, but it will be snatched
> away from you.[10]

Brooks Atkinson stated of Paul and Dirk that..."different as they may be as individuals, they represent the
purity of heart of the American. In the last act they win
a moral victory over the corruption of European culture."
However, Mr. Atkinson felt that after the second act...
"the mechanics of the craft truimph over common sense...
Mr. Barrows ties all the loose ends into a victorious conclusion. But it is a victory of dramatic composition."[11]

Paul V. Beckley of the New York Herald Tribune
said that the author "has proved able to create some living
characters, however, which should be a promise of something better to come once he takes a firmer hold on struc-
ture and plotting."[12]

The author, Robert Guy Barrows, was the recipient
of one of three $3,000. Rockefeller grants in playwriting
awarded in 1955 in the name of Kenneth Macgowan, former
Broadway producer and author. Barrows has an M.A. in
playwriting from UCLA.

Career by James Lee, made into a movie, is a
cynical and unusually truthful play about the hardwon victory
of an actor who wins success. At the conclusion of Career
his agent asks him if he thinks that the price he has paid
was worth it. He answers in the affirmative. The actor,
Sam, had twenty-five years of hard struggle during which
he averaged $20.00 a week. However, it is not money so
much as the loss of human decency and identification with
the rest of society which is the greatest price he has paid.

He has lost his first wife, who came with him to New York at the beginning of his quest for recognition. She wanted a typical midwestern home life, but Sam was not willing to give up his ambitions to take a regular job.

Although Sam is not a vicious person, in the final analysis he has sold his soul to the theater. The play emphasizes that the artist often has a lonely life and that there is no "formula" that fits him in with the rest of the life of the nation. The play was "well-written" and created "characters from the inside."[13] Lee was commissioned to write the screen version of his play when it was bought by Hollywood.

In the 1957-1958 season, Palm Tree in a Rose Garden, one of the most highly publicized new dramas now published by Dramatist's Play Service, was not given a very good review by Variety. Palm Tree already had a straw hat circuit history at the time it was produced Off-Broadway at the Cricket on November 26, 1957.

Meade Roberts, the author, is a New Yorker who has been writing since he was 18. This was his first work to be staged in New York. Since then he has done very well with his adaptation of Henry James' Wings of the Dove for TV's Playhouse 90 and with his film scenario for Williams' Orpheus Descending.

In A Palm Tree in a Rose Garden we are introduced to a cast of eccentric humans who live on the outskirts of the film industry. All of their lives they have been trying to break into the glamourous film world. Rose, who once had a "closeup;" Lila, her plain daughter; Jim, enamoured of his own physique; Alice, the wealthy spinster enamoured of Jim; and Mona, the fat old maid next door are at war with each other and with their imaginary world. Rose, the

owner of the Rose Garden, rents rooms to film hopefuls.
Her latest protegee, a pretty girl who feels that the world
has slipped away from her, slashes her wrists, whereupon
the star with whom she is in love takes her back.   Then
Rose's plain daughter, as out of place in this setting as the
palm tree which Rose displays in her garden, finds someone who loves her for her strength of character.

With the attempted suicide and her daughter's be-
trothal, Rose, overcoming these crises in her life, for the
first time rises above her ambitious fantasies. She comes
to an adult realization that she must give of her love in
order to receive love.

The pace of the drama depicting this bombastic life
is rapid. The personalities are well portrayed. The play,
also, is skillfully written even though the plot is rather
well-worn.[14]

The life of the late Bohemian poet, Max Bodenheim,
is presented in the play Winkleberg by Ben Heckt. Max
Bodenheim was a man who had the appearance of a Lord
Chesterfield and lived like a hobo. This play, presented
in February, 1958, is handled entertainingly, which may be
a fault in that "when one is summing up the life of a
stormy and passionate man" to be just entertaining is not
sufficient. No new insight is given into this "proud, tortured human being."

Bodenheim began his career as a resident poet in a
gangsters' Chicago night club until some of his poetry
finally got into print. After his short lived success he
went back down again to flop houses and even Communism
until he was murdered by a sailor. In this odyssey of his
life are included many quips delivered by the poet such as
the one that T.S. Eliot has made "dulness fashionable" and

his statement describing Faulkner as "just a bad writer."[15]

The Long Gallery by Ramsey Yelvington is "a moving
story of the lives of a few small town Texans between the
years 1931-1950." It is the recital of day-to-day events
through which the homely truths of human existence
emerge, "the things that make people laugh or cry, the
humdrum details of life." The play was a mature Off-
Broadway production.

Stella Holt produced The Long Gallery in March of
1958. Among her other productions by new playwrights
have been Me, Candido! and Simply Heavenly by Langston
Hughes, which was later taken on Broadway.

"Author Yelvington has a marked flair for the small
situation, plain conversation, simple truths, and in his
play these things accumulate into the overwhelming importance of living and dying." In the play there were no big
dramatic moments of tortured climaxes, or impassioned
attempts to "say something." It is in his restrained ob-
servations that Mr. Yelvington's success lies. Miss Holt's
production was sympathetic, ideal for this sensitively
wrought play.[16]

A Power of Dreams by Peter John Stephens was a
contest-winning play at the University of California and
produced Off-Broadway at the Sullivan St. Playhouse in
1958.

Mr. Stephens' wrote in the style of fantasy about
"a dog with silver eyes, a gypsy-like lover who may be
half man, half fox, and a dead man who walks abroad giv-
ing every evidence of flesh and blood although his drowned
body lies outside in a cart."[17]

Tennessee Williams presented Garden District Off-
Broadway in the 1957-1958 season in a 299 seat theater, the

York. He rather tactfully stated that he didn't feel that
the Broadway audience would have the stomach for his play.
After going to an analyst after the opening of Orpheus Descending on Broadway because of the tension involved in
putting on the play, he decided that he would present Garden District Off-Broadway where the audience was receptive and the financial risk not so overwhelming. Mr.
Williams felt after presenting Orpheus Descending that
some of the Broadway audience thought he had "become a
homicidal maniac, if not worse..."

He stated "I've always been a little startled by people who are antagonized by plays for reasons other than the
quality of the work. Some of my plays, I think, have
suffered from a reaction of ethical bias and an imposed and
conventional morality...I couldn't cope at this time with
doing another controversial play on Broadway."[18]

Garden District consists of two sections---"Something Unspoken," the first, is a "sketch of charm and
oddly persuasive pathos---." "Something Unspoken" is the
dialogue between an overbearing older woman whose little
world revolves around the politics of her social clubs, and
her submissive and suffering companion and secretary."[19]

The major plot line of Suddenly Last Summer involves a poet who through cannabalism finds a medium for
expression, an expression which leads to his horrible
death at the hands of a mob of vandals on a tropic island.
In this play Williams embodies with "directness and inten-
sity of symbolism the shape of the destructive element...no
other work made so undistracted a confession of belief in
the artist's lyric vocation, his impotence in the flow of
experience." The play and its poetry are compared in its
imagery to Lorca, especially the manner of its bold end-

ing.[20] Suddenly Last Summer was made into an award
winning motion picture.

George Panetta's comedy, Comic Strip, mirrors a
section of the real New York rather that the city visitors
say is a swell place to visit but not to live in.   The
action takes place in an Italian neighborhood of Washington
Square where we meet many friendly people. A similar
story might have been gleaned from "the tumultuous life
of Harlem, of any Catholic parish or a block of Puerto
Ricans."[21]

Comic Strip a dramatization of Jimmy Potts Gets a
Haircut, was first presented in New York City on May 14,
1958, at the Barbizon-Plaza theater. It is an amusing
spoof on life in the days of La Guardia, the Little Flower,
Mayor of New York. Ignatio Romani, a little boy of ten,
is the central figure. He has a series of adventures with
the police and his parents; all created by the fact that he
wrote the word CAT on the forehead of a little neighbor
boy just before one of the dozing old women in the neighborhood, abruptly awakened, thought she saw the little boy
run over by a truck. What follows is a comedy of errors,
which includes satirical commentaries on doctors, the police and the government, caused as   direct result of the
lack of communication between the world of grown-ups and
that of children.[22]

The collection of characters includes a suspicious
barber, a tough sergeant and Hippo, the patrol man with
tired feet. They "get themselves into absurd situations and
their offbeat answers to casual questions are deliciously
humorous."

Included in the drama is a hospital scene which
finds a little Negro boy, one of the patients, passing out

his father's business card to other patients "while sub-
mitting a novel program for improving race relations. His
father, a mortician, thinks Negroes and white people should
bury each other." There is another scene "in which an
Italian boy and his dad decide how to make a good confession..."[23]

Before 1958, the critics were reluctant about writing
a review because they did not know how much of a con-
cession to make to Off-Broadway. They did not want to
judge it by the same standards as those set for Broadway
shows. In fact, one critic, John Chapman, solved his
dilemna by not reviewing any Off-Broadway shows. Therefore it was a major achievement when Richard Watts reported in Theater Arts that it was no longer necessary to
lower standards in judging the acting or the production
quality of Off-Broadway. He said that while the new plays
presented were not as good as one would hope, "the performances in general are just as good as those we see on
Broadway..."[24] Off-Broadway, he said, "is one of the
most promising phenomena in the contemporary American
theater."[25]

An auspicious beginning to the 1958-1959 season was
the production of U.S.A. based on the novel by John dos
Passos, which was first presented at the Martinique Theater, on October 28, 1958. It is a dramatic narrative depicting a cross section of American life from the turn of
the century until around 1931.

Narration is presented from lecterns at the side of
the stage. Each player, distinguished by a letter of the
alphabet, plays many parts. Music is used to bridge
scenes which generally begin with a narrative or the newspaper headline technique of Piscator. Antedotes and short

biographical sketches are given from the lives of such outstanding persons as the Wright Brothers, Eugene V. Debs,
Rudolph Valentino, Henry Ford and Isadora Duncan.

The tone is one of hope for a better life to come,
a wish expressed universally at the turn of the century and
mirrored in all of the newspaper headlines and speeches.
The hero of the American success story in this drama,
J. Ward Moorehouse, comes from humble origins and begins his career in a real estate office, from which he
rises through ambitious opportunism to our necrophilic
world's idea of success. In following his life the drama
compares it disparagingly with that of an Isadora Duncan
or the Wright Brothers by means of the rapid narrative
and newspaper broadcasting technique. Moorehouse's rapid
narrative and newspaper broadcasting technique. Moorehouse's wife, whose background was one of wealth, is
eventually committed to a mental institution by her husband
when she becomes sickly. In one scene she asks: "Do people ever wonder how a big man like you can be so empty?"[26]

The play has an echo of Brecht in its satirical
study that bites cuttingly into our American moralistic
hypocrisy. Phrases, funny yet disturbing, reveal an emptiness in the "successful" characters. The statements of the
degenerates and hopeless souls of the drama heighten the
unpleasant truth in all of their lives---that all built a life
based upon a foundation of untruth.

With the demise of J. Ward Moorehouse, public relations counsel and assistant to the President, the saga
comes full circle---the Crash of the '30's in the final scene
bring on stage a poor, unidentified, but hopeful young man,
thumbing a ride on a highway in the U.S.A.[27]

Although Maxwell Anderson gave the grand gesture

of acceptance in allowing his last and final play, The Golden
Six, to be produced by an Off-Broadway group, it was unfortunately not well received. Anderson had written about
the period of Rome during the years when Augustus was
emperor and reigned with his powerful wife, Livia.

It was presented Off-Broadway in the fall of 1958
and shows us the history of Rome at this time through a
"brace of reigns, amid dedicated and degenerate heirs,
with Livia the hidden, misdirecting hand." People die all
over the stage as in the "last act of Hamlet." The
speeches are oratorical and the role of Claudius is one
with a great deal of stammering.[28]

The Blackfriars' Guild felt in 1958 that they had
found a playwright in Fred J. Scollay. The discovery,
Father Carey remarked in an intermission speech at the
opening of the play, Listen to the Quiet, "may be of in-
calculable significance to Catholic theater---and the American stage as well." Father Carey regarded the benefits
from Catholic oriented playwrights to be the infusion that
our theater needs,. as it would serve to reflect "the Catholic attitude toward life and human destiny."

Listen to the Quiet is a drama of "spiritual fortitude
in the frame of a thrill play." The setting is the cell of
a prison behind the Iron Curtain. The characters are a
mute pickpocket, a blind girl, an alcoholic, an unlucky A-
merican tourist and a priest. All the inmates are sub-
jected to inhuman cruelty which first only the thief and the
drunkard withstand.

The playwright is master of his craft with the
characters "sharply etched and vividly portrayed..."[29]

The criticism of Emory Lewis of Cue and Henry
Hewes of Saturday Review were split as to the play by

Meade Roberts-Maidens and Mistresses At Home in the Zoo.
Lewis found it "jejune sex stuff" and said the only suspense
found in the play was to which "sexual deviation the playwright" would turn next.   Lewis felt it was Tennessee
Williams' Garden District in a Pasadena setting.[30] In contrast, Hewes felt it was the "most burning and hypnotic
piece of theater seen in New York this season."

The play was presented on a double bill with an elegant and minor playlet by Giraudoux on mistresses and
marriage. The story of Maidens and Mistresses reveals
the devotion and loyalty of a wife, Lucy, to her husband
who became paralyzed as a result of a life of debauchery.
They have a handsome young servant named Tonio who was
bought as a slave by Lucy's husband in North Africa.   This
slave has been both she and her husband's lover. The trio
had been members of the International Set and had traveled
the circuit from Paris to Rome to Morocco but are now reduced to Pasadena.   Another character in this no-exit type
of play is Isabella who is "obviously the sort of woman who
can commit the most inhuman acts under the guise of some
socially acceptable excuse."

Forced to earn a living for the three, Lucy offers
the Arab boy to her friends for a fee. A question of moment is why the three stay together after their betrayal of
each other: Tonio, because of his Islamic philosophy of
surrender; the husband because he is comfortably taken care
of rather than being placed in an institution; and Lucy
because she can both punish her husband and prove her
love for him.

The playwright seems to be conveying the idea that
"the act is less important than the attitude of its doer. The
one pure thing in this menage is Lucy's love for her hus-

band...her motives and her courage are honorable." Hewes
felt that Roberts had suggested these things with "poetic
insight and ironic touches of humor..."[31]   Roberts wrote
this play shortly after completing the scenario for Orpheus
Descending which seems to have left an impression upon
him that is evident in Maidens and Mistresses.

        The Man Who Never Died by Barrie Stavis recalls
in certain aspects the protest drama so popular on Off-
Broadway during the '30's.   Dealing with the underdog, the
question of justice is raised as it would be by an I.J.
Golden.   Mr. Stavis went to a great length to research
material on Joe Hill.   This he began while on a fellowship
from the National Theater Conference.   Five years went
into the difficult search for the material and the writing of
the book.

        The Man Who Never Died was presented at the Jan
Hus Theater on November 21, 1958.   This drama is proof
that the stage can still be a powerful and potent weapon---
one of the greatest proponents of freedom of speech.

        Joe Hill, a poet of labor, is accused of murder.
Through inside information the courts build a case against
him on circumstantial evidence that sends him to his death.
Joe's character is well developed in the prison scenes and
throughout the trial while the other characters appear to be
convenient instruments by which to expound philosophic demands for a new world.   It becomes evident as the drama
unfolds that the state wants not so much to grant a fair
trial as to rid itself of a nuisance.   Political opportunism
builds the case against Joe Hill.

        The drama grows in intensity, pitch and fervor
until the execution shots ring out.   At the final ordeal,
the workers are heard singing the songs which Joe Hill

wrote to aid them in their battle for equal opportunity. The
dedication to Joe Hill which concludes the play is appropriate to the theme---"And blessed is the man who works."

The play is powerful as a drama of protest in the
same way as the Crucible or An Enemy of the People. In
the use of dramatic technique, The Man Who Never Died,
also employs the crowd in the audience, spilling onto and
from the stage. All three plays are involved with questions of social significance and the quality of justice which
appeal to an Off-Broadway audience, but not particularly to
the wealthy audience of Broadway.[32]

Stavis, started with Joe Hill as "a simple man" who
rose to great heights and in the process became a "very
complex and noble man, larger than life-size..." "This,"
says Stavis, "is not a play about a strike, about a union
leader. It's about something which rises above that-about
justice and truth!"

The play has been published in two editions here in
the United States; was being translated into the 15th language,
French, in 1961, for a production at the Theater Du
Noveau Monde to be directed by Jean Gascon; was being
prepared as an opera to be done at Die Komische Oper in
Berlin; and has been presented on radio and television in
half a dozen countries.

Stavis has written three other plays in his search
for an understanding of these men who rose above the
average in their societies. The plays by Stavis are The
Sun and I, about Joseph of the Old Testament, produced by
the Federal Theater in the '30's; Lamp at Midnight, about
Galileo and produced by the Old Vic in England in 1956;
and a play about John Brown---Banners of Steel.

Although it was written in 1941, the initial produc-

tion of **Many Loves** was at the Living Theater on January
13, 1959. The evening consisted of a series of scenes
which "demonstrate how love in our time is often a mask
for selfishness and bestiality, and how pitifully unable we
are to communicate more than superficially with those
whom we profess to love." The doctor in one scene
exclaims, "Talk, talk, talk! And all the shyness and all
the prudery and all the moral carpings are no more than
so much heartburn from our chronic emptiness."

The playlets are tied together by presenting them as
the work of an earnest young playwright, who is showing
them to a rich and sophisticated but homosexual friend.
It all develops into a triangle. The playwright falls in love
with the leading lady of his company. The homosexual expresses his jealousy of this by violently criticizing the plays
as they are performed for him. In the play the earnest
young playwright occassionally suggests an "attempt to use
theater in a new way, to draw life as it recognizably is,
messy and vulgar, but to avoid the theatrical convention of
oversimplification so that each member of the audience will
be provoked to build his own play out of it."[33] The three
acts are called: Serafina, The Funnies, and Talk. The
play was, on the whole, well received.

To continue presenting new theater, the facilities to
house new drama must be found and often a difficult task.
In February, 1959, Elia Kazan at an ANTA conference said,
"Off-Broadway shouldn't try to imitate Broadway. I'm not
for a totally subsidized theater, but I would like to know
that there were perhaps three houses available for experimental work."[34] This problem has been a continually growing one---how will the new and original playwright find a
live and professional producing organization which will pre-

sent his drama. In 1959, Show Business reported a jump
of 53% in Off-Broadway shows while Broadway decreased
slightly. Off-Broadway had 72 shows in 1958.[35]

Among the theaters presenting new playwrights is
the Theater Marquee where Lonny Chapman's The Buffalo
Skinner was previewed in February, 1959. The play was
reminiscent of other plays such as William Inge's Picnic
and, especially, Heaven's My Destination by Thornton
Wilder. It is about Woody Royal, a farm boy from Okla-
homa, former football hero who, after all of his football
triumphs, is rapidly disillusioned with a world which is a
hollow mockery to him even though he is still remembered
for his past prowess on the gridiron. His disillusionment seems to stem from his hatred of his father, a grim-
visaged hellfire fundamentalist. His father has succeeded
in stifling all of the gaiety in his mother, whom Woody
seems to prefer to the women who throw themselves at
him.

Eventually he rides the rails through the West with
his frequent companion in his travels, an esoteric bum
with a degree in history, from Cornell, who is more disillusioned than Woody. In these wanderings Mr. Royal
meets a lovely hymn-singer, Lois Mae, the daughter of a
revivalist, who proves more pure and more passionate than
all the rest of the women Woody has known. Somehow
Lois Mae seems to solve all of his problems and he re-
turns---although without Lois Mae---to his home to become a decent and God-fearing man.[36]

Sister Mary Francis, a cloistered Poor Clare Nun
of Roswell, New Mexico, was the author of a new play produced in February, 1959. It is in a sixteenth century Spain
in which everyone is so very sure of God's existence and

love that "to conceive and talk of Him was about the easiest
thing possible. Being a modern man with whom the picture
of the image of God is so framed by guilt, doubt, and
tension, " the only solid reference the reviewer could relate
to with his typically twentieth century mind was a "contemporary sorority house."

The play, set in a Sixteenth Century Carmelite Con-
vent depicts an order which at that time had become in-
fected with worldliness. The play relates the attempts of
Saint Teresa of Avila to return the order to the primitive
observances upon which it was founded. She must overcome the obstacles of monastic politics and a spoiled princess, among others, to succeed, but we find her sitting
humbly in the Prioress' chair by the final curtain. The
atmosphere of Sixteenth Century Spain is successfully re-
created by the author in this play presented at the Blackfriars' Guild.[37]

The Power and the Glory[38] is a dramatization by
Denis Cannan and Pierre Bost of Graham Greene's novel.
Although it has many extremely moving individual scenes
the whole is less effective than the parts.

It is set in southern Mexico during the early 1930's
and treats both sides with equal understanding. This is
difficult for a playwright to accomplish in a story which
pits a priest against an anticlerical government. This is
the drama of a country's last priest who, after escaping
twice returns in order to administer the last rites to his
people, to a totalitarian state which condemns priests to
death.

The priest is shown as a human being who does his
duty despite his many human weaknesses. He is a "whiskey
priest" and one who has yielded to the temptations of the

flesh as well as to those of the bottle. "He is a thoroughly weak man in many respects...when he is about to face a firing squad he is far from composed by the thought that he is dying as a consequence of doing his professional duty." The priest has done his duty in the face of grave consequences "at a time when he might legitimately have looked the other way, and we know there is much good in him."

On the side of the government is a lieutenant who is a "practical seeker of heaven on earth, and if destroying religion is a necessary part of that system, he accepts it as a means to what he honestly believes is a good end."[39] The lieutenant is not portrayed as a stock heavy.

The contest is ill-matched but in this struggle the priest finds his ultimate redemption. As he is taken to his death a new priest enters upon the scene. The play was a credit to the Phoenix.

The Smokeweaver's Daughter, by Thomas Barbour, was presented by the Fourth Street Theater in April, 1959. There are five fascinating characters in this production: a Count, whose characterization reveals a masterly glibness; a country boy; a good-natured and tolerant Countess; a soft-spoken Smokeweaver, who is genuinely amusing; and the Smokeweaver's daughter. Barbour "has given them magnificent lines to speak; his linguistic faculty is quite obviously highly developed."[40]

Another of the highlights of the spring season at the Phoenix in 1959 was the new production, Once Upon a Mattress. It was presented on a modest scale for a musical, but with George Abbott as its director and with good young talent, it had "an impression of spontaniety." Once Upon a Mattress was a "shining fairy tale." Atkinson felt that

there was "a dilettante libretto by Jay Thompson, Marshall
Barer and Dean Fuller, who seem to be in love with their
own cleverness...But Mary Rodgers' bountiful score, set
to pithy lyrics by Mr. Barer, uses the libretto as a point
of departure and lightly carries the burden of the party."
Miss Rodgers, a daughter of Richard Rodgers, has a "vigorous musical intelligence." The show was "a small, light,
genial musical by young people of fresh talent."[41]

Once Upon A Mattress was a marvel of unexpected
success. It began as an amateur effort at a summer camp
in the Poconos where in the space of three weeks it was
put together as a musical burlesque of the Andersen fairy
tale, The Princess and the Pea. After its initial success
with the Tamiment audience the play was put on again to
an invited audience from New York. Norris Houghton and
T. Edward Hambleton from the Phoenix offered to produce
it, and in only six weeks a full-length book for a musical
was produced by three people who had never attempted to
write anything of the kind before. Also nine songs were
written and the producers, two of them William and Jean
Eckhart, managed to raise $100,000.

The play opened to good but not rave reviews and at
first, possibly because of the hot weather, just got by, but
by the fall it was doing well. Unfortunately with the fall
season and the beginning of the already scheduled Phoenix
subscription series the play found itself without a theater.
The cast in a fit of simulated pique, went on strike, one of
the signs reading ---"Our kingdom for a house!"

With a felicitous piece of luck a house did show up
and then began the show's wanderings from one theater to
another---from the Phoenix to the Alvin to the Winter Garden
to the Cort to the St. James and then onto the road. Mary

Rodgers summed it up in describing the show as "The Little Train That Could"---and did.[42] "The Little Train" later had a successful engagement on the road. It had a performance in 1961 at Chicago's Encore Theater.

The Cricket Theater presented one of its protegées
works---The Redemptor by James Dey in May, 1959. Dey
treats satirically man's insane destruction of his own world.

Included in the cast is a mild-mannered scientist, a
gentleman of advanced age, who is completing work on a
bomb with which he hopes to blow up the world, and his
wife, a gentle lady who passes most of her time working
puzzles, and who has enthusiasm for her husband's project.
Upon completion of the bomb the couple toast each other
with sherry as they prepare to leave for Washington, D. C.
---one of the two places on earth, in the scientist's opinion,
appropriate for detonating it.

A neighbor woman, whose sensitive boy sees visions
and talks to voices in the refrigerator, visits them at this
point. The scientist's wife confides their plans to the
neighbor, who calls the police.

When the police arrive at the door, the couple aban-
don their plans to go to Washington. (The bomb is wrapped
in a baby's blanket in the manner of a new-born infant.)
As the curtain falls the scientist lights the fuse. Mr. Dey
also designed the set for this production of this one-act
play.[43]

A brief review of other new plays of the 1958-1959
season includes Valgene Massey's Chaparral, about a degenerate Texas family; Frank Merlin's Foenix in Choir,
which takes place after the A-bomb has fallen; Wade Dent's
A Good Place To Raise A Boy which attacks the South upon
its attitude on segregation, John Wulp's The Saintliness of

Margery Kempe, a comedy set in the fourteenth century;
and Bernard Evslin's The Geranium Hat, which is a children's play suitable for adults about a puppet master who
could and did change people into tiny puppets.[44]

The Connection, by Jack Gelber, is the first play
of a 27 year-old author. It has been more roundly con-
demned and more loudly hailed than almost any other recent Off-Broadway play by an American author. Directed
by Judith Malina, it opened at the Living Theater on Sixth
Avenue on July 15, 1959.

Excellent jazz was included in the evening's entertainment when the play was presented at the Living Theater. A quartet of musicians are among the guests at
Leach's pad, the setting of the drama.

This is one of the latest truly experimental dramas
to be a success Off-Broadway, a success mostly through
word of mouth advertising. The action is presented as if
the producer and writer had gathered a real group of addicts together to improvise on the given theme.

The tecnhique is reminiscent of that employed in
Haven in the Dark by Paul Nord, as the audience is included in a bewildering world of superimposed reality.
The characters' identities are transitory: the 1st and 2nd
Photographer's for example, as the play unfolds, become
dope addicts and exchange their clothing, symbolically,
piece-by-piece. The audience is the more involved in the action as two "squares" who are part of the audience in the
beginning---the writer and a photographer--get hooked into
the habit by the persuasion of the "actors." Certainly, the
abstract, experimental approach by this Beat Generation
author, Jack Gelber, gives us a more perceptive view of
dope addiction than such a purely realistic approach as

that in Harold Cobin's Annie's Son or even A Hatful of
Rain, a Broadway play about dope addiction.

The Connection has also been compared to Waiting
for Godot by Samuel Beckett and in its mood to Gorky's
Lower Depths. The characters talk in the passive yet almost poetic language of the hipster. They are waiting for
their connection, Cowboy, who is supposedly accompanied
by Leonard the Locomotive. The passive resistance of the
hipster and his philosophy of non-existence in existence is
well expressed. The squares in the audience are being let
in on the system by the slaves of the addiction but not willingly.

Most interesting of the addicts is Solly, who of all
of them obviously has the mental capacities which would indicate ability to conform and to be accepted by society.

The first act is concluded with the ironic revelation
by Jim Dunn, the producer, that he is to pay the junkies
with a fix for their performance. At the second act the
actors are getting their fix. Little happens in the second
act except that Leach, at whose pad the action takes place,
gives himself an overdose of stuff, causing the other addicts a nervous moment from the fear that he will die. As
Jaybird, the new hipster, says, at the second act's conclusion; it all fits, but now as an addict there is a wall
between him and the producer and the audience. We leave
the addicts at the drama's conclusion in their same existence of non-existence. The impression the play gives is
that of a visit to a nether world where the people are as
"nebulous and transitory as the speeding beam of light."[45]

Jackknife, by Rock Anthony, was presented at the
Royal Playhouse in 1959. After a truck jackknifes close to
the roadhouse of Maude Dade in Pennsylvania, she and her

Uncle Ned become hosts to the strange trio which emerges
from the wreakage---a young Southern farm girl who is
pregnant, supposedly by the driver of the truck; Sailor, the
driver and a he-man; and Sailor's twenty-one year-old
companion, Danny,

    The intrigue begins when Sailor, who jackknifed to
avoid hitting the drunken driver of a Cadillac, decides to
pretend injuries in order to collect insurance. To further
complicate matters, Sailor's cunning is matched in Maude,
a robust and clever woman. Matters are rapidly getting
out of hand when the police catch up with Sailor and arrest
him for violating the Mann Act. Lolly, the Southern girl,
repents and confesses that she is not pregnant and is really
in love with Danny.

    All ends well with Maude and Sailor collecting the
insurance to start a business. One of the most amusing
sections of the play is the sequence in which an insurance
lawyer investigates the claim made by Sailor. This play is
a full evening of entertainment. [46]

    In a study of the Off-Broadway play some contend
as Popkin did in the Reporter in 1959, that it is mainly
an amateur theater, but "often enough courage, imagination
and professional playwriting can make it as exciting as anything on Times Square."[47]

    Viewing the scene with less optimism about the A-
merican Off-Broadway playwright was Gerald Weales of
Commonweal, who said:

> Finally, there is the business of new American play-
> wrights. If the Off-Broadway theater were to be judged
> on the basis of the native talent it has turned up, then
> its grade would have to be a low one. [48]

    The old problem of Off-Broadway theater is that it

is geared to a different public than that of Broadway, but continues to be judged by Broadway-oriented reviewers. A Beckett play that ran successfully through six weeks of previews was closed by bad reviews.

Nevertheless, new shows by American playwrights such as Dinny and the Witches, by the well-known playwright William Gibson, continue to attract attention. Dinny and the Witches, a fantasia produced for $15,000. Off-Broadway in the last half of 1959, was originally written in 1945 as a one-act play and produced by a Topeka community theater.

The reviews on the opening were not good, four out of seven finding the play a pretentious bore. However, one reviewer felt it to be..."the funniest, most original play to come around in a long time."

Dinny and the Witches takes place in Central Park. The interesting proposition upon which the plot rests is that in the world governed by evil forces (in the play presented in the form of witches) man in his attempt to arrest time and mold the world to his ambitions will never succeed in finding happiness or the satisfaction of his wants.

Dinny outwits the destiny of death administered by the witches when he plays a song of pure feeling which causes their clock of eternal time to stop---thus the power to run the world is placed in Dinny's hands, the answer to his earlier quest for knowledge.

The second act opens on the hundredth year of Dinny's administration. A simplified Faustian personality, Dinny has in his search for perfection in the world left it in a shambles without progress because of the state of timelessness. One mother has been having a baby for the whole hundred years.

There is much truth in this play. Gibson seems
to find man in a basically evil world which is torn by con-
flicting idealogies that have created a world which washes
its hands in "gore and love and fraud---,"[49] to be resolved
through the love of a purified woman. Gibson resolves
this matter of life and death for our civilization in an a-
musing and fanciful fashion which gives being to an otherwise unendurable topic.

As Dinny and Amy, his love, plan to live happily
ever after, safe because of a miscalculation by the forces
of fate; Zenobia, a witch, in a pleasantly devasting manner
holds the clock up to the audience and tells them that each
tick is one heartbeat less for them and to go home and be
about their---"nuclear business. Savor the world, while
you have it."[50]

A booming hit among Off-Broadway musicals was
Little Mary Sunshine. As Off-Broadway became more commercial it is noticeable that fortune seemed to smile on the
musicals in agreement with the Broadway pattern. Some
critics feel that the public is tired of being fed its "medi-
cine" in straight dramas in which there is so little humor
to be found, only psychological probings into the ills of an
already over-tense era. What playwright dares to poke
fun at people who eye you coldly as soon as a little humor
is exposed. For instance, a perfectly delightful Broadway
farce by Noel Coward, Look after Lulu, failed.

One of the musicals holding sway Off-Broadway is
Little Mary Sunshine, a sort of Rose Marie "transplanted
to Colorado, with handsome forest rangers, comic Kadota
Indians, demure maidens from finishing school and Little
Mary herself, beautiful and beatific, spreading sunshine
as the owner of a Rocky Mountain Inn." Although the play

started slowly it became the "surprise bonanza of the Off-
Broadway season." Nobody would have predicted its success.

Broadway theater owners urged the show to move
uptown but it stayed in the village. Rick Besoyan was the
author of this surprise hit. He had been coaching voice in
Stella Adler's studio and had previously coached Kim Stanley
for her "That Old Black Magic" number in Bus Stop. He
hopes someday to write a musical for Kim.

With Little Mary Sunshine and other plays..."Off-
Broadway's future as a significant factor in the American
theater lies in the new plays that the commercial theater
uptown does not dare to tackle.[51]

An outstanding play, The Prodigal, was first performed at the Downtown Theater in New York on February
11, 1960. The theme is the Orestes legend of ambitions,
politics and vengeance. Jack Richardson, very modern and
sophisticated in his treatment, was the recipient of the
Vernon Rice and Obie awards for it.

Jack Richardson was 24 at the time that The Prodigal was written as an academic exercise while he was in
Germany on a fellowship. In his drama are incisive and
provocative discussions of the relative merits of men's
ambitions.[52]

Time called Richardson, "the season's best new playwright." Richardson may be the hope for the American
theater---its answer for a Giradoux or Annouilh. He has
written into the drama such gems of dialogue as "I have
nothing against collective misery being turned to someone's
advantage and called Religion..."[53] and ..." a curio of
folly to be placed under glass and studied to be avoided."[54]

Orestes is characterized as a seeker and philosopher;

he views life as one set apart, not as participant nor partisan. His is not a personality of diplomacy and tact but
one which outspokenly reveals the festering truth.

Agammenon, as the symbol of a way of life for
which his followers no longer care, is ultimately assassi-
nated. He represents a military and heroic authority from
which his followers turn to the less demanding but totalitarianistic rule of Aegisthus. This rule promises them
sympathy and equality without regard to individual merit.

Orestes, who will not stand by his father while he
is alive to strike the "fresh blow of the future"[55] must later battle for his fathers' causes alone, not being able to
escape the responsibilities imposed by fate. Orestes is
judged by the standards of the world that supported Agammenon and its dictates force him to take a hero's revenge.
The premise that there is no place in life for the prodigal
concludes the drama with Orestes returning to Argos.
Complementing the style of the drama is the staging technique used in the third act in which the sea and the audience area become one.

Come Share My House, by Theodore Epstein, formerly on the dramatic arts staff at Columbia University and
also a member of the New Dramatist's Committee, was
rewritten after a strawhat tryout at the Barn Theater in
Augusta, Michigan. Variety felt that it never rose "above
the soap opera classification."[56] It opened at the Actors'
Playhouse on February 18, 1960. The setting is one of
the seven-story buildings between Broadway and Riverside
Drive in the Nineties. The play uses the scrim-flashback
method to show scenes in Mexico which occurred before
Amparo and Tom arrived in New York; he to study at
Columbia University, she to bear a child. Amparo, the

young Mexican wife, is a delightful, strong person. She
must suffer for her marriage for reasons which the Negro
superintendent of the building aptly states as..."If you step
out of your place, if you don't do it like everybody else
around you, you got trouble...is it worth the pain and the
fight or ain't it?"[57]

Amparo continues fighting when Joe has turned to
drink and dominoes. He is ashamed of her since he married her only because she was to bear his child. Through
her employment as a servant Amparo sees Tom back at
Columbia University. Tom, realizing her true value, also
becomes aware that he does love her and that it is she who
should be ashamed of him. This drama, like Sign of Winter and Me, Candido!, deals with the problems which con-
front different racial groups which dare to integrate.

Marshall Young of the Theater Guild Staff is execu-
tive producer of Studio Three, a non-profit foundation that
plans to sponsor the works of unproduced playwrights for
brief runs before invited audiences. The project's first
venture was Answered the Flute, a first play by Sam Robins, which had been making the rounds of the offices in
manuscript form for a number of seasons.

Although the aim of producing new plays was worthwhile, it seems the group's initial offering of March, 1960,
was a weak one. The plot centered around domestic up-
heavals in the household of a drab candy store proprietor.
He is a father with faded dreams of success as a flute
player. He is in conflict with his daughter, who challenges
him to turn his illusions into reality. Other characters in
the play are a mother who lusts after her 22-year old
boarder, the son of an old flame, and a neighborly matron
who is an alcoholic.

Climaxes follow rapidly upon one another. The
father auditions for a symphony and fails. The daughter
succeeds in persuading the boarder to rob her of her vir-
ginity. The mother trys to seduce the boarder but he
announces that he is moving out. Then the daughter runs
away from home with a young neighbor but is persuaded to
return home by the police. At the final curtain the parents
are reconciled.[58]

The Secret Concubine, an Oriental fable by Aldyth
Morris was presented in April, 1960. Into this delicate
and unreal world presented by the playwright are inter-
jected arguments for pacifism and brotherhood.

The central character, a concubine, gives an imperious emperor the son he always wanted. The emperor
is ruthlessly militant and in order to temper his militarism,
the concubine abandons that which he loves most---his son,
to a stranger. "Now they're all your sons," she says,
applying some of the thoughts of Arthur Miller on human
responsibility to the world of ancient China.[59]

The Ignorants Abroad by William A. Guthrie was
written as a farce in an artificial, highly stylized manner
resembling that of Oscar Wilde. At a time when most
playwrights are abandoning conventional theatrical forms,
the play was something of an "anachronism, but an often
amusing one..." The characters are a brash Texas oil
millionaress and her sweet, 17 year-old daughter who are
going through England in search of a title. They sight the
goal in the 28 year-old scion of an ancient manor house,
Abbotts Crumbling. The young man is wonderfully naive
and docile. One of his more memorable lines is, "I say,
Mummy, am I old enough to marry?"

The narrative involves the scion's imperious mother,

his long-lost father, who reappears much in the manner of
Miss Prism's satchel, and an elegant butler with firm opin-
ions on upper and lower case society. There are epigrams
such as the one of Lady Umbridge, "Respectability is the
curse of a dull life." "Nonsense," says her husband, "respectability is the cause of it." Or, "A woman goes to her
dressmaker to be saved, to church to be seen."

The daughter elopes and the mother, Mrs. Pearce,
exclaims, "I gave her the best years of my life, the best
comic books money could buy. It was I who saw that she
had her first permanent as soon as her hair was thick
enough to absorb chemicals." The style of the play, produced in June, 1960, was "generally consistent but the quality was not." The Ignorants Abroad was a "skillful imita-
tion concocted by a writer of talent."[60]

The Laughing Academy, with its atmosphere reminiscent of Tobacco Road, was presented in June, 1960. The
setting is in the patio of the Sunset Point Motel on the
Southern California coast, surrounded by a collection of
dilapidated cabanas. Characters are hard-drinking, sluttish
and moronic. They often live in corrugated iron shacks.
One has, as his home, the luggage compartment of a broken-
down car. The dialogue is rough, but colorful. Inevitably,
drink is the main topic of conversation. A second favorite
subject is how to dodge the rent collector, known as the
money man. Another topic consists of advice to the one
young girl to stay away from romance, advice she is ultimately forced to ignore.[61]

Off-Broadway, fortunately, continues to produce
writers for the theater. As long as there are organizations
such as the Cricket and Originals Only dedicated to the
encouragement and nurture of the new playwright, we can

hope that a theater will continue to flourish which consists of more than merely realistic presentations or "psychological" studies. Off-Broadway must maintain its place as a stage that gives expression to the experimental and the unusual "avant-garde" piece. In the financial situation of today we cannot deny that the existence of the art form becomes more difficult to realize. Even playwrights must bow to the necessities of making a living. However, Off-Broadway continues as a theater which is more than merely a "celebration of technique."

An encouraging fact is that Off-Broadway has given Broadway such playwrights as Tad Mosel and Leslie Stevens. A genuine impetus to the Off-Broadway producer to present new playwrights is the latest success by Michael Shurtleff, Call Me By My Rightful Name. The critics commented "A man who knows how to write for an intelligent audience!" (Davis of the News), "Shurtleff has the feel of the theater in His Blood!" (Taubman, New York Times) "Fine comedy! Quivering with vitality and full of humor." (Morgenstern of the Herald Tribune) And, finally, "A Hit is Born!" (Mc Lain, Jr. of the American).[62]

Off-Broadway is of age at a time when unrest and tension has robbed the world of much of its spontaniety. It started with productions put on for practically nothing, with costumes and scenery made at home, the free expression of those devoted to the theater. It has had at its service the talent of many of the greatest names in American theater who brought the idea of a theater of experiment alive and gave impetus to others who wished to show new expression, to protest at a time when protest was needed against injustice or suppression of the truth.

Although, today Off-Broadway has attracted the most

expert professionals and the experienced guidance of the
commercial and moneyed interests of the theater, and is
previewed like Broadway by such reviewers as Alan Pryce-
Jones, it nevertheless, as shown by the cast of <u>Little
Mary Sunshine,</u> in the midst of all of its recognition and
sometimes splendor, does not altogether lose its identification as truly representative American theater. This is a
theater built of the ideas of the people or of the, wants of
an intellegentsia which wishes to view new and untried
forms of drama which feels the pulse of the United States,
its ideas, its hopes, its aspirations, its trials, and its people.

A play presented Off-Broadway may be noticed by
films and television and reviewed by the major critics. Although remuneratively Off-Broadway is not what it could be,
to the playwright there is always the hope that the play may
move on Broadway or be bought by the more expensive
media, TV and films.

With Broadway talent, including playwrights, using
Off-Broadway as a means for expression, production costs
are steadily rising. Due to these rising costs, tomorrow
the young hopefuls may be paradoxically, off Off-Broadway.
Although the new playwright who has never been produced
still continues to have the opportunity to be heard, there is
a new need for expansion to free the stage to all the developing talent to be found in the United States.

Notes

1.   "Calendar of the Theater Arts," <u>Theater</u> Arts, Vol.
      XL, No. 2, February, 1956, p. 4.

2.   Walker, Gerald, "Theater: Third Person," <u>The
      Village Voice,</u> January 25, 1956, p. 10.

3.   Rosenthal, Andrew, Third Person, MSS, c/o David
      Clive, Clerrman Productions.

4.   "Theater: The Thorntons," The Village Voice,
      February 22, 1956, p. 9.

5.   Anderson, Walt, Me, Candido!, Dramatists Play Ser-
      vice, Inc., Copyright 1950, 1958, p. 64.

6.   Driver, Tom F., "Lane Beyond the River," Criti-
      cism, Christian Century, July 24, 1957, 74:895.

7.   The Villager, Greenwich Village, New York, Feb-
      ruary, 7, 1957, Vol. XXIV, No. 45, p. 8.

8.   Barrows, Robert Guy, Bivouac at Lucca, MSS, 11-14.

9.   Hayes, Alfred, The Girl on the Via Flaminia, the
      Off-Broadway Theater, Edited by Richard A. Cordell
      and Lowell Matson, Random House, New York.

10.   Barrows, Robert Guy, Bivouac at Lucca, MSS,
      III-23.

11.   Atkinson, Brooks, "Theater: Drama in Italy," The
      New York Times, Wednesday, October 30, 1957.

12.   Beckley, Paul V., "Off-Broadway," New York Herald
      Tribune, October 30, 1957.

13.   Lee, James, "Career: Drama," Theater Arts,
      November, 1957, 41:36-61.

14.   Roberts, Meade, A Palm Tree in a Rose Garden,
      Dramatists Play Service, Copyright 1955, 1958.

15.   Hewes, Henry, "Criticism," Saturday Review of
      Literature, February 1, 1958, 41:25.

16.   "Legitimate," Variety, Wednesday, March 12, 1958,
      p. 74.

17.   Ibid.

18.   Gelb, Arthur, "News and Gossip of the Rialto,"
      Drama, The New York Times, Sunday, December
      15, 1957, Section 3.

19.   "Off-Broadway," Theater Arts, March, 1958, Vol.
      XLII, No. 3, p. 13.

20.   Williams, Tennessee, "Garden District," Common-
      weal, May 30. 1958, 68:232-3.

21.   "Criticism," America, June 21, 1958, 99:359.

22.   Panetta, George, Comic Strip, Samuel French, Inc.,
      Copyright 1958.

23.   America, June 21, 1958, op. cit.

24.   Watts, Richard, Jr., "Off-Broadway's Season in
      Summary," Theater Arts, July, 1958, Vol. XLII,
      No. 7, p. 18.

25.   Ibid., p. 70

26.   Passos dos, John and Paul Shyre, Theater Arts,
      June, 1960, Vol. XLIV, No. 6, p. 44.

27.   Passos dos, John and Paul Shyre, USA, Theater
      Arts, June, 1960, Volume XLIV, No. 6, pp. 23-50.

28.   "Criticism---Golden Six," Time, November 3, 1958,
      72:50.

29.   "Criticism," America, Nov. 8, 1958, 100:174.

30.   Lewis, Emory, "The Theater," Cue, Jan.31, 1959, p.13.

31.   Hewes, "Criticism," Saturday Review, November
      15, 1958, 41:27.

32.   Stavis, Barrie, The Man Who Never Died, Drama-
      tists Play Service, Inc., Copyright 1959.

33.   "Many Loves, Criticism," Saturday Review, January
      31, 1959, 42:24.

34.   "Elia Kazan Calls for More Experimental Theaters
      in the U.S.," Show Business, February 23, 1959,
      Vol. XIX---No. 8, p. 1.

35.   "Bigger B'way Stage Season Seen; Grosses Up; 53%
      Jump Off-B'way," Show Business, Vol. XIX---No. 5,

February 2, 1959, p. 1.

36.   Tallmer, Jerry, "Theater: The Buffalo Skinners,"
      The Village Voice, February 25, 1959, p. 9.

37.   Schleifer, Marc D., "Theater:" The Village Voice,
      February 25, 1959, p. 8.

38.   Cannan, Denis and Pierre Bost, The Power and the
      Glory, Samuel French, Inc., Copyright 1956, 1959.

39.   "Off-Broadway," Theater Arts, February, 1959,
      p. 67.

40.   Pomex, Lee, "Off-Broadway Reviews," Show Busi-
      ness, Monday, April 20, 1959, p. 8.

41.   Atkinson, Brooks, "On Off-Broadway," The New
      York Times, Sunday, May 17, 1959, Section 2, p. 1.

42.   Rodgers, Mary, "From Pillow to Post," Theater
      Arts, July, 1960, pp. 21-24.

43.   Meehan, Thomas, The Villager, Greenwich Village,
      New York, Vol. XXVII, No. 5, May 7, 1959, p. 16.

44.   The Burns Mantle Yearbook, The Best Plays 1958-
      1959; Edited by Louis Kronenberger; Dodd, Mead and
      Company; New York, 1959, Toronto, p. 50.

45.   Gelber, Jack, The Connection, Evergreen Books, Ltd.,
      Grove Press, Inc., London, New York, Copyright
      1957.

46.   Anthony, Rock, Jackknife, Samuel French, Inc.,
      Copyright, 1957.

47.   Popkin, H. "It's Big on Bleecker Street," Reporter,
      July 9, 1959, 21:46-7.

48.   Weales, Gerald, "Box Office and the Muse is Off-
      Broadway Theater," Commonweal, September 25,
      1959, 70:541.

49.   Gibson, William, LDinny and the Witches, Atheneum
      Publishers, New York, Copyright 1950, 1960, p. 77.

50.   Ibid., p. 155.

51.   "Bright-eyed with Hope; Off-Broadway," Newsweek, February 22, 1960, 55:95.

52.   "Legitimate," Variety, Wednesday, March 2, 1960, p. 72.

53.   Richardson, Jack, The Prodigal, E.P. Dutton & Co., Inc., New York, Copyright 1960, p. 17.

54.   Ibid., p. 74.

55.   Ibid., p. 81.

56.   "Legitimate," Variety, Wednesday, March 2, 1960, p. 72.

57.   Apstein, Theodore, Come Share My House, Samuel French, Inc., Copyright 1960, p. 56.

58.   "Legitimate," Variety, Wednesday, March 30, 1960, p. 74.

59.   "Legitimate," Variety, Wednesday, April 6, 1960, p. 80.

60.   "Legitimate," Variety, Wednesday, June 1, 1960, p. 72.

61.   "Legitimate," Variety, Wednesday, June 29, 1960, p. 70.

62.   "Drama," The New York Times, February 5, 1961, 4X.

Chapter IX

Views Of Current Off-Broadway Leaders
Jerry Tallmer
Leo Garen
Ted Mann
Gene Frankel
Kip Hastings
James Spicer
Judith Malina

The following chapter is a compilation of authoritative interviews with prominent personalties who are leaders of the Off-Broadway stage. Their views substantiate the impression of Off-Broadway as it has emerged from the preceding chapters.

---Jerry Tallmer---

Jerry Tallmer is drama critic and associate editor of The Village Voice which, since its appearance in 1955, has followed the Off-Broadway scene.

The first question I presented in our interview was why original plays were not being produced.

"For financial reasons. When it costs $5,000-$20,000. to produce a play Off-Broadway, it is rather hard to get a production."

My next query was whether unions were causing the difficulty.

"Phyllis Anderson at 2nd Ave. and 5th St. had 12 stage hands for Girl of the Golden West...crushed by stage hands. Union imposes terribly big loads on the Phoenix Theater, too."

I asked if there were enough new playwrights or
whether the new authors couldn't reach the producers.

"Not much talent in playwrights. Most of the interesting writing European---Beckett, Ionesco, Genet, Behan, Kops."

The remaining conversation reviewed the general
Off-Broadway picture as of 1959, its problems and possible
solutions. Tallmer noted that "7 out of 200 shows break
even Off-Broadway." "Very long runs" are necessary to
make a profit. "New playwrights must contact New York.
They must have the push because theater does not have
enough cash to send people out like baseball scouts."

Tallmer said that some of the new productions Off-
Broadway of that year had left a definite impression on him.
One playwright he felt had promise was Bernard Evslin,
although he declared that he "tried to do too much." His
play, No Face Is Evil, was "about atom bombs." "The
writer has a feel for fantasy; it was a charming play, well
directed and well staged."

Other plays of the 1958-1959 season mentioned by
Tallmer included The Automobile Graveyard by John Clellan
Holmes, GO by Arrabal, Graham Greene's The Power and
the Glory, The Buffalo Skinner by Lonny Chapman, And the
Wind Blows by Tanjo Stewart, The Golem which was "semi-
professional," and Heloise which he felt was the "dreariest
of bores." He described it as a play, based on history,
in which a "brilliant student made love to a girl who was
his student, is castrated, and devotes his life afterwards to
study---becomes a brilliant scholar."

Listen to the Quiet by Fred J. Scollay was "terrible,"
about "prisoner in solitary and priest." Mead Roberts'
Maidens and Mistresses "mocks Williams." A Clearing in

the Woods by Arthur Laurents was "the best thing Off-Broadway." Tallmer felt George Hitchcock's Housewarming was "very much like Ionesco." He really liked The Hamlet of Stephney Green by Bernard Kops. He mentioned The Young Provincials by Ben Levinson, The Failures, Songs of Walt Whitman, The Midnight Caller by Horton Foote, Lulu by Frank Wedekind, Ullyses in Nighttown, (an adaptation of James Joyce which Mr. Tallmer called a "mishmash with music and dance"), The Quare Fellow by Brendan Behan, "a beautiful play, done very badly," and Two Masks by Louis A. Lippa which was "very promising." Tallmer felt that Lippa may be one of the "future hopes of the theater." He also discussed the experimental production presented on June 18, 1959, The Make of Moo which was "about religion in Africa" and stated that "all religion corrupts."

Finally, he commented that most writers, directors, and actors are trying to go on Broadway. This trend is supported partly by such organizations as Circle-in-the-Square that has people who are definitely "trying to rival Broadway." However, Tallmer feels that the Broadway audience would never go Off-Broadway.

---Leo Garen---

My next interview was with Leo Garen whom Jerry Tallmer had recommended as one of the most promising of young directors. His direction of The Deathwatch by Jean Genêt was outstanding. At the time that I visited him he was working on his next production---The Automobile Graveyard, the second play by Arrabal, a Spaniard who has been writing in Paris for the last few years. Richard Howard translated the play, which is about the "nilhilism and terrorism of modern times."

Garen, at 23, is young for a director. His future
assignments at that time included a Broadway play. On
June 18, 1959, I found him busily typing in his apartment
on Central Park South.

Immediately he launched into a discussion of his
views of Off-Broadway. He felt that there was "a greater
restiveness on Broadway because of Off-Broadway." An
audience of "2,000 to 3,000 who go to Off-Broadway each
night can be discounted. He felt "Off-Broadway has been
overdue as there was already such a movement established
in Paris, Mexico City and Germany." Off-Broadway has
made "theater more exciting than before. In some plays
the line gets thin between Broadway and Off-Broadway.
Also Off-Broadway opens possibilities for Broadway which
never existed before." Mr. Garen stated that "Off-Broadway exactly like Broadway in that you have a hit or a flop."
But at the same time "it has expanded horizons which were
commercially unfeasible." "Off-Broadway has done extra-
ordinary things; however, one needs perserverance and
courage."

"The Theater Guild deserves distinction in the '20's
in that they were first similar to Off-Broadway theater.
They presented such works as Karel Capek's The Insect
Comedy, which is similar to what Off-Broadway is doing
today."

I asked him about the format of repertory theater
which many Off-Broadway groups tried to institute. He
felt that repertoire was a great American fantasy. "One
needs incredible control and taste. Also, you need someone with talent and drive and strength."

"Most people throw up their hands in disgust after

a while. For instance Kazan could run a repertory theater but he does as he wishes. I would be happy if the government would subsidize theater. But stage of government as far as theater concerned, at about level of Robert Montgomery as far as kind of theater government would do. The Columbus Square project may be a very good thing but the Phoenix is a mess.

"Only good things Phoenix has done was when people from outside came in such as the Ionesco play done by Tony Richardson. Houghton and Hambleton, producers, were at fault because they have no point of view. For instance, their latest list of plays in their subscription drive. Who the hell wants to do Lysistrata and Winterset?"

I asked whether it is difficult to obtain an original play. Mr. Garen replied that plays with excellent quality usually fall into hands of agents and one has to "break his back to get it from them." Sometimes a playwright with obvious potential is successful in doing them Off-Broadway, but it is, however, a gamble. Many times, Mr. Garen stated, that revivals are done Off-Broadway because of unavailability of safe plays and a lack of imagination in those working Off-Broadway.

"If Threepenny Opera had run with another edition, it would have lasted 3 days. Carmen Capalbo showed some theater nerve. Intellectual qualities theater has are secondary, after feeling. First point of theater is that it is a sensory experience to affect you. There must be humanity in drama. Theater must be sharp and clear, show sincere human nature. The content of plays on Off-Broadway are richer and fuller."

Mr. Garen was the first to admit that Off-Broadway "has much incompetence. In fact the "vast majority are

terrible." He even suggested people should learn and experiment away from Off-Broadway. "But at the same time
a small handful of people Off-Broadway keep oroducing
something very good."

"People are beginning to accept Off-Broadway. They
are beginning to look on Off-Broadway in the light of Broadway."

Mr. Garen made clear that Broadway has certain
advantages. For one, a star often supports a play on
Broadway. Also, there is usually six to ten weeks to prepare on a Broadway play. An enormous amount of publicity
is sent out before the opening and the play is publicized by
such magazines as Life and Time.

Today, fortunately, such papers as The Village
Voice and The Villager are encouraging Off-Broadway. But
still, during the run of a production, Off-Broadway theaters
often turn away 50 or 60 people from the door during the
weekend while only 60, 70, or 80 seats are filled during
the week. As yet not enough people "are interested in
going to see Genet."

Garen felt a "sameness to all Broadway things while
Off-Broadway is tending to raise the cultural level throughout the country." He felt Off-Broadway began to be accepted "sometime in the last three or four years. In
1955 it was still on the brink of being accepted." Off-
Broadway is "still not accepted completely by the press."

"There is a crying need for Off-Broadway. Broadway and pressure getting worse. True, pressure on individual greater Off-Broadway, but greater freedom in
terms of what you want to do."

"Off-Broadway and Broadway shouldn't be that different an expression. Many plays by Williams have not been

done on Broadway."

---Ted Mann---

On June 15, 1959, I had an appointment with Ted
Mann, one of the producers of Circle-in-the-Square, and
a member of the board of directors for the Off-Broadway
Theater League. We opened our discussion with the
League. Anyone may join who has produced or is planning
to produce an Off-Broadway show. Mann feels that Off-
Broadway is gaining many benefits from it although it no
longer has a joint advertising and joint ticket office, one
of its former major assets.

Mann felt that the League, by unifying Off-Broadway
theaters, had enabled them to work together in negotiating
with the unions. This had proved most beneficial. Mann
noted that during the time of the newspaper strike, the
League had kept the name of the shows in front of the public. He felt that the policy initiated at that time should be
continued.

"They banded together that time with advertising---
presented lists of productions on same listings. This was
desirable."

(I recalled that at the time of which Tallmer had
spoken, four shows which opened at the same time Off-
Broadway advertised their combined bill on the side of a
bus.)

---Gene Frankel---

On June 22, 1959, I met with Gene Frankel at his
successful theater school atop the Players Theater on Mac-
Dougal Street. He had left a never-to-be-forgotten impression on New York theater with his direction of "Volpone"

at the Rooftop Theater two seasons back. This feat won
for him both the Obie and Lola d'Annunzio Awards as best
director of the year. Since then he has directed the successful Arthur Miller adaptation of An Enemy of the People
at Actors Playhouse.

We began our interview with a discussion of the
financial aspects of Off-Broadway.

"More courage is needed in doing certain things
Off-Broadway because not as much money involved. For
instance, it cost $16,000. to do Volpone and $14,000. for
An Enemy of the People. I didn't make money with Volpone
but I did with An Enemy of the People."

He mentioned that "many pipe dreams held Off-
Broadway and one is to make a success and bring it on
Broadway and capitalize there. A few successes keep the
idea going. The Fourth Street theater is starting Chekhov
again because it is a successful investment. One always
needs to draw an audience."

He felt that in the preceding five years Off-Broadway
had changed and that it had become intensified. For instance, "comparatively speaking," for a production like Nat
Turner---"there was not much expense." This was "prior
to the opening of Circle-in-the-Square." Nat Turner stayed
eight months at a cost of $2,000.

"Then they were not interested in investment in theater. They were interested in supporting experimental theater."

"Investment in Off-Broadway theater is getting too
stiff to leave too much room for experiment. Now it is
commercial operation on lesser scale than Broadway. Most
money invested on the basis that they will get their money
back."

"Successes are usually those formerly on Broadway, which won't do revivals. For successes formerly on Broadway, there is now an audience Off-Broadway. By and large, though, uptown Broadway audience not coming downtown. People that keep uptown shows running don't keep Off-Broadway running."

He mentioned the production of Summer and Smoke which, a failure on Broadway, was very theatricalized in the Off-Broadway version. Mr. Frankel feels:

"Theatricalization for itself and by itself is pointless. Within the framework of point of view of what play is about rather than for sake of theater. If it helps meaning of play, then valuable directorial contribution can be made, otherwise it makes no contribution to Off-Broadway."

As to the future, Frankel feels that producers Off-Broadway will continue to choose plays not as much for experimentation as "with eye for successes." He feels the day is gone when producers will "produce plays for just doing theater."

He would think ten times before doing an original play Off-Broadway. Audiences prefer to go to see revivals, classics, and so on. New plays are dangerous to do because new plays get a shorter visit. Some critics go, but not the first string. New playwrights who are successful Off-Broadway are practically non-existant. The new plays produced are mainly by established writers such as Clerambard, Ionesco and Beckett.

Mr. Mann claims that Off-Broadway has succeeded in that certain productions have been allowed to open up their prosceniums. He felt the "nature of play houses on Broadway has stultified production." J.B. was the most "inventive"of the 1959 season. A play which preceded this

production was Off-Broadway in 1949---They Shall Not Die,
and had the same type of staging as J.B. It had a "raked,
circular platform stage in exactly the same style as on
Broadway."

Then, too, Frankel felt that Off-Broadway "had extended the subway circuit." Possibly because "of dwindling
commercial theater as we know it, Off-Broadway fills a
vacumn."

"More theater not more opportunities are what is
needed. Off-Broadway fills a necessary vacumn.

"Some producers would assist that which was truly
different, and in developing theaters some would like to see
a sort of Off-Broadway which was truly a breeding ground
for latent theater. Experimentation is needed in the establishment of new kinds of theater."

He conceded that with Kazan and others, directorially,
some of the theater forms on Broadway are more creative.
For instance, the Broadway productions of Annouilh,
Giradoux and Beckett.

"It just isn't feasible to do modern classic on Broad-
way and it isn't feasible to do a revival on Broadway.
Revivals and classics don't work."
Perhaps in his last statement lies the answer to why Off-
Broadway exists.

One reason Broadway no longer has as large a production schedule is that "theater houses are dwindling" and
a good reason for that is "theater owners get 30% off the
top and there is a stop clause which can ask a show to
leave if it isn't running to capacity."

When asked about original writers today, Frankel
said that most write for other media. William Carlos
Williams wrote for the stage only in the "twilight of life."

"Off-Broadway capitalizes on these writers and winds up with plays written by writers with training in other fields. We should encourage writers in college and community theater."

On the whole Frankel feels that "they are as commercial Off-Broadway as on and we need an off Off-Broadway theater today."

---Kip Hastings---

During an interview on June 22, 1959, I found Kip Hastings of the Herbert Berghof studios to be a very gracious and charming person. Her first remark affirmed what Frankel had said: Circle-in-the-Square and the Phoenix theater operations were the most successful Off-Broadway. Most Off-Broadway theater, she stated, "was not commercial."

She commented that Summer and Smoke was the forerunner of the successful Off-Broadway theater of today, and resulted in the discovery of Geraldine Page.

As to my constantly repeated inquiry about new Off-Broadway scripts, Miss Hastings said new scripts are presented more often in summer stock, because Off-Broadway's experimental period is more or less over. Of 1950-1955, "there were not many good scripts starting Off-Broadway even at this time." Now with production costs Off-Broadway at from "$10, 000-$12, 000, it is even harder to put on a script.

She felt that Broadway was worse off with the minimum Broadway production costing about $40, 000.

"It is absolutely crazy about theater rentals. The equity minimum going up. It only leaves room for Arthur

Miller's and T. William's plays---only room for these
writers.   Other scripts are mutilated because of so many
outside interests who know nothing about the theater having
their say so.   Young producers with money haven't appren-
ticed themselves to the theater."
Having studied the fundamentals of directing with Berghof,
I found Miss Hasting's analysis reviewed some of the
statements he had made in the class.

As to Off-Broadway's advantages she felt it was "a
place where actors get the greatest opportunity."   Then,
too, it was a "marvelous idea to get the theater less cen-
tralized."

As to the ever-pressing question of finances, Miss
Hastings "thinks prices on Broadway may drive audiences
Off-Broadway."   She said that the "tax deductible audience
is on Broadway."   To quote her, "the snobs patronize
Broadway."

"If Geraldine Page would be Off-Broadway, tax
deductible would go see her.   However, the star system is
failing at the Phoenix.   There it doesn't seem to be working.
It is a combination of repertory Broadway and Off-Broadway.   But tax deductible audience doesn't necessarily need
stars as they live in a world of stardom."

Miss Hastings felt that "Off-Broadway would have to
go for broke before union problems would be better."   This
financial situation was worse on Broadway and she felt that
the "Off-Broadway movement is desirable because it would
stimulate more creative activity away from all of the stifling
necessities of financing productions on Broadway."

"Herbert Berghof was doing Twelfth Night and wanted
to put in some of their students.   He got four in but they
had to pay the union, 132 dollars, so that they could have

walk-on parts.

"Schools such as Berghof's are trying to create
their own theater where artists can truly create. I feel
that the Broadway crowd won't venture to go Off-Broadway
unless something such as intellectual appeal will draw them."

Miss Hastings also discussed the lethargy that she
found in the theater today. However, she speculated that
one reason for that may again be financial. If prices were
lower more people would be able to go.

"In England where I started I went to the theater
for our equivalent of $.35. I went to several shows several
times. The West End theaters in London were the avant-
garde there as some of our Off-Broadway theaters are in
the United States."

---James Spicer---

James Spicer, public relations director of the Living Theater staff, sat at his huge desk on June 18, 1959
in the uniquely modern premises of the theater, and stated
that he, unfortunately, was too busy to see many of the
other plays on or Off-Broadway.

He could give a great deal of information about his
own group---The Living Theater. It is interested in "modern poetic theater" and is primarily a membership organization which began its "repertory system" on July 8, 1959.

Spicer felt "financial costs shouldn't affect the
theory behind the theater---400 odd people have been on
our payroll in the last two or three productions." By
making an organization a "membership organization and
non-profit, cost wouldn't be so high."

One very revealing comment made by Spicer was

that: "the living theater doesn't belong to the Off-Broadway
Theater League because it is not really Off-Broadway theater but poetic theater, with the exception of Circle-in-the-
Square, the Living Theater is the only group with a repertory series."

Living Theater considers itself "experimental avant-
garde." Such plays as The Cave at Machpelah by Paul
Goodman and The Connection, a play with jazz, by Jack
Gelber, would not be done on Broadway. "The type of
play done in Living Theater would not be sent to agents."
Playwrights send in plays to Living Theater which sometimes must wait years before Miss Malina and Mr. Beck
get a chance to look at them.

One of the Living Theater's most interesting projects
is its special events program, which includes concerts of
classical music, readings by leading poets, dance recitals,
poetry and jazz sessions, a film program, and publication
parties---all of which "extends and finds the Living theater
programs which will attract other people." The program
"expresses all artists rather than simply exclusively drama."

In conclusion, Spicer stated that there was a "sympathy between the ideas of Artaud particularly in music,
dance, poetry." He warned "don't strain comparison too
much, but a definite relationship exists."

---Judith Malina---

On June 22, 1959, I had the privilege of meeting and
talking to Miss Malina in her dressing room between rehearsals for the Living Theater's new repertory. I found
her a dedicated, sparkling woman who revealed her vibrant
personality even under the grotesque makeup of a very old

woman which she had applied for her role in The Cave of
Machpelah.

Judith Malina was born in a theater in Kiel, Germany, and made her first stage appearance at the age of
two. In 1948 she founded The Living Theater with Julian
Beck and has directed, among other plays, Dr. Faustus
Lights the Lights, and Ubu Roi. Another of her major
accomplishments in her varied acting assignments was the
creation of the role of Phaedre in New York City's first
professional production of Racine's play in English which
The Living Theater presented in 1955.

My first question after our preliminary conversation
was what qualities she considered to be necessary to a
good script.

"Producing a good evening's entertainment which extends the boundaries of dramatic event. Experiment in
original ways, which in some way extends the boundaries of
drama. It is almost certain such a script will not find production on Broadway."

"A great many scripts, about two a week, come in.
I look at all of them, but don't have time to read them all.
Jack Gelber brought in his script of The Connection himself.
Julian Beck and I decided to do it immediately."

The Living Theater did one show which could be
considered dangerous to produce---a French classical farce
of 1898, Ubu Roi by Alfred Jarry. After viewing the show,
the landlord had them turned out because they repeatedly
used the word "shit."

When they presented Paul Goodman's The Young
Disciple, the most avant-garde script that the Living Thea-
ter so far has presented, the chorus used the word "fucking!"
The first time the audience walked out, but later when it

was said in an off-hand way, no one objected. Obscenity
is one kind of thing "people are most easily touched on
for no real reason."

Judith Malina feels strongly about the fact that on
Off-Broadway "one kind of thing needed is willingness to
sacrifice."

"Willingness needed to feel the thing through; to go
through the ordeal. There are many ambitious actresses
but all should be so."

Miss Malina says that among the scripts that are
sent to them, many are not for Living Theater. She definitely feels that "good writing is stimulated by Off-Broadway."

Another problem of the experimental theater is how
much the public will allow in a script which is unconven-
tional.

"Shakespeare was the first of his type with the
illusion stage. Always the first, the dawn is the greatest
work. It always has been in the first burst that one finds
the important work. But the danger of doing something
original is that people will call you a fool and idiot and a
dilettante. The review in Times the second time Living
Theater did Dr. Faustus Lights the Lights was in this
vein. To present an original, one does it like diving off
a board into cold water."

"Experimenting is cautious today or else on the level
of fantasy. Fantasy often causes the extremely experimental, in which one has ghosts, but that does not make it
poetic or experimental.theater   Fancy is found in Anouilh
and Giradoux."

"Fancy is not avant-garde in sense that it will tread
on toes of people. The more one treads on their toes the

more it will be effective. The equation of the amount of
mockery and effectiveness pretty much equalizes. There is
a Dangerous point, though, where one merely gains shock
value."

Our discussion then led to a consideration of the
audience, particularly that of the Living Theater, where one
finds an artist's audience. Miss Malina stated that one
must have something to attract an audience and one needs
"artistic courage to do this." One must have something to
attract an audience away from Broadway and other influences.

"Off-Broadway needs to do very dangerous things.
Anyone can say they will do something but need artists who
will do it."

"One danger of doing new things is that the charge
of obscene theater may be leveled against the very theater
which is experimental."

In conclusion Judith Malina quipped that when she
and Julian Beck received the Drama Critic's Award, Julian
said, "Time for us to move on." This statement proved to
be prophetic. In the summer of 1961 they did just this
when the Living Theater Company toured in Europe.

Let us hope that Off-Broadway will continue to develop with people who are not afraid to perform and create
that which is advanced for its time. In the field of drama
there is an Off-Broadway for those with the talent and the
courage to produce experimental theater. Each of the people in the preceding study were able successfully to extend
their own dramatic creativity despite privations. Theirs is
an earned and honorable insight into the problems and
opportunities inherent in an advanced theater. Theirs is
also a prophetic vision of that which may be the theater of the
future.

Off-Broadway Productions 1950-1960

A Bibliography and Checklist

This is a preliminary checklist of plays presented Off-Broadway between 1950 and 1960. It includes, in separate listings, both new American plays and revivals of all kinds. Many of the original plays have not been published, and many of the others have appeared in numerous editions. Where it would be helpful, I have tried to include brief information beyond the author and title, but this is not intended to be consistently done.

New Plays by American Authors, 1950-51

1. The Fine Old Wine of Monsieur Nuche by Paul Willems.

2. The Doctored Wife (based on Moliere's Physician In Spite of Himself).

3. The Mourner's Bench by Maire Nolan (NY: Master Institute, Sept. 21, 1950).

4. Hidden House by Dr. Robert Bachman.

5. Angel with Red Hair by Ted Farah.

6. The Cat That Hated Christmas.

7. A House In Berlin by Max Frisch.

8. Season in Hell by Rae Dalvin.

9. Sky High by Powers Moulton.

10. Roots in the Wasteland by Alvin Keller.

11. Giants in the Earth by Arnold Sundgaard, based on O. E. Rolvaag's novel, with music by Douglas Moore.

12. You Twisted My Arm (New York: Master Theater,

April 12, 1951).

13. The Family of Shirokov by Sergei Masimov.

14. Apartment for Rent by Jon Griffin.

15. Crew #55 by Marvin Silbersher.

16. Christopher Columbus Brown by Horace W. Stewart
    (New York: Henry St. Playhouse, October 15, 1950).

17. Etched in Granite by Ivan Becker (New York, Originals
    Only Theater, July 18, 1950).

18. Haven in the Dark by Paul Nord (under option to Eddie
    Dowling).

19. The House of Pierrot by Ch. A. Dunleary.

20. Ninth Life by Sidney E. Porcelain (New York: Bleecker
    St. Playhouse, October, 1951).

21. The Caller.

22. The Pot Boils by Frank Wilson (N.Y.: Actor's Theater,
    June, 1950).

23. Sky High by Powers Moulton (formerly Broadway
    musical title, too, but different author) (NY: Province-
    town Playhouse, January, 1951).

24. The Thirteenth God by Richard Gerson (New York:
    Cherry Lane Theater, March, 1951).

25. Turnstile by James A. Cavan (N.Y.: Cherry Lane
    Theater, Nov. 29, 1950).

26. The Warrior's Return by Jules Koslow

27. Blind Alley by James Warwick.

Revivals, 1950-1951

1. Master Builder Solness by Henrik Ibsen.

2. A Trip to Chinatown (America's Lost Plays, Vol. 9---
   Princeton Univ. Press).

3. Nat Turner by Paul Peters (Negro History in 13 Plays
   ---Associated Publishers).

4. Ubu Roi by Alfred Jarry (Gaberbocchus Press, London).

5. Earth Spirit by Frank Wedekind.

6. The Beggar's Opera by Mark Bucci.

7. Right You Are If You Think You Are by Luigi Pirandello.

8. King Lear by Wm. Shakespeare.

9. Alchemist by Ben Jonson.

10. Naked by Luigi Pirandello.

11. Family Reunion by T. S. Eliot.

12. Mrs. Warren's Profession by George Bernard Shaw.

13. Dangerous Corner by J. B. Priestley.

14. Dark of the Moon by Berney and Richardson.

15. Electra by Euripides.

16. Colombyre by Gabriel Marcel.

17. Pillars of Society by Henrik Ibsen.

18. The Merchant of Venice by Wm. Shakespeare.

19. Miranda by Peter Blackmore.

20. Major Barbara by G. B. Shaw.

21. Murder in the Cathedral by T. S. Eliot.

22. Lady Precious Stream (Goodman Theater in Chicago produced in 1959) by S. I. Hsiung.

23. Stalag 17 by Edmund Trazciuski and Don Hovan.

24. Pirates of Penzance by Gilbert and Sullivan.

25. Trial by Jury by Gilbert and Sullivan.

26. Dope by Maryat Lee.

27. The Streets of New York (As performed at Wallack's Theater, Dec., 1857).

28. Creditors by August Strindberg.

29. The Father by Strindberg.

30. The Silver Tassie by Sean O'Casey.

31. Dr. Faustus Lights the Lights by Gertrude Stein (Living Theater).

32. Beyond the Mountains by Kenneth Rexroth (Living Theater).

33. Faustina by Paul Goodman (Living Theater).

34. Desire by Pablo Picasso (Living Theater).

35. Burning Bright by Steinbeck.

36. Bonds of Interest by Jacinto Benevente.

37. Frankie and Johnny by John Huston.

38. Summer and Smoke by Tennessee Williams (Loft Players, Circle-in-the-Square, April 24, 1952).

39. The Land of Promise by Somerset Maugham.

40. A Sleep of Prisoners by Christopher Fry.

41. All The King's Men by Robert Penn Warren.

42. Antigone by Sophocles.

43. Billy Budd adapted from Herman Melville's novel.

44. Cross Purpose by Albert Gamus.

45. The Circle of Chalk by Brecht.

46. The Private Secretary by Charles Hawtrey.

47. The Flies by Jean Paul Sartre.

New Plays by American Authors, 1951-52

1. Dark Legend by Helen Fraenkel (President Theater, Opened March 24, 1952; Closed March 29, 1952 (8 perf.)

2. The Victim by Leonard Lesley (adapted from novel by Saul Bellow, New York, President Theater, May 2, 1952).

3. The King's Darling by Ivan Becker.

4. The Cruelest Month by Susan MacPherson.

5. The Lion Hunters by Tad Mosel.

6. Laura by Vera Caspary.

7. The Restless Flame by Louis de Wohl.

8. Dear Barbarians (recent Broadway failure, Samuel French publishers, MS).

9. The Way the Cat Jumps by Denison Clift (New York: Originals Only, November, 1951).

10. Acres of Sky based on book by Charles Morrow Wilson.

11. Surprise Package by Tom Hill.

12. Aegean Fable by Bill Long.

13. All Around the Town by Larry Parke, Dick Miles and Paul Secon (Barbizon-Plaza Theater, March 25, 1952).

14. Bed of Neuroses by A. P. Mollison (N.Y.: Originals Only Playhouse, April, 1952).

15. Bundle from Heaven by Deborah Frankel.

16. The Strong Feeling by Ilf & Petrov.

17. People You'll Want as Distant Friends.

18. Everywhere I Roam by Sundegaard & Connoly.

19. The Nightingale Sang Too Late by John Richards.

20. October in the Spring by Joseph G. Stockdale.

21. The Patchwork Heart by Roberta Hadley.

22. The Sea Serpent by Elwood Hoofman.

23. Spippin House by Ted Tiller.

24. Starfish by William Noble.

25. Story Teller by Ben Levinson (NY: President Theater, Dec. 14, 1951).

26. Yours Till Yesterday.

27. The Ladder.

28. Difference in God.

29. The Daughters of the Late Colonel by Ben Morse and Louis Beachner.

30. Ride the Right Bus by Harry Wagstaff Gribble and James Proctor.

31. Nothing But the Truth by James Montgomery.

32. Amata (Circle-in-the-Square).

Revivals, 1951-1952

1. The Rehearsal by Buckingham.

2. The Enchanted by Jean Giradoux.

3. Shadow of a Gunman by Sean O'Casey.

4. Ghosts by Henrik Ibsen.

5. Detective Story by J. B. Priestley.

6. Billy the Kid.

7. Othello by Wm. Shakespeare.

8. Candida by George Bernard Shaw.

9. Desire Under the Elms by O'Neill.

10. Macbeth by Wm. Shakespeare.

11. The Year of Pillar by Lynn Riggs.

12. In the Zone, Bound East for Cardiff, The Long Voyage Home by E. O'Neill.

13. Ladies' Voices by Gertrude Stein.

14. Sweeney Agonistes by T. S. Eliot.

15. This Happy Breed by Noel Coward.

16. Rain by Somerset Maugham.

17. The Madwoman of Chaillot by Jean Giradoux.

18. Dr. Jekyll and Mr. Hyde by Richard Abbott.

19. Faustina by Paul Goodman.

20. Measure for Measure by Wm. Shakespeare.

21. Ascent of F6 by Isherwood.

22. The Inspector by Nicolai Gogol.

23. Hall of Healing by Sean O'Casey.

24. The Playboy of the Western World by Sean O'Casey.

25. Rope by Patrick Hamilton.

26. La Ronde by Schnitzler, adapted by Eric Bentley.

New Plays by American Authors, 1952-1953

1. Fortress of Glass by Daniel Polis.

2. The Barrier by Langston Hughes.

3. Love in Our Time by Anita Granniss.

4. Dakota by Tom Hill, Music by Jane Douglas (NY: Originals Only Theater, Oct. 9, 1950).

5. First Love by Edward Caulfield.

6. Hey, You! by Norman Meranus and June Carroll.

7. Noone by Gil Orlovitz.

8. Monday's Heroes by Les Pine.

9. Which Way Is Home? taken from writings of Stephen V. Benet, Gertrude Stein & Mark Lodge.

10. Alice in Wonder by Ossie Davis.

11. The Other Foot by Julian Mayfield.

12. A World Full of Men by Julian Mayfield.

13. The Big Ideal by Ossie Davis.

14. The Devil in Boston by N. Buckwald.

15. Thespis by W. S. Gilbert (Complete Plays of Gilbert & Sullivan, Random House).

16. Faith and Prudence by Lottie Michelson.

17. Angelic Doctor by Brendan Larnen.

18. The Heroes by John Ashberry (NY: Cherry Lane Theater, August 5, 1952).

19. Merry-Go-Round by Ben Victor New York: Amato Opera Theater, January, 1953.

20. Three in One by Ken Parker.

21. Peking Man by Reginald Lawrence (Adapted from a play by Tsao Yu, New York; Studio Theater; April, 1953).

22. Sambatian by Abrahan Goldfaden.

23. The Year Round by Sidney Bernstein.

24. Surprise Package.

25. Mrs. Moonlight by Ben W. Levy.

26. Legend of Lovers.

27. Distant Star by Stanley Richards.

28. Hobson's Choice by Harold Brighouse.

29. One Foot to the Sea by Harold Levitt, Opened Wed., July 1, 1953, Closed April 11, 1954 (249 perf.)

Revivals, 1952-1953

1. Summer and Smoke by T. Williams.

2. The Grass Harp by Truman Capote.

3. Down in the Valley, libretto by Arnold Sundegaard.

4. The Rivals by Sheridan.

5. Widowers' Houses by G. B. Shaw.

6. Thespis by W. S. Gilbert.

7. The Marriage Proposal by Chekhov.

8. No Exit by Sartre.

9. You Never Can Tell by Shaw.

10. The Plough and the Stars by O'Casey.

11. The Heroes by John Ashbury.

12. Getting Married by Shaw.

13. Winterset by Anderson.

14. The Glass Menagerie by T. Williams.

15. Man and Superman by Shaw.

16. The Sea Gull by Ibsen.

17. The Tragical History of Dr. Faustus by Marlowe.

18. Trial by Jury, H.M.S. Pinafore, The Pirates of Penzance by Gilbert and Sullivan.

19. The Sacred Flame by Somerset Maugham.

20. Goodbye My Fancy by Fay Kanin.

21. Shirokov Family by Sergei Maksimov.

22. Belugin's Marriage by Alexander Ostrovski (New
     Russian Theater Assoc.).

23. Theater of the Soul by Nikolayevich Yvrerinov.

24. Night of January 16 by Ayn Rand (Chelsea Players).

25. Candida by Bernard Shaw (The Institute Players).

26. Vasilisa Melentyeva by Ostrovsky.

27. The Glass of Water by Scribe.

28. The Happy Time by Samuel Taylor.

29. Les Fourberies de Scapion by Moliere.

30. Within the Gates by Sean O'Casey.

31. Madame Favart by Offenbach, English libretto by John
     F. Grahame.

32. Portrait in Black by Goff and Roberts.

33. Phaedre by Jean Racine.

34. Mamba's Daughters by Dorothy DuBose Heyward.

35. The Clandestine Marriage by David Garrick.

36. Yerma by Garcia Lorca.

37. Camino Real by T. Williams.

38. The Birthday of the Infanta by Oscar Wilde.

39. Miss Julie by August Strindberg.

40. The Scarecrow by Percy MacKaye (Theater de Lys,
     Presented June 16-21, 1953; 7 performances).

41. The School for Scandal by Sheridan.

42. The Little Clay Cart by Shudraka.

New Plays by American Authors, 1953-1954

1. Moon in Capricorn by James Leo Herlihy, Incidental
   Music by Joseph Liebling (New York: Theater de Lys,
   October 27, 1953).

2. Penguin by Norman Vein.

3. Praise of Folly by John McGuire (New York: Blackfriar's Theater, February, 23, 1954).

4. Cyanamide by Burt Marnick.

5. The Time of Storm by Sheldon Stark.

6. End As A Man by Calder Willingham.

7. Haven in the Dark by Paul Nord (New York: Originals
   Only, Playhouse March 3, 1954).

8. Mood Piece by Stanley Richards (Banner Play Co.,
   Cincinnati, Ohio).

9. Zoom! by Fred Weiss, with music and lyrics by Paul
   Giasson and David Herzbrun.

10. The Wedding Present by Ken Parker.

11. St. Tithonus by James Merrill.

12. Building Blocks by Eugene Feist.

13. Stockade by Mark Appleman.

14. Bullfight by Leslie Stevens (Theater de Lys, Opened
    Tuesday, Jan. 12, 1954; Closed Feb. 28, 1954).

15. Emperor's Clothes by George Tabori.

16. American Gothic by Victor Wolfson, based on the
    author's book, The Lonely Steeple (Presented Nov. 10,
    1953 to Jan. 24, 1954) 77 perf.

205

17. The Girl on the Via Flaminia by Alfred Hayes based
     on his novel, Act of Love.

18. Maya by Simon Gantillon, (Theater de Lys, Opened
     Tuesday, June 9, 1953, & Closed June 14, 1953;
     7 perf.)

19. Late Arrival by Charles Oxton.

Revivals, 1953-1954

1. The Knight of the Burning Pestle by Beaumont and
   Fletcher (Theater de Lys, Opened Fri., October 23,
   1953.)

2. The Threepenny Opera by Bertoldt Brecht, (Opened
   Wed. March 10, 1954: Closed May 30, 1954---95 perf.

3. Ten Nights in a Barroom by William W. Pratt.

4. Everyman.

5. Othello by Wm. Shakespeare (Opened Thurs., Oct. 29,
   1953 by Shakespeare Guild Festival Company at Jan
   Hus Auditorium, Closed Jan. 31, 1954 -- 72 perf.

6. Hamlet by Wm. Shakespeare (Jan Hus Aud., Closed
   May 30, 1954---25 perf.)

7. Miss Julie by August Strindberg.

8. The Climate of Eden by Moss Hart (Current Stages,
   Oct. 6, 1953-March 14, 1954---138 perf.)

9. The Wise Have Not Spoken by Paul Vincent Carroll.

10. The World of Sholom Aleichem by Arnold Perl
    (Barbizon-Plaza Theater, Opened Fri., May 1, 1953;
    Closed May 23, 1954---305 perf.)

11. The Simpleton of the Unexpected Isles by G.B. Shaw.

12. The Infernal Machine by Jean Cocteau, (Club Theater,
    Inc.; Opened Fri., March 5, 1954; Closed March 28,
    1954---16 perf.)

13. Voice of the Turtle by John van Druten.

14. Home of the Brave by Arthur Laurents.

15. Volpone by Ben Jonson, adapted by George Antheil into
    satiric opera.

207

16. The Late George Apley by John P. Marquand.

17. The Second Mrs. Tanqueray by Arthur Wing Pinero.

18. The Fossils by Francois de Curel (done by Antoine's Theater Libre).

19. The Glass Menagerie by T. Williams.

20. Blithe Spirit by Noel Coward.

21. The Country Girl by Clifford Odets.

22. Family Portrait by Lenore Coffee.

23. Under Milkwood by Dylan Thomas.

24. The Ecclesiazusae by Aristophanes.

25. The Girl from Samos by Ida Lublenski Ehrlich.

26. Herod and Mariamne by Fredich Hebbel.

27. The Boy With a Cart by Christopher Fry (Broadway Tabernacle Church, Opened Sun., April 4, 1954).

28. Ethan Frome by Owen Davis.

29. The Sea Gull by Anton Chekhov (Phoenix Theater, Opened Tues., May 11, 1954).

30. La Parisienne by Henri Becque.

31. Beyond the Horizon by Eugene O'Neill.

32. Electra by Sophocles.

33. Madam, Will You Walk? by Sidney Howard, (Phoenix Theater, Opened Tues., December 1, 1953, Closed January 10, 1954).

New Plays by American Authors, 1954-1955

1. Sandhog by Earl Robinson and Waldo Salt (Phoenix Theater, Nov. 29, 1954-Jan. 2, 1954---48 perf.).

2. Bamboo Cross by Theophane Lee.

3. Slightly Delinquent by Leo Thomas.

4. The Chair by Tom Hill and Don Stuart.

5. Homeward Look by Effie Young and Ernest Pagano.

6. I Feel Wonderful by Jerry Herman and Barry Alan Grael (Theater de Lys).

7. High Named Today by David Z. Goodman (Theater de Lys, Nico Prods., Dec. 10, 1954-Dec. 19, 1954--- 13 perf.)

8. The Immortal Husband by James Merrill (5 Plays from the New Theater, New Directions).

9. Shoestring Revue by Ben Bagley (President Theater, Feb. 28, 1955-May 22, 1955---100 perf.)

10. In Splendid Error by Wm. Branch.

11. Circus by Harold Yablonsky.

12. When the Bow Breaks by Viola Swayne.

13. A Switch in Time by Lola Pergament.

14. Safari by Milt Kamen & Hans Holzer, Music by Ben Machan Blanche (NY: Barbizon-Plaza Theater, May 11, 1955).

15. I Believe in Rubble by Deric Riegen.

16. Highway Robbery by Moshe Shamir.

17. Almost Crazy by James Shelton, Hal Hackady &
    Robert A. Bernstein, Music & Lyrics by Portia Nel-
    son, Raymond Taylor & James Shelton (NY: Longacre
    Theater, June 20, 1955).

18. The Golden Apple by John Latouche and Jerome Moross
    (Phoenix Theater, published by Random House).

19. Mark Twain's America.

20. Annie's Son by Harold Cobin.

21. The Terrible Swift Sword by Arthur Steuer.

22. Trouble in Mind by Alice Childress.

23. La Flamme by Crane Johnson.

24. Song Out of Sorrow by Felix Doherty, Blackfriar's
    Guild, October 31, 1955).

25. The Last Love of Don Juan by Edwin Justus Mayer.

26. Teach Me How to Cry by Patricia Joudry (Theater de
    Lys, April 5, 1955-May 15, 1955, LPS Productions,
    Inc.---48 perf.).

27. Sing Me No Lullaby by Robert Ardrey, (Phoenix Thea-
    ter, Oct. 11, 1954-Nov. 7, 1954--32 perf.)

28. Phoenix '55 by Ira Wallach (Phoenix Theater).

29. See How They Run by Phillip King.

30. The Troublemakers by George Bellak (President Theater,
    March Productions).

31. A Stone for Danny Fisher by Leonard Kantor based on
    novel by Harold Robbins.

32. The Pony Cart by Roger Garis, (Theater de Lys).

Revivals, 1954-1955

1. Thieves' Carnival by Jean Anouilh (Cherry Lane Theater, Proscenium Productions, Feb. 1, 1955-June 12, 1955---150 perf.)

2. The Doctor's Dilemna by G.B. Shaw (Phoenix Theater).

3. The Master Builder by Henrik Ibsen (Phoenix Theater).

4. The White Devil by Webster (Phoenix Theater).

5. The Cretan Woman by Robinson Jeffers (The Players Theater, Provincetown Playhouse, Opened Wed., July 7, 1954-September, 26, 1954---95 perf.)

6. The Clandestine Marriage by David Garrick (The Players Theater, Provincetown Playhouse, Oct. 2, 1954-Nov. 7, 1954---41 perf.)

7. A Streetcar Named Desire by Tennessee Williams.

8. "Chair Endowed," "The No' Count Boy," "Supper for the Dead" under title Salvation on a String by Paul Green (Theater de Lys, Opened Tues., July 6, 1954-July 11, 1954---8 perf.)

9. The Way of the World by William Congreve.

10. Twelfth Night by Wm. Shakespeare, (Jan Hus Aud., Feb. 22, 1955-May 29, 1955--77 perf.)

11. Merchant of Venice by Wm. Shakespeare, (Jan Hus Aud., Feb. 22, 1955-May 29, 1955--77 perf.)

12. The Dybbuk by S. Ansky (Fourth St. Theater, David Ross, Oct. 26, 1954-Jan. 23, 1955---103 perfs.)

13. The Three Sisters by Anton Chekhov (Fourth St. Theater).

14. <u>Billy Budd</u> by Herman Melville, adapted by Louis O. Coxe & Robert Chapman, The Masques, May 2, 1955-May 21, 1955---23 perf.

15. <u>Major Barbara</u> by G. B. Shaw.

16. <u>Juno and the Paycock</u> by Sean O'Casey.

17. <u>Noah</u> by André Obey (Broadway Tabernacle Church, Broadway Chapel Players, Oct. 10, 1954-Jan 30, 1955--Sun. only, 14 perf.)

18. <u>In April Once</u> by Wm. Alexander Percy, (Broadway Tabernacle Church, March 13, 1955-May 8, 1955-Sun. only).

19. <u>The King and the Duke</u> by Francis Fergusson.

20. <u>Headlines from Paradise</u> by Walter Grotyohann.

21. <u>The Shy and the Lonely</u> by G. B. Shaw.

22. <u>Morning's at Seven</u> by John Osborn.

23. <u>La Ronde</u> by Schnitzler, adapted by Eric Bentley.

24. <u>The Silver Cord</u> by Sidney Howard.

25. <u>The Anniversary</u> by Anton Chekhov.

26. <u>Anna Lucasta</u> by Eugene O'Neill.

27. <u>Finian's Rainbow</u>.

28. <u>Tonight We Improvise</u> by Luigi Pirandello.

29. <u>Macbeth</u> by Wm. Shakespeare.

30. <u>Today is Friday</u> by Ernest Hemingway.

31. <u>Full Moon in March</u> by W. B. Yeats.

32. <u>Alice Through the Looking Glass</u> by Lewis Carroll.

33. <u>My Three Angels</u> by Sam & Bella Spewack.

34. <u>Village Wooing</u> by G. B. Shaw

35. A Pound on Deamand by Sean O'Casey.

36.   Oedipus at Colonus by Sophocles.

37. Highway Robbery by Moshe Shamir.

38. The Trial by Franz Kafka.

39. Electra trans. by Winifred Smith from Jean Giradoux
     (Opened April 18, 1954-April 25, 1954---8 perf.)

40. Coriolanus by Wm. Shakespeare, (Phoenix Theater,
     Setting: Donald Oenslager, Opened Tues., Jan 19, 1954,
     Closed Feb. 28, 1954---48 perf.)

41. The Typewriter by Jean Cocteau.

42. The Old Maid and the Thief by Gian Carlo Menotti.

43. The Philanderer by G. B. Shaw.

44. She Stoops to Conquer by Oliver Goldsmith.

45. Once Upon a Tailor adapted by Henry Sherman from a
     text by Baruch Lumet.

46. Spring's Awakening by Frank Wedekind.

47. The Cherry Orchard by Anton Chekhov.

48. As You Like It by Wm. Shakespeare.

49. Saint Joan by G.B. Shaw.

50. In A Garden by Gertrude Stein (Tempo Theater Prod.
     May 6, 1955,. Closed July 17, 1955---63 perf.)

51. Three Sisters Who Are Not Sisters by Gertrude Stein,
     Ibid.

52. The Maids by Jean Genet, Ibid.

53. Phaedra, trans. of Racine.

54. Two on an Island by Elmer Rice.

55. Tower Beyond Tragedy by Robinson Jeffers.

56. Amédeé by Eugene Ionesco.

57. The Cradle Song by the Sierras, trans. by J. C. Underhill.

58. The Damask Cheek by John van Druten & Lloyd Morris.

59. Six Characters in Search of an Author by Pirandello.

60. Dragon's Mouth by J. B. Priestley & Jacquetta Hawkes.

61. Out of this World by Cole Porter.

62. Venice Preserv'd by Thomas Otway.

63. Alcestis by Euripides.

64. Hour Glass by W. B. Yeats.

65. Salome by Oscar Wilde.

66. Uncle Vanya by Anton Chekhov.

67. The Plough and the Stars by Sean O'Casey.

68. The Dreaming Dust by Denis Johnston.

69. Sands of the Negev by Yigal Mossensohn, adapted by Shimon Wincelberg, President Theater).

70. The Three Sisters by Anton Chekhov, Fourth Street Theater, David Ross, Opened Fri., Feb. 25, 1955-May 22, 1955---102 perf.)

71. The Merchant of Venice by Wm. Shakespeare, Jan. 7, 1955-Jan. 30, 1955, The Club Theater (Clarence Derwent as Shylock) 19 perf.

72. The Way of the World by Wm. Congreve, Cherry Lane Theater, Proscenium Productions, Opened Oct. 2, 1954-Jan. 23, 1955---122 perf.)

73. The Grass Is Always Greener by Sholom Aleichem, (Downtown National Theater).

74. The Miser by Moliére.

New Plays by American Authors, 1955-1956

1. <u>Dakota</u> by Tom Hill (Originals Only).

2. <u>Annie's Son</u> by Harold Cobin (Royal Playhouse) .

3. <u>Phillip of Macedon</u> by Clark Wiswell (Concert reading, St. John's Theater Group).

4. <u>Nona Crabtree</u> (psychological drama of an actress, Originals Only).

5. <u>Trouble in Mind</u> by Alice Childress (Greenwich Mews).

6. <u>See How They Run</u> by Phillip King (Hudson Guild).

7. <u>The Women of Trachis</u>, the Ezra Pound translation of the Sophocles play (Living Theater).

8. <u>Tom Thumb, the Great</u> by Henry Fielding (Living Theater).

9. <u>The Terrible Swift Sword</u> by Arthur Steuer (New Directors' Series at the Phoenix Theater).

10. <u>The Last Love of Don Juan</u> by Edwin Justus Mayer (Rooftop Theater).

11. <u>Song Out of Sorrow</u> by Felix Doherty (Blackfriars Guild, 316 W. 57th St.)

12. <u>The Last Minute</u> by George Whitney (Finch Theater, 52 E. 78th St.)

13. <u>The Sword Without</u> by Aurel Keating (Open Door, 55 W. Third St.)

14. <u>The Carefree Tree</u> by Aldyth Morris (Phoenix Theater).

15. <u>The Third Person</u> by Andrew Rosenthal.

16. The Dreaming Dust by Denis Johnston.

17. Green Sleeves by Marian Johnson (children's play for YW-YWHA).

18. A Day at Doubleday by Kenn Sylvia (St. Peter's Parish House).

19. Are Diamonds---? by Kenn Sylvia (St. Peter's Parish House).

20. Harlequinesque by Larry Vide (St. Peter's Parish House).

21. A Cloth of Gold by Kenn Sylvia.

22. Grab Bag by Kenn Sylvia.

23. The Perry Committee by Harry Wagstaff Gribble (Originals Only).

24. A Family of Waiting by Deric Riegen (verse play, Originals Only).

25. The Thorntons by Millie Fredrick and Irving Strouse (Provincetown).

26. The Peons by Philip Freund (Columbia Theater Associates).

27. The Neophytes by Bown Adams (Bown Adams Studio).

28. Desires of Four by Bown Adams.

29. The Grand Gesture by Bown Adams.

30. Only the Troubled by Bown Adams.

31. Scars and Stripes by Deric Riegen (Originals Only).

Revivals, 1955-1956

1. The Trial by Franz Kafka.

2. The Typewriter by Jean Cocteau (Tempo Theater).

3. The Threepenny Opera by Bertolt Brecht and Kurt Weill.

4. Amedee by Eugene Ionesco (Tempo Theater).

5. As You Like It by Shakespeare (Shakespearean Theater Workshop, 729 East 6th St.)

6. The Great Theater of the World by Pedro Calderon (Concert readings, St. John's Theater Group).

7. Spring's Awakening by Frank Wedekind.

8. The Shepherd King by Leizer Treister.

9. The Cradle Song by the Sierras (Circle-in-the-Square).

10. The Mountbanks by Gilbert and Cellier (St. John's Theater).

11. The Trial of Mary Dugan by Bayard Veiller (Equity Library Theater).

12. The Damask Cheek by John van Druten and Lloyd Morris (Liederkranz Dramatic Circle, 6 East 87th Street).

13. Out of This World by Porter, Lawrence and Taylor (Actor's Playhouse).

14. The Children's Hour by Lillian Hellman (Capitol Hotel).

15. Camino Real by Williams (92nd Street YM-YWHA).

16. Boy Meets Girl by the Spewacks (ELT).

17. The Cherry Orchard by Chekhov (Fourth Street Theater).

18. The Hour Glass by W. B. Yeats (Chapel Players).

19. A Village Wooing by G. Bernard Shaw (Davenport).

20. Macbeth by Shakespeare (Jan Hus Auditorium).

21. Six Characters In Search of An Author by Pirandello (Phoenix Theater).

22. Venice Preserv'd by Otway (Phoenix Theater).

23. Highway Robbery (primitive comedy from Israel, President).

24. She Stoops To Conquer by Oliver Goldsmith (Provincetown).

25. Thesmophoriazusae by Aristophanes (Rooftop Theater).

26. The Wedding March (Second Avenue Theater).

27. The Cricket on the Hearth by Dickens (St. John's Theater).

28. The Brothers Ashkenazi (Yiddish Art Theater).

29. Dragon's Mouth by J. B. Priestley (Cherry Lane Theater).

30. Oedipus at Colonus by Sophocles (Labor Temple, 242 E. 14th Street).

31. Highway Robbery by Moshe Shamir (President Theater, 247 W. 48th St.)

32. John Ferguson by St. John Ervine (Alhambra Hall, 15 Second Ave.)

33. The Two Gentlemen of Verona by Shakespeare (Shakespearean Theater Workshop).

34. The Cherry Orchard by Chekhov (Fourth Street Theater).

35. La Ronde by Schnitzler, adapted by Eric Bentley (Circle-in-the-Square).

36. Climate of Eden by Moss Hart (Actors Playhouse).

37. The Diary of a Scoundrel, an adaptation by Rodney
     Ackland (Phoenix).

38. No Time for Sergeants by Ira Levin (Alvin Theater).

39. The World of Sholom Aleichem by I. L. Peretz (YM-
     YWHA, Lexington Ave., at 92nd St.)

40. Measure for Measure by Shakespeare (Columbia Players).

41. Antigone by Jean Anouilh (Columbia Players).

42. The Shewing-up of Blanco Posnet by G. B. Shaw
     (Columbia Players).

43. The Medium by Gian Carlo Menotti (YW-YMHA).

44. Uncle Vanya by Anton Chekhov (Fourth Street Theater).

45. Romeo and Juliet by Shakespeare (Jan Hus Auditorium).

46. He Who Gets Slapped by Andreyev (Actors Playhouse).

47. Opera, Opera; The Pot of Fat; Apollo and Persephone
     (After Dinner Opera).

48. Thunder Rock by Robert Ardrey.

49. Island of Goats by Ugo Betti.

50. The Admirable Bashville, The Dark Lady of the
     Sonnets by G. B. Shaw (Cherry Lane Theater).

51. Candida by G. B. Shaw (Downtown Theater).

52. The Shadow of the Glen by J. M. Synge (Labor Temple).

53. Mason by Nahum Yablonovitz (Labor Temple).

54. The Private Life of the Master Race by Brecht,
     adapted by Eric Bentley.

55. Miss Julie, The Stronger by Strindberg.

56. Rosmersholm by Ibsen (Provincetown).

57. Overruled by G. B. Shaw (Senior Dramatic Workshop).

58. The Evil Eye by Luigi Pirandello (Senior Dramatic Workshop).

59. The Insect Comedy by Karel and Josef Capek (Senior Dramatic Workshop).

60. Much Ado About Nothing by Shakespeare (Shakespearean Workshop).

61. Dangerous Corner by J. B. Priestley (Studio Theater).

62. L'lle des Chevres by Ugo Betti (French Art Theater, Carl Fischer Hall).

63. Mandragola by Nicoli Machiavelli (Prince Productions, Pantomime Theater, 122 Second Ave.)

64. American Blues by Tennessee Williams (Dramatic Workshop).

65. Best Foot Forward by James Nygren (ELT)

66. The Grand Duke by Gilbert and Sullivan (Chamber Opera Players).

67. The Beaver Coat by Gerhardt Hauptmann (Greenwich Mews).

68. The Curious Savage by John Patrick (Equity Library Theater).

69. Miranda by Blackmore (St. Paul's Church, 86 and West End Ave.)

70. The Petrified Forest by Robert Sherwood (Tompkins Square Playhouse, 287 E. 10th St.)

71. Queen After Death by Montherlant (Phoenix Theater).

72. Down in the Valley by Kurt Weill (Actor's Playhouse).

73. Rustic Rivalry, music by Mascagni (Cleff Theater).

74. Baron Almost, music by Strauss (Cleff Theater).

75. La Flamme (Royal Playhouse).

76. L'Apollon de Bellac by Giradoux (French Art Theater).

77. Le Pain de Menage by Julee Renard (French Art Theater).

78. Gros Chagrins by George Courteline (French Art Theater).

79. Salome and the Florentine Tragedy by Oscar Wilde (Davenport Theater).

80. The Son-in-Law of Mr. Pear by Emile Augier and Jules Sendesu (Everyman's Theater).

81. Age and Grace by Dominic Rover (Blackfriars Guild).

82. Murder in the Cathedral by T. S. Eliot (St. Paul's Chapel, Columbia University).

83. The Affected Young Ladies by Moliere (Afternoon Theater, Inc., 353 West 57th St.).

84. The Young Disciple by Paul Goodman (Living Theater).

85. Antigone by Jean Anouilh (Mazda Productions).

86. The Queen's Gambit by Eugene Scribe (Columbia Theater Associates, Columbia University).

87. The Ascent of F6 by Christopher Isherwood (Davenport Theater, Markaren Productions).

88. The Three Sisters by Chekhov (Fourth Street Theater, David Ross presents).

89. Thieves' Carnival by Jean Anouilh, adapted by Lucienne Hill (Proscenium Productions, Cherry Lane Theater).

90. Down in the Valley by Kurt Weill (Actor's Playhouse, 100 Seventh Ave.).

91. Floyada to Matador by William Saroyan (Amato Theater, 159 Bleecker St.)

92. Hello, Out There; The Hungerers; Opera, Opera (Amato Theater).

93.   The Richelieu Conspiracy by Bulwer-Lytton (Daven-
      port Theater, 138 E. 27th).

94.   Our Town by Thornton Wilder (Henry Street Playhouse,
      466 Grand St.)

95.   Side Show (Phoenix Theater, 12th St. and Second Ave.)

96.   Antigone Revisited, adapted from Sophocles' Antigone
      by Bown Adams.

97.   A Midsummer Night's Dream by Shakespeare (Jan Hus
      Auditorium).

98.   A Month in the Country by Turgeniev (Phoenix Thea-
      ter, directed by Michael Redgrave).

99.   A Doll's House by Ibsen (Greenwich Mews Theater).

100. The Beautiful People by William Saroyan (Theater
      East, 211 East 50th).

101. Pantaloon, based on Andreyev's He Who Gets Slapped
      (opera, Columbia Theater Associates).

New Plays by American Authors, 1956-1957

1. Trouble in Mind by Alice Childress (Directed by Clarice Taylor and Alice Childress, Greenwich Mews Theater, 141 W. 13th).

2. Golden Alley by Burt Marnik (Argo Players present, The Clubhouse, 150 W. 85th Street).

3. The Perry Committee by Harry Wagstaff Gribble (Staged by Tom Hill, Originals Only, 430 Ave. of Americas, at 9th St.)

4. The World's My Oyster (Actor's Playhouse).

5. The Merry-Go-Rounders (Phoenix Theater, 2nd Ave. at 12th St.)

6. Shoestring '57 by Ben Bagley (musical revue, Barbizon-Plaza Theater, 58th St. & 6th Ave.)

7. The Death of Don Juan by Edwin Justus Mayer (Rooftop Theater, 111 E. Houston St.)

8. Annie's Son by Harold Cobin (Royal Playhouse, 62 E. 4th St.)

9. Third Person by Andrew Rosenthal (Yiddish Theater).

10. The Neophytes, Desires of Four by Bown Adams (Bown Adams Studio, 306 W. 81st St.)

11. Me, Candido! by Walt Anderson (Greenwich Mews Theater).

12. A Land Beyond the River by Loften Mitchell.

13. The Shadow Years by Kenneth Sylvia (a drama about Mary Todd Lincoln).

14. Career by James Lee.

15. A Box of Watercolors by G. Wood.

16. Simply Heavenly by Langston Hughes (Harlem-set musical play).

17. Tom Sawyer, with book, lyrics and music by Jack Urbont and Bruce Geller (Phoenix Theater).

223

Revivals, 1956-1957

1. The Lesson by Eugene Ionesco (Tempo Theater).

2. Escurial by Michel de Ghelderode (Tempo Theater).

3. Johnny Johnson by Paul Green, music by Kurt Weill (Carnegie Hall Playhouse).

4. Camille, an adaptation (Cherry Lane Theater).

5. Hamlet by Shakespeare (The Shakespearwrights, St. Ignatius Church, 214 West 87th Street).

6. The Seagull by Anton Chekhov (Fourth Street Theater).

7. The Diary of a Scoundrel by Ostrovsky (Phoenix Theater).

8. Thor, With Angels by Christopher Fry (Broadway Congregational Church).

9. Out of This World by Cole Porter (Actors' Playhouse, 103 Seventh Ave. S., Sheridan Square).

10. The Cherry Orchard by Anton Chekhov (Fourth St. Theater, 83 East 4th St.)

11. Romeo and Juliet by Shakespeare (Shakespearean Theater Workshop 729 E. 6th St., New York 9).

12. As You Like It by Shakespeare (Shakespearean Theater Workshop).

13. The House of Bernarda Alba by Lorca (Village Repertory Players Workshop).

14. Dandy Dick by Sir Arthur Wing Pinero (Directed by Warren Enters, Cherry Lane Theater, 38 Commerce St.)

15. H.M.S. Pinafore and Trial by Jury by Gilbert and Sullivan (Provincetown Playhouse, 133 MacDougal St.,

224

21st season of Comic Opera Repertory).

16. The Private Life of the Master Race by Bertolt Brecht
     (Open Stage, 15 Second Ave., near First Street).

17. Man of Destiny by G. B. Shaw (Downtown Theater, 85
     E. 4th St.)

18. The Evils of Tobacco by Anton Chekhov (Downtown
     Theater).

19. Arms and the Man by G. B. Shaw (Downtown Theater).

20. Patience by Gilbert and Sullivan (Provincetown Play-
     house).

21. Rendezvous in Wien by Fritz Eckhardt (Barbizon Plaza
     Theater).

22. No Exit by Jean Paul Sartre (Theater East).

23. Picture of Dorian Gray (Bleecker St. Theater).

24. I Am A Camera by John Van Druten (Directed by
     Phillip Pruneau, Actors Playhouse, Sheridan Square,
     165 W. 57th St.)

25. The Misanthrope by Moliere (Stephen Porter presents
     Theater East, 211 E. 60th St., new translation by
     Richard Wilbur.

26. Boy With A Cart by Christopher Fry (St. John's Hall,
     224 Waverly Place).

27. The Anniversary by Anton Chekhov (St. John's Hall).

28. Titus Andronicus by Shakespeare (Shakespeare Theater
     Workshop).

29. Easter by Strindberg (translated by Elizabeth Sprigge,
     Fourth St. Th.)

30. Purple Dust by Sean O'Casey (Cherry Lane Theater).

31. The Duchess of Malfi by John Webster (Phoenix Thea-
     ter).

32.   The Eagle Has Two Heads by Jean Cocteau.

33.   Exiles by James Joyce (Renato Theater).

34.   The Lower Depths by Maxim Gorki (Alhambra Hall).

35.   Volpone by Ben Jonson (Rooftop Theater).

36.   Lady from the Sea by Ibsen (Tempo Theater).

37.   The Doctor In Spite of Himself by Moliere (Tempo
      Theater).

38.   Riders to the Sea, The Tinker's Wedding and In the
      Shadow of the Glen by J. M. Synge (Theater East).

39.   The Lady's Not For Burning by Christopher Fry (Car-
      negie Hall Playhouse).

40.   Right You Are by Pirandello.

41.   Idiot's Delight by Sherwood.

42.   The Crucible by Miller.

43.   The Hasty Heart by John Patrick.

44.   La Boheme and La Traviata (Amato Opera Theater).

45.   In Good King Charles Golden Days by G. B. Shaw.

46.   Take a Giant Step by Louis Peterson (Jan Hus Audi-
      torium).

47.   The Duchess of Malfi by John Webster (Phoenix,
      Directed by John Landau).

48.   Another Language by Rose Franken (Equity Library
      Theater).

49.   Supplement au Voyage de Cook by Jean Giradoux
      (French Art Theater).

50.   La Lecon by Eugene Ionesco (French Art Theater).

51.   The Anatomist by Ravenscroft (Royal).

52. The Importance of Being Earnest by Oscar Wilde
    (Musical version, Actors Playhouse).

53. Exiles by James Joyce (Renata Theater).

54. Utopia Ltd. by Gilbert and Sullivan (Savoyards at St.
    Ignatius).

55. Electra, The Trojan Women and Agamemnon (Theater
    Marquee).

56. Apollo of Bellac, The Victorious Island by Jean Gira-
    doux (Produced by Leo Shull, Carnegie Playhouse).

57. La Paiz Chez Soi by Courteline (French Art Theater)
    (Carl Fischer Hall).

58. La Plus Forte by Strindberg (French Art Theater).

59. Sisyphe et la Mort by Merle (French Art Theater).

60. The Iceman Cometh by Eugene O'Neill (winner of
    New York Drama Desk Award, Circle-in-the-Square.)

61. Saint Joan by G. B. Shaw (starring Siobhan McKenna,
    Phoenix Theater).

New Plays by American Authors, 1951-1958

1. Palm Tree In a Rose Garden by Meade Roberts (Directed by Warren Enters, Cricket Theater).

2. Bivouac at Lucca by Robert Guy Barrows (Royal, 62 E. Fourth St.)

3. Garden District, "Something Unspoken" and "Suddenly Last Summer" by T. Williams.

4. Comic Strip by George Panetta.

5. The Brothers Karamazov, dramatized by Boris Tumarin ---Jack Sydow (Gate Theater, 162 Second Ave., ran 165 perf.)

6. Winkelberg by Ben Hecht (Renata Theater, 144 Bleecker St.)

7. The Trial of Dmitri Karamazov (Jan Hus Aud., 351 E. 74th St.)

8. Clown Face, a play with music for children (Theater East).

9. Obligato by Jane Hinton Gates, based on the novel Une Ombre by Paul Violar (Theater Marquee, 110 East 59th St.)

10. Portofino, a new musical comedy (Adelphi Theater).

11. Pale Horse, Pale Rider by Katherine Ann Porter (Jan Hus Auditorium, 351 E. 74th St.)

12. Speak to Me, Sam by Keith McClelland.

13. The Transposed Heads by Peggy Glanville-Hicks and Thomas Mann (New York premiere, Phoenix Theater).

14. Heaven and Helen, Musical comedy adapted from Offenbach's La Belle Helene (Provincetown Playhouse).

228

15. A Power of Dreams by Peter John Stephens (Sullivan St. Playhouse).

16. The Long Gallery by Ramsey Yelvington (RNA Theater, B'way at 91st St.)

17. The Saturday Night Kid by Jack Dunphy (Provincetown Playhouse, 133 MacDougal St.)

18. Sign of Winter by Ettore Rella (Theater 74 at 334 E. 74 St.)

19. Truce of the Bear by Pat Wilmot (Blackfriar's Guild).

20. Light A Penny Candle by Jack Dunphy(Circle-in-the-Square).

21. A Part of the Memory by James Van Lare.

22. Rigmarole by Harold Levitt.

23. Tevya and His Daughters, adapted by Arnold Perl from stories by Sholom Aleichem.

Revivals, 1957-1958

1. The Quare Fellow by Brendan Behan.

2. Our Town by Thornton Wilder (Circle-in-the-Square).

3. Ivanov by Anton Chekhov (Directed by William Ball, Renata Theater).

4. Clerambard by Marcel Ayme (Rooftop, Second Ave. and Houston St.)

5. Julius Caesar by Shakespeare (Shakespearewrights).

6. The Will and the Way by Michael Molloy (Theater East).

7. The Chairs by Eugene Ionesco (Phoenix Theater).

8. The Lesson by Ionesco (Phoenix Theater).

9. Everyman (Phoenix Theater, Religious Drama Series).

10. The Cocktail Party by T. S. Eliot (Equity Library Theater).

11. Endgame by Samuel Beckett (Directed by Alan Schneider, Cherry Lane Theater, 38 Commerce St.)

12. The Threepenny Opera by Brecht-Weill (Theater de Lys).

13. The Boy Friend (New Princess Company, Cherry Lane, 38 Commerce St.)

14. The Crucible by Arthur Miller (Martinique, 32nd St. at Broadway).

15. The Playboy of the Western World by J. M. Synge (Irish Players, Tara, 120 Madison Ave.)

16. You Never Can Tell by G. B. Shaw (Downtown, 85 E. Fourth St.)

17. Children of Darkness by Edwin Justus Mayer (Direct-
    ed by José Quintero, Circle-in-the-Square).

18. Ulysses in Nighttown dramatized by Padraic Colum
    from Joyce's Ulysses (Rooftop, Second Ave. and
    Houston St.)

19. The Bald Soprano and Jack by Eugene Ionesco (Sullivan
    St. Playhouse, 181 Sullivan St.)

20. Othello by Shakespeare (Central Park at the Belvedere
    Tower).

21. The Iceman Cometh by E. G. O'Neill (Circle-in-the-
    Square).

22. Purple Dust by Sean O'Casey (Cherry Lane).

23. The Girl of the Golden West by Belasco.

24. The Makroupoulos Secret by Karel Capek (Phoenix,
    189 Second Ave.)

25. The Trip to Bountiful by Horton Foote (Equity Library
    Theater).

26. The Wild Duck by Ibsen (Equity Library Theater).

27. Herod the Great by David Demarest (Broadway Chapel
    Players, Broadway Congregational Church).

28. Ardéle by Anouilh (Cricket Theater, 2nd Ave. at 10th
    St.)

29. Fools Are Passing Through by Friedrich Duerrenmatt
    (Jan Hus Aud.).

30. Dark of the Moon by Richardson and Berney (Carnegie
    Hall Playhouse).

31. The Alchemist by Ben Jonson.

32. The Beaux Stratagem by Farquhar.

33. Edward II by Christopher Marlowe.

34. An Enemy of the People by Ibsen.

35. Gil Blas by Victor Hugo.

36. The Lady's Not for Burning by Christopher Fry
    (Carnegie Hall Playhouse).

37. Oedipus Rex by Euripides (55th St. Playhouse).

38. The Shrike by Joseph Kramm (Carl Fischer Hall).

39. The Infernal Machine by Jean Cocteau, new adapta-
    tion by Albert Bermel (Phoenix Theater).

40. The Servant of Two Masters by Carlo Goldoni (Daven-
    port Theater).

41. Asmodée by Francois Mauriac (Theater 74, 334 E.
    74th St.)

42. Blood Wedding by Lorca (Actor's Playhouse, 100 7th
    Ave.).

43. The Philanderer by G. B. Shaw (Downtown Theater,
    85 E. 4th St. at 2nd Ave.)

44. The Sisterhood and One Autumn Evening by Madolin
    Cervantes (The Alhambra, 15 2nd Ave.)

45. Bonds of Interest by Jacinto Benavente (Sheridan
    Square Playhouse, 99 Seventh Ave. South).

46. Conversation Piece by Noel Coward.

47. All My Sons by Arthur Miller.

48. An Italian Straw Hat by Eugene Labiche and Marc-
    Michel (4th St. Theater).

49. Beaux Stratagem by George Farquhar (Downtown Theater).

50. Pink String and Sealing Wax by Roland Pertwee (Lon-
    don success).

51. The Clandestine Marriage (David Garrick's production,
    Provincetown).

52. The Judge by H. C. Branner, a Danish author, trans-
    lation by A. I. Roughton, (Theater Marquee).

New Plays by American Authors, 1958-1959

1. Maidens and Mistresses at Home at the Zoo by Meade Roberts.

2. The Buffalo Skinner by Lonny Chapman.

3. Chaparral by Valgene Massey.

4. Foenix in Choir by Frank Merlin.

5. A Good Place To Raise A Boy by Wade Dent.

6. Jackknife by Rock Anthony.

7. Listen to the Quiet by J. Fred Scollay.

8. The Man Who Never Died by Barry Stavis (Jan Hus Auditorium).

9. The Saintliness of Margery Kempe by John Wulp.

10. Season of Choice by Nathaniel Banks.

11. The Smokeweaver's Daughter by Thomas Barbour.

12. The Geranium Hat by Bernard Evslin.

13. The Redemptor by James Dey.

14. Diversions by Stephen Vinaver.

15. The Golden Six by Maxwell Anderson (final play).

16. A Palm Tree In a Rose Garden by Meade Roberts (Cricket Theater, Second Ave. and 10th Street).

17. Comic Strip by George Panetta (Barbizon Plaza, 106 Central Park S.)

18. Garden District, "Something Unspoken" and "Suddenly Last Summer" by Tennessee Williams (York, 64th St.

and First Ave.)

19. The Young Provincials by Ben Levinson (Cricket, 162 Second Ave.)

20. Shield for Medusa by Bill Packard.

21. The Liars by Walter Beakle.

22. Many Loves by William Carlos Williams.

23. La Madre by Sister Mary Francis, P.C. (Blackfriar's Guild).

24. The West Wind Blows by Niki Juston (Washington Players' Studio, 50 West 13th Street).

25. Mink and Honey by Anthony Asnato and Jean Flynn (music play, Encore Theater, 224 Waverly Place).

26. Fallout by David Panich, Abe Goldsmith, Jerry Goldman, Martin Charnin (musical revue, Renata Theater, 144 Bleecker St.)

27. The Connection, a jazz play by Jack Gelber (Living Theater).

28. Once Upon A Mattress by Jay Thompson, Marshall Barer and Dean Fuller, with music by Mary Rodgers (Phoenix Theater).

29. Chic (musical revue, Orpheum Theater, 2nd Ave. & 8th St.)

30. Eddie Fey, comedy drama by Paul W. Clark (Jan Hus Auditorium).

31. The Girl Who Misplaced Herself by Story Talbot (Washington Square Players).

32. The 25¢ White Hat by Arnold Weinstein (Sr. Dramatic Workshop).

33. The Tortoise and the Hare by Thomas Kiernan (Sr. Dramatic Workshop).

34. Single Man At A Party by Richard Kayne (Theater Marquee).

35. The Power and the Glory, adapted by Denis Cannan and Pierre Bost from Graham Green's novel (Phoenix Theater).

Revivals, 1958-1959

1. Captain Brassbound's Conversion by G. B. Shaw
(Players West, Grace and St. Paul's Lutheran Hall,
123 W. 71st St.)

2. Ardele by Anouilh (formerly Cry of the Peacock,
Cricket Theater).

3. As You Like It by Shakespeare (New York Shakespeare
Festival).

4. Richard III by Shakespeare (presented by Joseph Papp's
Shakespearean Company).

5. Mary Stuart by Schiller.

6. The Courageous One by Maxim Gorky.

7. The Enchanted by Giradoux.

8. Blood Wedding by Lorca.

9. Mark Twain Tonight, stories from Mark Twain dramatized by Hal Holbrook, 34 year old TV actor).

10. Heloise by James Forsyth.

11. The Making of Moo by Nigel Denis.

12. Deathwatch by Jean Genet (Directed by Leo Garen,
Theater East).

13. The Death of Cuchulain by Yeats (world premiere by
Sunday Night Theater Club).

14. The Play of Daniel (medieval, Trinity Church, with
narration written by W. H. Auden).

15. Electra by Sophocles.

16. Philoctetes by Sophocles.

17. Tis Pity She's A Whore by John Ford (The Players Theater, 115 MacDougal Street).

18. A Clearing in the Woods by Arthur Laurent.

19. The Innocents by William Archibald (Gramercy Arts Theater).

20. An Enemy of the People by Arthur Miller (Actors Playhouse).

21. The Cave Dwellers, Separate Tables, The Rope Dancers, The Matchmaker, Night of the Auk, Orpheus Descending and Billy Budd (ELT).

22. Salad Days, British musical (Barbizon-Plaza).

23. She Shall Have Music, musical version by Stuart Bishop and Dede Meyer of The Country Wife.

24. On The Town (Carnegie Hall Playhouse).

25. A Party, program of material by Betty Comden and Adolph Green (Cherry Lane Theater, later moved successfully on Broadway).

26. Street Scene by Elmer Rice-Kurt Weill (City Center).

27. Lute Song by Sydney Howard, Will Irwin, book; Bernard Hanighen, lyrics; Raymond Scott, score.

28. The Hamlet of Stepney Green by Bernard Kops.

29. A Streetcar Named Desire by T. Williams (Carnegie Hall Playhouse).

30. Cock A Doodle Dandy by Sean O'Casey.

31. The Time of the Cuckoo by Arthur Laurents (Actors Playhouse).

32. Ole!, based on La Chulapona (Spanish Variety of musical comedy, Greenwich Mews, 141 W. 13th Street).

33. Arms and the Man by G. B. Shaw (Provincetown Playhouse).

34. Electra by Sophocles (Rita Allen Theater).

35. Harlequinade by Terrence Rattigan (Rita Allen Theater).

36. The Beaux' Stratagem by George Farquhar (Phoenix Theater).

37. The Golem by H. Leivick (St. Mark's Playhouse).

38. The Trip to Bountiful by Horton Foote (Theater East).

39. Widowers' House by G. B. Shaw (Downtown Theater).

40. Fashion by Anna Cora Mowatt (Royal Playhouse, 62 E. 4th St.)

41. A Grasshopper, as adapted by Corinne Jacker from two stories by Anton Chekhov (Theater Club).

42. The Quare Fellow by Brendan Behan (Circle-in-the-Square).

43. The Waltz of the Toreadors by Jean Anouilh (Cricket Theater, 2nd Ave. at 10th St.)

44. Drunkard, musical version by E. W. Smith (Gate Theater).

45. The Children's Hour by Lillian Hellman (Washington Players Studio).

46. The Magistrate by Arthur Wing Pinero (The Ring, 169 Allen St.)

47. The Well of the Saints by J. M. Synge (Gate Theater, Second Ave. and 10th St.)

48. Leave It to Jane, musical by Kern, Bolton, and P. G. Wodehouse (Sheridan Square Playhouse, 99 Seventh Ave.)

49. The Boy Friend by Sandy Wilson (Cherry Lane Theater, 38 Commerce St.)

50. Our Town by Thornton Wilder (Pulitzer Prize winning play, Circle-in-the-Square).

51. Faust by Goethe (Judson Memorial Baptist Church, 55
     Washington Sq. S., Part I).

52. Bouyant Millions, Getting Married by G. B. Shaw
     (Provincetown Playhouse).

53. La Traviata (Amato Opera Theater).

54. The Cave at Machpelah by Paul Goodman (Living Thea-
     ter).

55. The Young and the Beautiful, adapted by Sally Benson
     from Scott Fitzgerald (Theater East).

56. The Billy Barnes Revue (York Theater).

57. Lysistrata, adapted from Aristophanes (East 74th St.
     Theater).

58. Dr. Willy Nilly, adapted from Moliere by Alfred
     Drake and Edward Eager (Barbizon-Plaza Theater).

59. The Romancers by Edmond Rostand (Washington Square
     Players).

60. The Precious Debutants, adapted by Story Talbot from
     Moliere (Washington Square Players).

61. A Sunny Morning by Serafin and Joaquin Alvarez Quin-
     tero (Washington Square Players).

62. Night Talk With a Contemptible Visitor by Friedrich
     Durrenmatt (Senior Dramatic Workshop, 1639 Broadway.

63. The Theater of the Soul by N.N. Evreinov (Sr. Dra-
     matic Workshop).

64. The Devil's Disciple by G. B. Shaw (Provincetown
     Playhouse).

65. Before the War with the Eskimos, For Esme: With
     Love and Squalor, Catcher in the Rye, from the
     stories of J. D. Salinger (Herbert Berghof Studio).

66. Fidelio by Ludwig von Beethoven (Gate Theater, 162
     Second Avenue).

67. Ivanov by Chekhov (Renata Theater).

68. The Royal Gambit by Herman Gressieker (Sullivan St.
     Playhouse, 181 Sullivan St.)

69. The Failures by H. R. Lenormand (Fourth St. Theater).

70. Ping Pong by Arthur Adamov (French comedy).

71. Candida by Shaw (Provincetown Playhouse).

72. Look Back in Anger by John Osborne (Chelsea revival,
     41st St. Theater).

73. The Adding Machine by Elmer Rice (Actors Repertory
     Theater Workshop).

74. The Curious Savage by John Patrick.

75. On Borrowed Time by Paul Osborne (Players Theater),
     115 MacDougal St.)

76. The Workhouse Ward by Lady Gregory (Gate).

77. Come Play With Me, a musical adapted by Haila
     Stoddard and Tamara Geva from Marcel Achard's
     Voulez Vous Jouer avec Moi? (York, 64th St. and
     First Ave.)

New Plays by American Authors, 1959-1960

1. Many Loves by William Carlos Williams.

2. The Connection by Jack Gelber.

3. Once Upon A Mattress by Jay Thompson, Marshall Barer, Dean Fuller, music by Mary Rodgers.

4. Vincent by Francis Gallagher, based on the life of Vincent Van Gogh (Cricket Theater, 162 Second Ave.)

5. Dinny and the Witches by William Gibson (Theater One, 1 Sheridan Square).

6. Misguided Tour by James Allen Reid.

7. Between Two Thieves by Warner LeRoy, based on Diego Fabbri's Processo a Gesu---(Provocative work in form of a discussion, York Playhouse).

8. The Birthday Party by Harold Pinter (Living Theater).

9. Ernest in Love, a musical version of The Importance of Being Earnest, with book and lyrics by Ann Croswell and Music by Lee Pockriss.

10. Little Mary Sunshine by Rick Besoyan (Orpheum, Second Ave. and E. 8th).

11. The Marrying Maiden by Jackson MacLow (Living Theater).

12. Alley of Sunset by John Duff Stradley (Jan Hus, 351 E. 74 St.)

13. Follies of 1910, revue with sketches, lyrics and music by Albert Moritz.

14. Parade, a revue by Jerry Herman (Players Theater).

15. Sappho, dramatization of Alphonse Daudet's novel by Ernest Silverman and Rex Williams (Renata, 144 Bleecker St.)

240

16. Come Share My House by Theodore Apstein (Actors Playhouse).

17. The Prodigal by Jack Richardson (Downtown, 85 E. 4th St.)

18. A Banquet for the Moon by John Cromwell (Theater Marquee, 110 E. 59 St.)

19. The Fantasticks, score by Harvey Schmidt, book and lyrics by Tom Jones (Sullivan St. Playhouse).

20. The Moon in the Yellow River by Denis Johnston.

21. The Sudden End of Anne Cinquefoil by Richard Hepburn.

22. The Breaking Wall by Louis A. Lippa (St. Marks Playhouse).

23. The Crystal Heart, musical comedy by William Archibald (East 74th St. Theater).

24. USA by John Dos Passos (Martinique Theater).

25. Answered the Flute by Sam Robins.

26. Rosemary and the Alligators by Molly Kazan.

27. The Apple by Jack Gelber (Living Theater).

28. The Shoemaker and the Peddler, book and lyrics by Trmand Aulicino, music by Frank Fields (based on Sacco-Vanzetti).

29. Greenwich Village, U.S.A., with music by Jeanne Bargey, lyrics by Jeanne Bargey and Frank Gehrecke.

30. The Laughing Academy by Charles Hamblett.

31. The Ignorants Abroad by William A. Guthrie.

32. The Secret Concubine by Aldyth Morris.

33. Stewed Prunes, a revue written and acted by Mac Intyre Dixon, Lynda Segal and Richard Libertini.

34. The Summer Pygmies by Gerard Marchette.

Revivals, 1959-1960

1. The Threepenny Opera, Marc Blitzstein's adaptation.

2. The Boy Friend by Sandy Wilson.

3. The Crucible by Arthur Miller.

4. An Enemy of the People, adapted from Ibsen by Arthur Miller.

5. Leave It to Jane, book by Guy Bolton, lyrics by P.G. Wodehouse, music by Jerome Kern.

6. The Waltz of the Toreadors by Anouilh.

7. The Cave at Machpelah by Paul Goodman.

8. The Billy Barnes Revue.

9. Buoyant Billions and Getting Married by G. B. Shaw.

10. Our Town by T. Wilder.

11. Share My Lettuce, a Gottlieb, Garnett, Levin production.

12. Simone, adaptation by George Morris of a comedy by Georges Roland (Gate, 162 Second Ave.)

13. The Drunkard, musical version by E. V. Smith.

14. Shakuntala by Kalidasa (St. Marks Playhouse).

15. Overruled by G. B. Shaw.

16. All the King's Men by Robert Penn Warren (East 74th Street Theater).

17. Deidre of the Sorrows by J. M. Synge.

18. Iphigenia in Tauris (Jan Hus Auditorium).

19. Legend of Lovers by Jean Anouilh (Classics Production
    41st St. Theater, 41st Street east of Broadway).

20. Lysistrata by Aristophanes (Phoenix Theater).

21. No Trifling With Love by DeMusset (St. Marks Play-
    house).

22. Orpheus Descending by Williams (Gramercy Art Play-
    house, 27th St. and Lexington Avenue).

23. Shadow and Substance by Paul Vincent Carroll (Tara
    Theater).

24. Tonight We Improvise by Pirandello (Living Theater).

25. Henry IV, Part I and Henry IV, Part 2 by Shakes-
    peare (Phoenix Theater).

26. Krapp's Last Tape by Samuel Beckett (Players Theater,
    115 MacDougal).

27. Machinal by Sophie Treadwell (Gate, 162 Second Ave.)

28. A Bride in the Morning by Hugo Claus, translated by
    Jean Robbins (Maidman Playhouse, 416 W. 42 St.)

29. Camino Real by T. Williams.

30. A Country Scandal by A. Chekhov, Adapted by Alex
    Szogyi (first American professional production, Green-
    wich Mews, 141 W. 13).

31. La Ronde by Schnitzler.

32. The Women of Trachis, Ezra Pound's translation of
    Sophocles (Living Theater).

33. He Who Says Yes and He Who Says No, Lesson in
    Understanding by Bertolt Brecht (Living Theater).

34. The Three Sisters by Chekhov (Fourth Street Theater).

35. Peer Gynt by Ibsen (Phoenix Theater).

36. John Gabriel Borkman by Ibsen (repertory, Sullivan
    St. Playhouse).

37. Time of Vengeance by Ugo Betti, adapted by Charles
     Wasserman (York Playhouse, 64th St. and First Ave.

38. Marching Song by John Whiting (Gate Theater).

39. The Tempest by Shakespeare (E. 74th St.)

40. Measure for Measure, The Taming of the Shrew (New
     York Shakespeare Festival, Central Park).

41. Ballet Ballads by Jerome Moross and John Latouche
     (East 74th St. Th.)

42. Barrabas by Michele de Ghelderode.

43. Donogoo by Jules Romains (Greenwich Mews, 141 W.
     13th St.)

44. Drums Under the Windows by Sean O'Casey, adapted
     by Paul Shyre (Cherry Lane Theater).

45. Epitaph for George Dillon by John Osborne and Anthony
     Creighton (Actor's Playhouse, 100 Seventh Ave. S.)

46. Montserrat by Lillian Hellman (Gate Theater).

47. The Mousetrap by Agatha Christie (Maidman Playhouse).

48. The Rules of the Game by Luigi Pirandello (American
     premiere, Gramercy Arts, 138 E. 27 St.)

49. Hedda Gabler by Ibsen (Fourth St. Theater).

50. The Balcony by Jean Genet (Circle-in-the-Square).

51. Tonight We Improvise by Pirandello (Living Theater).

52. Dr. Knock by Jules Romain.

53. Henry V by Shakespeare (New York Shakespeare
     Festival).

54. Oh, Kay! by the Gershwins (74th St. Theater).

55. Dream Play by Strindberg (Theater East).

56. Man and Superman by G. B. Shaw (Gate Theater).

57. Here Come the Clowns by Phillip Barry.

58. Dance of Death by Strindberg.

59. The Sign of Jonah by Guenter Rectenborn, German au-
    thor, adapted by George White.

60. The Life of Galileo by Bertolt Brecht.

61. The Mother by Bertolt Brecht.

62. Jeannette by Anouilh.

63. The Killer by Ionesco.

64. The Women by Clare Booth Luce.

65. Under the Sycamore Tree by Sam Spewack.

66. The King's Standards by Helen A. Goubert, adapted
    from the French.

67. King Lear by Shakespeare.

68. Five Posts in the Market Place by Algirdas Iandsber-
    gis (won an award for the best play by a Lithuanian
    author living in the free world, 1957).

New Plays by American Authors 1960-1961

1. The Tattooed Countess, a new musical comedy with book, music and lyrics by Coleman Dowell, based on the book by Carl Van Vechten (Barbizon Plaza Theater).

2. Little Mary Sunshine by Rick Besoyan.

3. Call Me By My Rightful Name by Michael Shurtleff (One Sheridan Square, 4th St. between 6th and 7th Ave.)

4. Gallows Humor by Jack Richardson (Gramercy Arts Theater, 138 E. 27 St.)

5. The American Dream, The Death of Bessie Smith, by Edward Albee (York Playhouse, 64th St. and 1st).

6. The 7 at Dawn (Actor's Playhouse).

7. The Connection by Jack Gelber (The Living Theater).

8. The Fantasticks with score by Harvey Schmidt, book and lyrics by Tom Jones (Sullivan St. Playhouse, 181 Sullivan St.)

9. The Marrying Maiden by Jackson MacLow (The Living Theater, 530 Sixth Ave.)

10. Marcus in the High Grass by Bill Gunn (Greenwich Mews, 141 W. 13 St.)

11. Rosemary and the Alligators by Molly Kazan (York, 64 St. & First Ave.)

12. The Shoemaker and the Peddler (East 74 St. Theater 334 E. 74 St.)

13. Whisper to Me, a comedy by Greer Johnson, based on a short story by William Goyen (Players, 115 Mac Dougal St.)

14. What a Killing! a musical with book by Fred Herbert
     (based on a story by Jack Waldron) music and lyrics
     by George Harwell.

15. The Premise, improvisations on topics suggested by
     the audience during the performance.

16. A Fig Leaf in Her Bonnet, a new play by Jesse Torn,
     based on George Bernard Shaw's and Mrs. Patrick
     Campbell's relationship. (Gramercy Arts, 138 E.
     27 St.)

17. Meet Peter Grant, a musical comedy (based on Ibsen's
     "Peer Gynt") with book and lyrics by Elliot Arluck
     and music by Ted Harris (Folksbiene Playhouse, 175
     East Broadway).

18. Paradise Island, a musical comedy with music and
     book by John Jacob Loeb and Carmen Lombardo
     (Jones Beach Marine Theater).

19. The Red Eye of Love, a comedy by Arnold Weinstein
     (Living Theater, 530 Sixth Ave.)

20. Emmanuel by James Forsyth (Gate, 162 Second Ave.)

21. Greenwich Village, U.S.A., revue with sketches by
     Frank Gehrecke, music by Jeanne Barzy, (One Sheri-
     dan Square).

22. The Zoo Story by Edward Albee (Cricket Theater).

Revivals, 1960-1961

1. Under Milk Wood by Dylan Thomas (Circle-in-the-Square).

2. The Balcony by Jean Genet (Circle-in-the-Square).

3. The Blacks by Jean Genet.

4. Hedda Gabler by Ibsen (4th St. Theater).

5. Dance of Death by August Strindberg (Key Theater, 4 St. Marks Place).

6. Drums Under the Windows by Sean O'Casey (Cherry Lane Theater).

7. Here Come the Clowns by Phillip Barry (Actor's Playhouse, 100 Seventh Ave. S.)

8. Leave It to Jane with book and lyrics by Guy Bolton and P. G. Wodehouse, music by Jerome Kern.

9. The Mousetrap by Agatha Christie (Maidman Playhouse).

10. The Plough and the Stars by Sean O'Casey (Phoenix, 189 Second Ave.)

11. The Threepenny Opera, Marc Blitzstein's adaptation of the musical by Kurt Weill and Bertolt Brecht.

12. In the Jungle of Cities by Bertolt Brecht (The Living Theater).

13. King of the Dark Chamber by Rabindranath Tagore (Jan Hus Theater).

14. Much Ado About Nothing by Shakespeare (Wollman Memorial Skating Rink, Central Park).

15. L'Ecole des Femmes by Moliere (Vieux Colombier--- Barbizon Plaza Th.)

248

16. The Mikado, The Grand Duke, The Princess Ida,
    Iolanthe, H. M. S., Pinafore, by Gilbert and Sullivan
    (Greenwich Mews Theater).

17. George Maxim Ross' Philoktetes (One Sheridan Square).

18. The Women at the Tomb by Michel de Ghelderode
    (One Sheridan Square).

19. Krapp's Last Tape by Samuel Beckett (Cricket Theater).

20. Women of Trachis by Sophocles, version by Ezra
    Pound (The Living Theater).

21. Noontide by Howard Hart, based on "Partage de Midi"
    by Paul Claudel (Theater Marquee, 110 E. 59th St.)

22. Evenings with Chekhov: The Anniversary, The Wedding
    and On the High Road (Key Theater).

23. King Richard II by Shakespeare (Wollman Memorial
    Skating Rink, Central Park).

24. The Pirates of Penzance by Gilbert & Sullivan (Phoenix
    189 Second Ave.)

25. Misalliance by G. B. Shaw (Sheridan Square Play-
    house, Seventh Ave. and W. 4th St.)

26. Ghosts by Ibsen (4th St. Theater, 83 E. 4th St.)

27. O Marry Me, the musical comedy version of Oliver
    Goldsmith's "She Stoops to Conquer." Book and lyrics
    by Lola Pergament, music by Robert Kessler (Gate,
    162 Second Ave.).

28. Happy Days by Samuel Beckett (Cherry Lane Theater).

29. One Way Pendulum by N. F. Simpson (East 74th
    Street Theater).

30. The Thracian Horses by Maurice Valency (Orpheum
    Theater.)

New Plays by American Authors, 1961-1962

1. The American Dream by Edward Albee. (Cherry Lane Theater).

2. The Apple by Jack Gelber. (Living Theater)

3. Clandestine on the Morning Line by Josh Greenfield. (Actors Playhouse).

4. The Fantasticks by Harvey Schmidt and Tom Jones. (Sullivan St. Playhouse).

5. I Want You, musical comedy by Stefan Kanfer and Jess J. Korman. (Maidman Theater).

6. Little Mary Sunshine by Rick Besoyan. (Players).

7. The Connection by Jack Gelber, Many Loves by William Carlos Williams. (Living Theater).

8. The Red Eye of Love by Arnold Weinstein. (Province-town Playhouse).

9. The Sap of Life, a musical by Richard Maltby and David Shire in collaboration with William Francisco. (One Sheridan Square.)

10. Another Evening with Harry Stoones, revue. (Gramercy Arts Theater).

11. Death of Bessie Smith by Edward Albee (Cherry Lane Theater).

12. The Premise, improvisations. (154 Bleecker St.)

13. The Secret Summit by H. G. Merz. (Take-3 Theater, 149 Bleecker St.)

14. The Banker's Daughter, a musical by Edward Eliscu and Sol Kaplan (Jan Hus Theater).

15. The Cantilevered Terrace by William Archibald.
    (41st Street).

16. Dumbell People in a Barbell World by Daniel Blue.
    (Cricket).

17. Fly Blackbird, a musical comedy by C. Jackson and
    James Hatch.   (Mayfair).

18. The Jackhammer by Val Coleman.   (Theater Marquee).

19. Signs Along the Cynic Route, a revue by Will Holt,
    and Dolly Jonah.   (Actors Playhouse).

20. Who'll Save the Plowboy?   by Frank D. Gilroy.
    (Phoenix-E. 74th St.)

21. Sing Muse! a musical by Joe Raposa and Erich
    Segal.   (Van Dam Theater).

Revivals, 1961-1962

1. The Blacks by Jean Genet. (St. Marks Playhouse).

2. The Buskers by Kenneth Jupp. (Cricket Theater).

3. The Balcony by Jean Genet, Under Milkwood by Dylan Thomas, (Circle-in-the-Square).

4. Diff'rent by Eugene O'Neill. (Mermaid Theater).

5. Ghosts by Ibsen. (4th St. Theater).

6. In the Jungle of Cities by Bertolt Brecht. (Living Theater).

7. Misalliance by George Bernard Shaw. (Sheridan Square Playhouse).

8. O Marry Me, musical comedy version of Oliver Goldsmith's She Stoops to Conquer. (Gate Theater).

9. One Way Pendulum by N. F. Simpson. (Phoenix-74th St. Theater).

10. The Threepenny Opera by Marc Blitzstein. (from the musical of Kurt Weill and Bertolt Brecht). (Theater de Lys).

11. The Automobile Graveyard by Arrabal. (41st St. Playhouse.)

12. Across the Board on Tomorrow Morning and Talking to You by William Saroyan. (East End Theater).

13. Gayden (Maidman Theater).

14. Ghosts by Leueen MacGrath. (4th Street Playhouse).

15. Shadows of Heroes by Robert Ardrey (York Playhouse).

252

16. Sharon's Grave by John B. Keane. (Maidman Theater).

17. Red Roses for Me by Sean O'Casey. (Greenwich Mews Theater).

18. Toinette, a musical farce by J. I. Rodale, based on Moliere's La Malade Imaginaire. (Theater Marquee).

19. All in Love, a musical comedy by Bruce Geller and Jacques Urbont, based on Sheridan's The Rivals. (Martinique Theater).

20. Androcles and the Lion and The Dark Lady of the Sonnets by G. B. Shaw. (Phoenix-74th St. Theater).

21. The Hostage by Brendan Behan. (One Sheridan Square).

22. The Long Voyage Home by E. G. O'Neill. (Mermaid Theater).

23. The Merchant of Venice by Shakespeare (Gate Theater).

24. Moon on a Rainbow Shawl by Errol John. (East 11th Street Theater).

25. Plays, from Thornton Wilder's two cycles (each cycle including seven plays: Infancy and Childhood from "The Seven Ages of Man" and Someone from Assisi from "The Seven Deadly Sins." (Circle-in-the-Square).

26. Creditors by August Strindberg. (Mermaid Theater).

27. The Golden Apple by John Latouche--Jerome Moross. (York Theater).

28. Happy Days by Samuel Beckett. (Cherry Lane Theater).

Index

Abbe Practical Workshop 46
Abbey Theater 97
Abbott, George 156
Abbott, Richard 199
Abe Lincoln in Illinois 17
Abel, Lionel 56, 73
Abie's Irish Rose 17
Achard, Marcel 239
Ackland, Rodney 219
Acres of Sky 197
Across the Board On
  Tomorrow Morning 252
Act of Love 206
Actor's Playhouse 124, 162,
  217, 219, 220, 225, 231, 233,
  236, 241, 246, 248, 250
Actor's Equity Assoc. 35, 39,
  105, 113, 115, 116, 124,
Actor's Repertory Theater
  Workshop 239
Adamov, Arthur 239
Adams, Bown 216, 222, 223
Adding Machine, The 239
Adelphi Theater 228
Admirable Bashville, The 219
Aegean Fable 51, 76, 80, 94,
  95, 103, 197
Affected Young Ladies,
  The 221
Afternoon Theater 221
Agamemnon 227
Age and Grace 221
Agee, James 49
Albee, Edw. 125, 246, 247, 250
Alcestis 214
Alchemist 194, 231
Aleichem, Sholom 214, 229
Alhambra Hall 218, 232
Alice in Wonder 201

Alice Through the Looking
  Glass 212
All Around the Town 197
Alley of Sunset 240
All God's Chillun 5, 6
All My Sons 232
All the King's Men 196, 242
All the Way Home 49
Almost Crazy 210
Amata 99, 198
Amato Opera Theater 56, 66,
  221, 226
Amedée 214, 217
America 172
American Blues 220
American Drama, The 250
American Dream, The 246
American Gothic 205
American Rep. Theater 35
Amram, David 91
An Enemy of the People 125,
  152, 182, 231, 236, 242
An Italian Straw Hat 232
Anatomist, The 226
Ancient Mariner, The 6
And So They Perish 37
And the Wind Blows 176
Anderson, Maxwell 17, 34, 44,
  148, 203, 233
Anderson, Phyllis 175
Anderson, Walt 105, 171, 203,
  223
Andreyev 219, 222
Androcles and the Lion 253
Angel with Red Hair 192
Angelic Doctor 201
Anna Lucasta 212
Annie's Son 65, 97, 99, 100,
  160, 210, 215, 223

Anniversary, The   66, 212,
                          225, 249
Another Evening With
    Harry Stoones   250
Another Language   226
Anouilh, Jean   61, 184, 211,
    219, 221, 231, 235, 237, 242,
                          243, 245
Antheil, George   207
Anthony, Rock   160, 173, 233
Ansky, S.   24
Answered the Flute   166, 241
Antigone   99, 196, 219,
                          221, 222
Apartment for Rent   193
Apollo & Persephone   219
Apollo of Bellar   227
Apple, The   241, 250
Appleman, Mark   205
Apstein, Theodore   105, 174,
                              241
Arcadia Revisited Group   6
Archibald, H.A.   22
Archibald, Wm.   236, 241, 251
Archipel Lenoir   61
Ardéle   231, 235
Ardrey, Robt.   63, 74, 210,
                          219, 252
Are Diamonds---?   216
Arent, Arthur   28
Argo Players   223
Aristophanes   208, 218, 238,
                              243
Arluck, Elliot   247
Arms and the Man   225, 236
Arrabal   176, 177, 252
Artef, The   23
Artist's Theater   68
Ascent of F6, The   200, 221
Ashberry, John   201, 203
As Husbands Go   17
Asmondée   232
Asnato, Anthony   234
Assoc. Players, Inc.   30
As You Like It   213, 224, 235
Athenian Women   4

Atkinson, Brooks   20, 30, 31,
    89, 94, 96, 107, 108, 109, 141,
                          154, 171, 173
Auden, W. H.   235
Augier, Emile   221
Aulicino, Trmand   241
Automobile Graveyard,
    The   176, 177, 252
Avlon Studio Theater   120
Avon Theater   23
Awake & Sing   17
Awakening of the American
    Theater   26
Ayme, Marcel   115, 230

Bachman, Robt.   192
Bagley, Ben   209, 223
Baker, George Pierce   22
Balcony, The   244, 248, 252
Bald Soprano, The   231
Ball, William   230
Ballantine, E. J.   3
Ballet Ballards   244
Bamboo Cross   208
Banners of Steel   152
Bandbox Theater   7
Banker's Daughter, The   250
Banks, Nathaniel   233
Banquet for the Moon, A   241
Barbizon-Plaza Theater   197,
    209, 220, 223, 225, 233, 234, 236,
                          238, 246, 248
Barbour, Thomas   156, 233
Barer, Marshall   157, 234, 240
Bargey, Jeanne   241
Barlow, Jane   20
Baron Almost   220
Barrabas   244
Barrett, Eliza. Mrs.   xi
Barrier, The   201
Barrows, Robt. Guy   139, 141,
                          171, 228
Barry, Phillip   245, 248
Barzy, Jeanne   247
Beachner, Louis   198

Beakle, Walter   234
Beaumont & Fletcher   207
Beautiful People, The   222
Beaux Stratagem 231, 232, 237
Beaver Coat, The   220
Beck, Julian   44, 104, 188,
                         189, 191
Becker, Ivan   47, 193, 197
Beckett, Samuel   160, 183, 190,
                    230, 243, 249
Beckley, Paul   141, 171
Becque, Henri   208
Bed of Neuroses   103, 197
Beethoven, von, Ludwig   238
Before the War With the
   Eskimos   238
Beggar's Opera, The   194
Behan, Brendhan   177, 230,
                       237, 253
Behn, Noel   115, 116
Behrman, S. N.   17
Belasco   231
Bellak, George   100, 210
Belugin's Marriage   204
Ben-Ami, Jacob   18
Benavente, Jacinto   232
Benet, Stephen   201
Benson, Sally   238
Bentley, Eric   200, 218, 219
Berghof, Hubert   185, 186,
                       187, 238
Berk, Marvin   132
Bermel, Albert   232
Berney & Richardson   194
Bernstein, Robt.   210
Bernstein, Stanley   202
Besoyan, Rick   127, 164, 240,
                      246, 250
Best, Charles   103, 105
Best Foot Forward   220
Best Plays of 1902-1912 and
   the Yearbook of Drama in
   America... 13, 29, 40, 41, 42,
        54, 70, 72, 108, 173
Betti Ugo   219, 244
Between Two Thieves   240

Beyond the Horizon   5, 208
Beyond the Mountain   195
Biancardo, Pascal   35
Biel, Nicholas   35, 105, 111
Big Ideal, The   201
Biggest Book in the World,
   The   24
Bijou Theater   21
Billion Dollar Baby   38
Billy Budd   196, 212, 236
Billy Barnes Revue, The   238,
                          242
Billy the Kid   199
Birthday of the Infanta,
   The   8, 204
Birthday Party, The   240
Bishop, Stuart   236
Bivouac at Lucca 139, 171, 228
Black Diamond   20
Black Souls   22
Blackfriars Theater   37, 52,
   58, 205, 207, 210, 215, 221, 229
Blackmore, Peter   45, 70
Blacks, The   248, 252
Blake, Ben   25, 31, 32
Blanche, Ben Machan   209
Bleecker St. Theater   225
Bldg. 222   46
Blind Alley   193
Blithe Spirit   208
Blitzstein, Marc   28, 242,
                       248, 252,
Block, Anita   29, 32
Blood Wedding   232, 235
Blue, Daniel   251
Blue Denim   51
Boal, Augusto   102
Bodenheim, Max   143
Bolton   237, 242, 248
Bonds of Interest   195, 232
Booth, Shirley   22
Bossick, Bernard   77
Bost, Pierre   155, 173, 234
Bound East for Cardiff   199
Bouyant Millions   238, 242
Box of Watercolors, A   223

Boy Friend, The 230, 237, 242
Boy Meets Girl   217
Boy With A Cart   208, 225
Bramhall Theater   9
Branch, Wm.   209
Branner, H. C.   232
Breaking Wall, The   241
Brecher, Egon   18
Brecht, Bertolt   196, 207, 217,
      219, 225, 230, 245, 248
Brennan, Eileen   127
Bride in the Morning, A   243
Brighouse, Harold   8, 202
Bromberg, J. Edw.   18
Brooklyn Repertory Theater
      The   10
Brothers Ashkenazi, The   218
Brothers Karamazov, The   228
Brown, Harry   34
Brown, John Mason 30, 31, 33
Bronx Theater Guild, The   18
Bronx Project Theater
      The   18
Bucci, Mark   194
Buckingham   199
Buckwald, N.   201
Buffalo Skinner, The 154, 176,
                                      233
Building Blocks 60, 61, 73, 205
Bullfight   59, 73, 124, 205
Bulwer-Lytton   222
Bundle From Heaven 103, 197
Burning Bright   99, 195
Burning Bush, The   46
Burnt Flower Bed   123
Bus Stop   164
Buskers, The   252

Caldwell, Erskine   37
Call Me By My Rightful
      Name   169, 246
Caller, The   193
Cameron, Donald   18
Camille   224
Camino Real   204, 217, 243
Campbell, Mrs. Patrick   247

Candida   199, 204, 219, 239
Cannan, Denis   155, 173, 234
Cantilevered Terrace, The 251
Capalbo, Carmen   179
Capek, Karel   178, 231
Capek, Karel & Josef   220
Capone, Al   19
Capote, Truman   99, 108, 203
Captain Brassbound's
      Conversion   235
Carb, David   3
Career   141, 171, 223
Carefree Tree   215
Carey, Father   149
Carl Fischer Hall   232
Carnegie Hall Playhouse 120,
      224, 226, 227, 230, 231, 236
Carroll, Jane   72
Carroll, Lewis   212
Carroll, Paul Vincent   207,
                                      243
Carson, William   xi
Caspary, Vera   37, 197
Catcher in the Rye   238
Cat that Hated Christmas
      The   192
Caulfield, Edw.   201
Cavan, James A.   193
Cave at Machpelah, The   188,
                                189, 238, 242
Cave Dwellers, The   236
Cert Theater   119
Cervantes, Madolin   232
Chair, The   209
Chair Endowed   211
Chair for Lorna, A   47
Chairs, The   230
Challenge of A Poetic
      Theater, The   75
Change Your Style   3
Changing World in Plays &
      Theater, The   29
Chanin Bldg. Theater   18
Chaparral   158, 233
Chapel Players   218
Chapman, Lonny   154, 176

Chapman, John   70, 147, 233
Chapman, Robt   212
Charnin, Martin   234
Chase, Mary   35
Chekhov, Anton   66, 106, 182,
203, 208, 211, 212, 213, 214, 217,
218, 219, 220, 224, 225, 230, 237
239, 243
Chelsea Players   204, 239
Cherry Orchard   213, 217, 218,
                             224
Chiarelli   16
Chic   234
Children's Hour, The   217, 237
Children of Darkness   46, 231
Childress, Alice   210, 215
Chlumberg   16
Christadora House   7
Christie, Agatha   244, 248
Christopher Columbus
    Brown   47, 193
Circle-in-the-Square   97, 99,
    123, 126, 127, 181, 195, 198,
    217, 227, 229, 230, 231, 237,
    248, 253
Circle of Chalk, The   196
Circus   209
Civic Repertory   19, 24
Clandestine on the Morning
    Line   250
Clandestine Marriage,
    The   204, 211, 232
Clark, James N.   84
Clark, Paul W.   234
Claudel, Paul   249
Claus, Hugo   243
Clearing in the Wood,
    A   176, 177, 236
Cleff Theater   220
Clerambard   115, 183, 230
Cleveland Armory   137
Clift, Denison   197
Climate of Eden, The   207, 218
Cloth of Gold, A   216
Clown, Face   228
Club Theater   207

Clurman, Harold   105, 110,
                        113. 130
Coastwise   22
Cobb, Irvin S   5
Cobin, Harold   65, 74, 160,
                     210, 215, 223
Cock A Doodle Dandy   236
Cocktail Party, The   230
Cocteau, Jean   209, 213, 217,
                        226, 232
Coffee, Lenore   208
Cole, Porter   224
Coleman, Val   251
Colleagues   9
Colombyre   194
Comden, Betty   236
Come Play With Me   239
Come Share My House   165,
                        174, 241
Comedy Theater   7
Comic Strip 146, 172, 228, 233
Cone, Rhett   103, 104
Congreve, Wm.   106, 211, 214
Conkle, E. P.   16
Connection, The 159, 160, 173,
        188, 189, 234, 240, 246, 250
Connell, Leigh   127
Conrad, Joseph   20
Constancy   3
Contemporaries   3
Conversation Piece   232
Cook, George Cram   3, 4
Cook, Jig   5
Cordell, Richard A.   72
Coriolanus   98, 114, 213
Cort Theater   157
Cotton, Fred   116, 131, 133
Country Girl, The   208
Country Scandal, A   243
Country Wife, The   236
Courageous One, The   235
Courteline, Geo.   221, 227
Coward, Noel   137, 163, 199,
                        208, 232
Coxe, Louis O.   212
Cradle Song, The   99, 217

Cradle Will Rock, The   28
Craig Theater   19
Crawford, Cheryl   35
Crawley, Sayre   18
Creditors   195
Creighton, Anthony   244
Crescendo   20
Cretan Woman, The   211
Crew≠55
Cricket Theater   97, 103, 110,
142, 228, 231, 233, 234, 237, 240,
                247, 249, 250, 252
Cricket on the Hearth, The
                               218
Cromwell, John   241
Cross Purpose   196
Croswell, Ann   240
Crothers   17
Crouse, Russel   34
Crucible, The   55, 152, 226,
                          230, 242
Cruelest Month, The   197
Cry of the Peacock   235
Crystal Heart, The   241
Cup of Tea, A   57, 72
Curel de, Francois   208
Current Stages   207
Cyanamide   205
Cyrenian   10

Dakota   36, 201, 215
Dalvin, Rae   48, 192
Damask Cheek, The   214, 217
Dance of Death   245, 248
Dangerous Corner   194, 220
Danny Dick   224
Dark Lady of the Sonnets,
    The   219, 253
Dark Legend   50, 69, 72, 197
Dark of the Moon   99, 194, 231
Daudet, Alphonse   240
Daughters of the Late
    Colonel, The   198
Dauphin, Claude   115
Davenport Theater   218, 221,
                          222, 231

Davis, Ossie   201
Davis, Owen   208
Day at Doubleday, A   216
Dear Barbara   71
Dear Barbarians   48, 69, 197
Death In The Family, A   49
Death of Bessie Smith,
    The   246, 250
Death of Cuchulain, The   235
Death of Don Juan   223
Death of Odysseus, The   56, 73
Deathwatch   177, 235
Debs, Eugene V.   148
De Gioa, Giuseppe   35
Deidre of the Sorrows   242
Demarest, David   231
Denis, Nigel   235
Dent, Wade   158, 233
Deputy of Paris, The   35
Desire   195
Desires of Four   216, 223
Desire Under the Elm   199
Detective Story   199
Deutsch, Helen Hanau,
    Stella   11, 12
Devil in Boston, The   201
Devil's Disciple, The   238
Dey, James   158, 233
Diary of a Scoundrel   219, 224
Dickens   218
Dickinson, Thomas H.   11, 12,
                               13
Difference in God   198
Diff'rent   252
Dinny & the Witches   162, 173,
                               240
Distant Star   202
Diversions   233
Dixon, Intyre   241
Doctor's Dilemna   211
Doctor In Spite of Himself,
    The   226
Doctor's Wife, The   192
Doherty, Felix   210, 215
Doll's House, A   222
Donogoo   244
Dope   195

Dowell, Coleman   246
Dowling, Eddie   43, 77
Down in the Valley   220, 221
Downtown Theater   18, 214,
    219, 225, 230, 231, 241
Dr. Faustus Lights the
    Lights   189, 190, 195
Dr. Jekyll & Mr. Hyde   199
Dr. Knock   244
Dr. Willy Nilly   238
Dragon's Mouth   214, 218
Drake, Alfred   114, 238
Drama Theater of
    Action   27, 28, 32
Dramatic Workshop   46, 97,
                             101, 238
Dramatist's Play Service,
    Inc.   171, 172
Dramatist's Guild   35
Dream House   36, 103
Dreaming Dust, The   61, 214,
                                 216
Dream Play   244
Dreiser, Theodore   64
Driver, Tom F.   171
Drums Under the
    Windows   240, 244
Drunkard, The   237, 242
Druten, van, John   207, 214,
                             217, 225
Duchess of Malfi, The   225,
                                 226
Duerrenmatt, F.   231, 238
Bumbell People in a
    Barbell World   251
Duncan, Isadora   148
Dunleary, Ch. A.   193
Dunphy, Jack   229
Dunsany, Lord   7
Dyas, James   36
Dybbuk, The   211

Eager, Edw.   238
Eagle Has Two Heads,
    The   226

Early Morning After Burial 9
Earth Spirit   194
East 11th St. Thea.   253
East 74th St. Thea.   241, 242,
                        244, 246, 249
East and West Players   9
East End Players   252
Easter   225
Ecclesiazusae, The   208
Eckhardt, Fritz   225
Eckhart, Jean & Wm.   157
Eddie Fey   234
Edge of the Sword, The   101,
                                 109
Educational Alliance Aud.   9
Educational Theaters   2
Edward II   231
Ehrlich, Ida Lublenski   61,
                             74, 208
Electra   194, 208, 213, 227,
                             235, 239
Eliot, T.S. 143, 194, 195, 199,
                             221, 230
Eliscu, Edw.   250
Emmanuel   247
Emperor Jones, The   5, 6
Emperor's Clothes, The   58,
                    63, 64, 69, 73, 205
Enchanted, The   99, 199, 235
Encore Theater   234
End As A Man   54, 65, 205
Endgame   230
Epitaph For George
    Dillon   244
Epstein, Theo.   165
Equity Library Thea. 226, 230,
                                 231
Ernest In Love   240
Ervine, St. John   218
Escurial   224
Etched in Granite   47, 193
Ethan Frome   208
Euripides   194, 214, 232
Evenings With Chekhov   249
Everyman   207, 230
Everywhere I Roam   198

Evil Eye, The   220
Evils of Tobacco, The   225
Evreinov, N.N.   238
Evslin, Bernard   159,176,233
Exiles   226,227
Experience   18
Experimental Theater   5

Failures, The   177,239
Faith   35
Faith and Prudence   51,70,
                            72,201
Fallout   234
Family of Shirokov   193
Family of Waiting, A   216
Family Portrait   208
Family Reunion   194
Fantasticks, The   125,241,
                            246,250
Farquhar, Geo   231,232,237
Fashion   237
Father, The   195
Faust   238
Faustina   104,195,199
Federal Theater   16,17,23,28
Feist, Eugene   60,61,
                         73,74,205
Fergusson, Francis   212
Fervent Years, The   110
Fidelio   238
Fielding, Henry   215
Fields, Frank   241
Fig Leaf in Her Bonnet,
    A   247
Finch Theater   215
Fine Old Wine of Monsieur
    Nuche   192
Finian's Rainbow   212
First Love   201
Fitzgerald, M. Eleanor   6
Fitzgerald, Scott   238
Five Posts in the
    Market Place   245
Flannagan, Hollie   33
Flies, The   196
Floyada to Matador   91

Fly Blackbird   251
Flynn, Jean   234
Foenix in Choir   158,233
Folks Theater   18
Folksbiene   6,232,247
Follies of 1910   240
Fools Are Passing
    Through   231
Foote, Horton 46,177,231,237
Ford, John   114,236
For Esme   238
Forsyth, James   235,247
Fortress of Glass   201
Fossils, The   208
Four Flights Up   50
Fourth St. Theater   214,218,
219,221,224,231,243,248,252
Fraenkel, Helene   50,72
Frankel, Deborah   103,197
Frankel, Gene   47,70,73,125,
133,134,175,181,183,184,185,
                                 197
Franken, Rose   226
Frankie & Johnny   195
Frederick & Strouse   216
Freedley, George   xi
French Art Theater   220,221,
                                 226
French, Samuel   48,173,174
Fresnell, Robt.   10
Freund, Philip   216
Friedman, Chas.   27
Frisch, Max   192
Fry, Christopher 44,208,224,
                 225,226,232
Fuller, Dean   157,234,240
Fuller, Bob   122
Full Moon in March   212

Gabriel, Gilbert   21,31
Gagey, Edmond M.   11,12,29,
                       32,33,41,42
Gallagher, Francis   240
Gallows Humor   246
Gammer Gurton's
    Needle   8

Gamus, Albert   196
Gantillon, Simon   206
Garden District   125,144,145,
                    150,228,233
Garen, Leo   175,177,178,179
                             180
Garis, Roger   210
Garfein, Jack   54
Garrick, David   204,211,232
Gascon, Jean   152
Gate Theater   228,237,238,
239,242,243,244,247,252,253
Gates, Jane Hilton   228
Gayden   252
Gehrecke, Frank   241,247
Gelber, Jack   133,134,159,
171,173,188,189,234,240,241,
                        246,250
Geller, Bruce   223
Genet, Jean   177,213,244,
                        248,252
George White Scandals   2
Geranium Hat, The   159,233
Gershwins   244
Gerson, Richard   193
Getting Married   203,238,242
Geva, Tamara   239
Ghelderode, de Michele   224,
                             244
Ghosts   16,199,249,252
Ghost Bereft   20
Giants in the Earth   192
Giasson, Paul   205
Gibson, William   162,175,240
Gilbert & Cellier   217
Gilbert & Sullivan   195,201,
        220,224,225,227,249
Gil Blas   232
Gilroy, Frank D.   251
Giradoux, Jean   99,184,199,
        213,221,226,227,235
Girl from Samos, The   61,74,
                             208
Girl of the Golden West,
    The   175,231

Girl On The Via Flaminia,
    The   54,73,123,171,206
Girl Who Misplaced Herself,
    The   234
Glanville-Hicks, Peggy   228
Glaspell, Susan   3,5
Glass Menagerie, The   203,
                             208
Glass of Water, The   204
GO   176
God's of the Lightning   17
Gods of the Mountain, The   8
Goethe   238
Goff, Madison   36
Gogol, Nicolai   200
Goldblatt, Mel   122
Golden Alley   223
Golden Apple, The   62,69,98,
                        210,253
Golden Doom, The   8
Golden, I.J.   20,21,22,124
Golden Six, The   149,233
Goldfaden, Abraham   202
Goldman, Jerry   234
Goldoni, Carlo   232
Goldsmith, Abe   234
Goldsmith, Oliver   213,218,
                             252
Golem, The   176,237
Goodbye My Fancy   203
Good Gracious Annabelle   11
Goodman, David Z.   209
Goodman, Paul   104,188,189,
        195,199,221,238,242
Goodman Theater   195
Good Place To Raise A
    Boy, A   158,233
Gordon Reilley   103,110
Gorky, Maxim   226,235
Gottleib, Garnett L   242
Goubert, Helen A   245
Goyen, Wm.   246
Grab Bag   216
Grael, Barry Alan   209
Grahame, John F.   204

Gramercy Arts Theater 236, 244, 246, 247, 250
Grand Duke, The 220, 249
Grand Gesture, The 216
Grand St. Players 35
Granniss, Anita 201
Granny Maumee 10
Grass Harp 99, 108, 203
Grass Is Always Greener The 214
Grasshopper, A 237
Great Theater of the World, The 217
Green, Adolph 236
Green, Graham 155, 176, 234
Green, Paul 211, 224
Green Sleeves 216
Greenberg, Ed 73
Greenfield, Josh 250
Greenwich House 120
Greenwich Mews Thea. 66, 75, 84, 215, 220, 222, 223, 243, 244, 246, 249, 253
Greenwich Village U.S.A. 241, 247
Greenwich Village Thea. 5
Gregor Players 48
Gressieker, H. 239
Gribble, Harry W. 198, 223
Griffin, Jan 193
Gros Chagrins 221
Grotyohann, Walter 212
Group Theater 105, 106
Gunn, Bill 246
Guthrie, Wm. A 167

Hackady, Hal 210
Hadley, Roberta 198
Hall of Healing 200
Hambleton, Edw. T. 98, 108, 157
Hamblett, Chas. 241
Hamilton, Patrick 200
Hamlet 207, 224
Hamlet of Stephney Green, The 177, 236

Hammond, Percy 31
Hanau, Stella 6
Hanighen, Bernard 236
Hapgood, Hutchins 3, 10
Happy Breed, The 199
Happy Days 249, 253
Happy Time, The 204
Harlequinesque 210, 237
Harris, Ted 247
Harrity, Richard 36
Hart, Howard 249
Hart, Moss 29, 207, 218
Hart, Walter 20
Harwell, George 247
Hastings, Kip 132, 175, 185, 186, 187
Hasty Heart, The 226
Hatch, James 251
Hatful of Rain, A 160
Hathaway, D. L. 30
Hauptmann, Gerhardt 220
Haven In The Dark 43, 55, 56, 57, 73, 76, 77, 78, 94, 102, 159
Hawkes, Jacquetta 214
Hawkins, Wm. 108, 109
Hawtrey, Charles 196
Hayes, Alfred 54, 123, 171
Headlines From Paradise 212
Healey, Robt. C. 37
He and She 9
Heaven and Helen 228
Heaven's My Destination 154
Hebbel, F. 208
Heckscher Theater 18
Heckt, Ben 143
Hedda Gabler 244, 248
Heiress, The 99
Helburn, Miss 100
Hellman, Lillian 217, 237, 244
Hello, Out There 221
Heloise 176, 235
Hennefeld, Edmund B. 35
Henry IV 39
Henry IV, Part I 243
Henry IV, Part II 243

Henry V   244
Henry VIII   35
Henry St. Settlement   8, 222
Hepburn, Richard   241
Herbert, Fred   247
Here Come the Clowns   245
                                        248
Herlihy, James   51
Herman, Jerry   209, 240
Herod and Mariamne   208
Herod the Great   231
Heroes, The   201, 203
Herridge, Frances   131
Herzbrun, David   205
Hewes, Henry   149, 171
He Who Gets Slapped   219, 222
He Who Says Yes And   243
He Who Says No   243
Hey You!   53, 72, 201
Heyward, Dorothy   204
H.H.H.   18
Hidden House   192
Hiel   215
High Named Today   209
Highway Robbery   209, 213,
                                        218
Hill, Tom   36, 110, 197, 201
Hilland, Tom   209
Hirshbein, Percy   9
History of the Federal
   Theater, A   33
History of the Fourteenth
   St. Theater   30
Hitchcock, George   177
Hitchcock   43
Hivnor, Robert   36, 66, 75
H.M.S.   203, 224, 249
Hobson's Choice   202
Holbrook, Hal   235
Holly, Ellen   84
Holmes, John Clellan   176
Holt, Stella   144
Holt, Will   251
Holzer, Hans   209
Home of the Brave   34, 207
Homecoming   46
Homeward Look   209

Hood, Henry   78
Hoofman, Elwood   198
Hope Deferred   101
Hope Is A Thing With
   Feathers   36
Hopp, Julius   1, 2
Hostage, The   253
Houghton, Norris   32, 75, 98,
                                  108, 157
Hour Glass   214, 218
House Across the Street   102
House In Berlin, A   192
House of Bernarda Alba   224
House of Pierrot, The   193
Houseman, John   28
Housewarming   177
Hovan, Don   195
Howard, Richard   177
Howard, Sidney   17, 56, 73,
                                  212, 236
Hudson Guild   37
Hughes, Langston   144, 223
Hugo, Victor   232
Hull, Stacey   37
Hungerers, The   221
Huston, John   195
Hutchens, John   30
Hutchinson, Josephine   18
Hutto, Ted   49, 71, 107

I am a Camera   225
I Believe In Rubble   62, 76, 85,
                                94, 95, 209
I Feel Wonderful   209
Iandsbergis, Algirdas   245
Ibsen, Henrik   194, 199, 203,
211, 219, 222, 226, 231, 242, 243,
       244, 247, 248, 249, 252
Ibsen Theater   18
Iceman Cometh, The   99, 127
                                  227, 231
Idiot's Delight   226
If Booth Had Missed   20
Ignor   168
Ignorants Abroad, The   167,
                                        241

Ilf & Petrov   197
Immortal Husband, The   67,
                                   209
Importance of Being
   Earnest, The   227, 240
In a Garden   213
In April Once   61, 212
In Good King Charles Golden
   Days   226
In Splendid Error   209
In the Jungle of Cities 248, 252
In the Shadow of the Glen   226
In the Zone   199
Infernal Machine, The   207,
                                   232
Inge, William   154
Ingersoll, H.   13
Innocents, The   236
Insect Comedy, The   178, 220
Institute Players   204
Inspector, The   200
Intl. Ladie's Garment
   Workers Union   28
Iolanthe   249
Ionesco, Eugene 183, 214, 217,
              224, 226, 230, 231
Iphigenia in Tauris   242
Irwin, Will   236
Isherwood, Christopher   200,
                                   221
Island of Goats   219
Its Your Move   36
Ivanov   230, 239

J.B.   183, 184
Jack   231
Jacker, Corinne   237
Jackhammer, The   251
Jackknife   160, 173, 233
Jackson, C.   251
Jacobson, Sol   108
James, Henry   142
Jan Hus Aud.   207, 211, 218,
   219, 222, 226, 228, 233, 234,
              240, 242, 250
Jarry, Alfred   44, 70, 189, 194

Jeanette   245
Jeffers, Robinson   211, 213
Jennings, Talbot   22
Jewish Worker's Thea.   23
Jimmy Potts Gets a
   Haircut   146
John, Errol   253
John Ferguson   218
John Gabriel Borkman 35, 243
Johnny Johnston   224
Johnson, Crane   210
Johnson, Greer   246
Johnson, Marian   216
Johnston, Denis   61, 214,
                              216, 241
Jonah, Dolly   251
Jones Beach Marine Thea. 247
Jones, Robt. E.   3, 5, 6, 10
Jones, Tom   125, 246, 250
Jonson, Ben 194, 207, 226, 231
Joudry, Patricia   62, 74, 210
Joyce, James   177, 226,
                              227, 231
Judge, The   232
Julius Caesar   230
June Moon   17
Juno and the Paycock   212
Jupp, Kenneth   252

Kafka, Franz   213, 217
Kalidasa   242
Kamen, Milt   209
Kane, Lawrence   41
Kanfer, Stefan   250
Kanin, Fay   203
Kantor, Leonard   210
Kaplan, Sol   250
Kaufman, George S   17, 29
Kayne, Richard   234
Kazan, Elia 130, 153, 179, 184
Kazan, Molly   207, 241
Keane, John B.   253
Keating, Aurel   215
Keating, John   110
Keller, Alvin   192

Kern, Jerome   237, 242, 248
Kerrigan, Jeff   35
Kessler, Robert   249
Key Largo   34
Key Theater   248, 249
Kiernan, Thomas   234
Killer, The   245
King and the Duke, The   212
King Argimines and the
   Unknown Warrior   8
King Lear   194, 245
King of the Dark Chamber 248
King Phillip   215
King Richard II   249
King's Darling, The   197
King's Standards, The   245
Knights of the Burning
   Pestle, The   207
Kops, Bernard   177, 236
Korman, Jess J.   250
Koslow, Jules   36, 103, 193
Kouger, Alma   18
Kramm, Joseph   232
Krapp's Last Tape   243, 249
Krone, Gerald S.   132
Kronenberger, Louis   72, 74,
                            108, 134
Krutch, Joseph Wood   58, 73
Kummer, Clare   11

L'Apollon de Bellar   221
L'Ecole des Femmes   248
L'lle des Chevres   220
La Belle Helene   228
La Bohene   226
La Chulapona   236
La Flamme   210, 220
La Lecon   226
La Madre   234
La Paig Chez Soi   227
La Parisienne   208
La Plus Forte   227
La Ronde 99, 200, 212, 218, 243
La Touche, John   62, 74, 210,
                            244, 253
La·Traviata   226, 238
Labiche, Eugene   232

Labor Temple   218, 219
Ladder, The   198
Ladies' Voices   199
Lady from the Sea   226
Lady Gregory   239
Lady Precious Stream   195
Lady's Not for Burning
   The   226, 232
Lamp at Midnight   152
Landau, John   226
Land Beyond the River   171,
                                 223
Land of Promise   195
Langley, Noel   46
Lare, van, James   229
Larnen, Brendan   201
Last Love of Don Juan 46, 65,
                          75, 210, 215
Last Minute, The   215
Last Resorts, The   137
Late Arrival   58, 70, 73, 206
Late Geo. Apley   208
Laughing Academy, The   168,
                                 241
Laura   37, 197
Laurents, Arthur   35, 177,
                            207, 236
Lawrence, Reginald   202
Le Gallienne, Eva   19, 25, 35
Le Pain de Menage   221
Le Roy, Warner   240
League of Worker's Thea. 25
Leave It To Jane 237, 242, 248
Leavitt, Max   122
Lee, Eleanor   78
Lee, James   141, 171, 223
Lee, Maryat   195
Lee, Theophane   209
Legend of Lovers   202
Leivick, H.   237
Lenormand, H. R.   239
Leomonde Opera   120
Lerner, Alan Jay   34
Les Fourberies de
   Scapion   204
Lesson, The   224, 230
Let Freedom Ring   17

Levin, Ira 219
Levinson, Ben 177, 198, 234
Levitt, Harold 202, 229
Levy, Ben W. 202
Lewis, Emory 149, 172
Lewisohn, Alice & Henry 8
Leyssac, Paul 18
Liars, The 234
Libertini, Richard 241
Libin, Zalmon 9
Life of Galileo, The 245
Life with Father 34
Light a Penny Candle 229
Light, James 6
Lighthouse Little Thea. 18
Lindsay, Howard 34, 105
Lion, Eugene 123
Lion Hunters, The 49, 71, 197
Lippa, Louis A. 177, 241
Little Clay Cart, The 204
Little Mary Sunshine 127, 163, 164, 170, 240, 246, 250
Little Theater 9
Listen to the Quiet 149, 176, 233
Living Theater 18, 153, 187, 189, 190, 191, 195, 221, 234, 238, 240, 241, 243, 244, 246, 247, 248, 249, 250, 252
Lockridge, Richard 20, 21, 23, 30, 31
Lodge, Mark 201
Loeb, John Jacob 247
Lombardo, Carmen 247
Long, Bill 51, 72, 80, 95, 103, 197
Long Gallery, The 144, 229
Longacre Theater 210
Longitude 49, The 46, 101
Long Voyage Home, The 199, 253
Look After Lulu 163
Look Back In Anger 239
Lorca, Garcia 39, 204, 224, 232, 235
Lortel, Lucille 123
Love Comes First 35

Love In Our Time 201
Lower Depths 160, 226
Luce, Clare Booth 245
Lulu 177
Lumet, Baruch 213
Lute Song 236
Lysistrata 179, 238, 243

Macbeth 199, 212, 218
Macgowan 5
MacGrath, Leueen 252
Machiavelli, Nicoli 220
Machinal 243
Machiz, Herbert 68, 75
MacKaye, Percy 53, 204
Mackay, Constance D' Arcy 11, 12
MacLon, Jackson 240, 246
MacMillan 7
MacPherson, Susan 197
Madam, Will You Walk 73, 98, 208
Madame Favart 204
Madwoman of Chaillot, The 199
Magistrate, The 237
Magnanimous Lover, The 20
Maidens 176
Maidens & Mistresses At Home In The Zoo 150, 151, 233
Maidman Theater 243, 244, 248, 250, 252, 253
Maids, The 213
Major Barbara 195, 212
Making of Moo, The 177, 235
Makroupoulos Secret, The 231
Maksimov, Sergel 204
Malina, Judith 44, 104, 159, 175, 188, 189, 190, 191
Malin Studios 102
Maltby, Richard 250
Maltz, Albert 22, 24
Mamba's Daughters 204
Man & Superman 203, 204
Mandelstran, A. 101

Mandragola   220
Man of Destiny   225
Man Who Never Died,
  The   151, 153, 233
Man Who Never Lived,
  The   36
Mann, Ted   175, 181, 183
Mann, Theo.   127
Mann, Thomas   173, 228
Many Loves   153, 234, 240, 250
Marcel, Gabriel   194
Marchand, Nancy   63
Marchette, Gerard   241
Marching Song   244
Marc-Michel   232
Marcus In The High
  Grass   246
Mark Twain's America   210
Mark Twain Tonight   235
Marlowe, Christopher   203,
                                    231
Marnick, Burt   205, 233
Marquand, John P.   208
Marriage & Morals   49
Marriage-Go-Round   60
Marriage Proposal, The   203
Marrying Maiden, The   240,
                                    246
Martinique Theater   241, 253
Mary Francis, Sister   154
Mary Stuart   235
Mascagni   220
Mask & the Face, The   16
Mason   219
Massey, Valgene   158, 233
Master Builder Solness   194,
                                    211
Master Inst. Theater   120, 193
Matchmaker, The   236
Matson, Lowell   72
Maugham, Somerset   195, 199,
                                    203
Mauriac, Francois   232
Mayer, Edwin Justus   65, 75,
              206, 210, 215, 231
Mayfair Theater   250
Mayfield, Julian   201

Mayne, Rutherford   8
McClelland, Keith   228
McGee, Harold   6
McGuire, John   205
Measure for Measure   199,
                                219, 244
Me, Candido!   137, 144, 166,
                            171, 223
Medium, The   219
Meet Peter Grant   247
Melville, Herman   196, 212
Menotti, Gian Carlo   213, 219
Meranus, Norman, Dr.   72
Merchant of Venice   194, 214,
                                    216
Meritz, Albert   240
Merle   227
Merlin, Frank   158, 233
Merrill, James   68, 205, 209
Merry-Go-Round   22, 23, 201
Merry-Go-Rounders
  The   223
Meyer, Annie Nathan   22
Meyer, Dede   236
Meyers, John Bernard   66
Merz, H. G.   250
Michelson, Lottie   72, 201
Midnight Caller, The   177
Midsummer Night's
  Dream, A   222
Mighty Nimrod, The   19
Mikado, The   249
Miles, Dick   197
Miller, Arthur   167, 182, 186,
              226, 230, 236, 242
Mink & Honey   234
Miracle at Verdun   16
Miranda   45, 70, 194, 220
Misalliance   249, 252
Misanthrope, The   225
Miser, The   214
Misguided Tour   240
Miss Julie   204, 207, 219
Mitchell, Loften   223
Molieré   204, 214, 221, 225,
                226, 238, 248, 253
Mollison, A. P.   197

Molloy, Michael   230
Monday's Heroes   201
Montgomery, James   198
Month in the Country, A   222
Montserrat   244
Mood Piece   205
Moon In Capricorn   205
Moon In The Yellow
  River, The   241
Moorehouse, J. Ward   148
Montherlant   220
Morning At Seven   100
Morningside Players   10, 20
Moross, Jerome   62, 74, 210,
                               244
Morris, Aldyth   167, 215, 241
Morris, George   224
Morris, Lloyd   214, 217
Morris, Wm. Agency   49, 71,
                          75, 107
Morse, Ben   198
Morse, Leon   35
Morton, Frederick   108
Mosel, Tad   49, 71, 100, 169,
                               197
Mossensoh, Yigal   214
Mother, The   245
Moulton, Harold   18
Moulton, Powers   192, 193
Mountbanks, The   217
Mourner's Bench, The   192
Mousetrap, The   244, 248
Mowatt, Anna Cora   237
Mrs. Moonlight   202
Mrs. Warren's Profession
                               194
Much Ado About Nothing   220,
                               248
Mullally, Don   22
Murder in the Cathedral   195,
                               221
Musset, de, Alfred   128, 243
Myers, John Bernard   56, 68
My Three Angels   212

Naked   194
Nat Turner   37, 47, 182, 194
Negro Playhouse   10
Neighborhood Playhouse   8, 9,
                                13
Nemetz, Lee   122
Neophytes, The   218, 223
New Dramatic Comm. 105, 165
New Playwright's   101
New Stages   36
New Theater   61, 97
Next Half Hour, The   35
Nichol, Anne   17
Night of the Auk   236
Night of January 16   204
Night   9
Night Talk With A
  Contemplible Visitor   238
Nightingale Sang Too
  Late, The   198
Ninth Life   43, 193
Noah   212
Noble, William   51, 72, 198
No'Count Boy, The   211
No Exit   203, 225
No Face Is Evil   176
No More Frontier   22
Nolan, Maire   192
Nona Crabtree   215
Noone   53, 69, 72, 201
Noontide   249
Nord, Paul   43, 55, 56, 57, 73,
76, 77, 86, 94, 102, 159, 193, 205
Nothing But The Truth   198
Nygren, James   220

O'Brien, Charles   19
O'Brien, Joseph   3, 103
O'Casey, Sean   97, 195, 199,
200, 203, 204, 212, 213, 225, 230,
                 236, 244, 248, 253
O'Harra, Michaela   104, 105
O Marry Me   249, 252
O'Neill, Eugene 2, 3, 5, 6, 15,
 99, 127, 199, 208, 212, 227, 231,
                          252, 253

Obey, André   212
Obligato   228
October in the Spring   198
Odetts, Clifford   17, 28, 208
Oedipus at Colonus   213, 218
Oedipus Rex   232
Oenslager, Donald   213
Off Broadway Thea.
   Association   120
Offenbach   204, 228
Oh, Kay!   244
Old Maid and the Thief,
   The   213
Ole!   236
On Borrowed Time   239
On the High Road   249
On the Town   236
Once Upon A Matress   156, 157,
                          234, 240
Once Upon a Tailor   213
One Autumn Evening   232
One Day More   20
One Foot to the Sea   202
One Sheridan Square   246, 247,
                     249, 250, 253
One Way Pendulum   249, 252
Only the Troubled   216
Open Door   215
Opera, Opera   219, 221
Originals Only   36, 41, 77, 97,
102, 103, 124, 193, 197, 201, 205,
                     215, 216, 223
Orlovitz, Gil   53, 72, 207
Orpheum Theater   118, 120,
                          240, 249
Orpheus   145, 151
Orpheus Descending   236, 243
Osborn, Paul   100, 239
Osborne, John   212, 239, 244
Ostrovski, Alexander   204
Ostrovsky   224
Otway, Thomas   214, 218
Othello   199, 207, 231
Other Foot, The   201
Our Lan'   35
Our Town   222, 230, 237, 242
Out of this World   214, 224

Overruled   219, 242
Oxton, Charles   58, 73, 206

Packard, Bill   234
Pagano, Ernest   209
Page, Geraldine   99, 185, 186
Pale Horse   228
Pale Rider   228
Palma, Anthony   46, 101
Palm Tree In A Garden   103,
                142, 171, 223, 228
Panetta, Geo.146, 172, 228, 233
Panich, David   234
Pantaloon   222
Parade   240
Paradise Island   247
Park Theater   27
Parke, Larry   197
Parker, Kenneth 50, 51, 70, 72,
                          100, 202
Part of the Memory, A   229
Party, A   236
Passion of Judas, The   18
Passos dos, John   147, 172,
                               241
Patchwork Heart, The   198
Patrick, John   220, 226, 239
Payne, Virginia   139
Peace on Earth   24, 25, 26
Pearn, Violet   8
Peer Gynt   243
Peking Man   202
Penguin   205
Peons, The   216
People You'll Want As
   Distant Friends   197
People's Drama   37, 47, 124
Percy, Wm. A.   61, 212
Percy, Isaac   9
Peretz, I. L.   219
Pergament, Lola 66, 75, 82, 84,
                95, 209, 218, 249
Perl, Arnold   229
Perry, Antoinette   35
Perry Comm., The   216, 223
Pershoff, Nehemiah   36

Personal Island   36
Pertwee, Roland   232
Peterson, Louis   226
Peters, Paul   26, 47
Petrified Forest, The   220
Phaedra   204, 213
Philanderer, The   213, 232
Phillip of Macdeon   215
Philoctetes   235
Philoktetes   249
Phoenix '55   62, 210
Phoenix Theater 56, 62, 64, 65,
  86, 87, 97, 98, 114, 124, 156, 157,
  179, 186, 207, 209, 210, 211, 213,
  215, 218, 219, 220, 222, 223, 224,
  225, 225, 227, 230, 231, 243, 248,
                  249, 250, 252
Picasso, Pablo   195
Picnic   154
Picture of Dorian Gray   225
Pihonda, Joe   110
Pillars of Society   194
Pinafore   203, 224, 249
Pine, Les   201
Pinero, Arthur W.   208, 224,
                                  237
Ping Pong   239
Pink Jungle   60
Pink String and Sealing
  Wax   232
Pins & Needles   28
Pinter, H.   240
Pirandello, Luigi   39, 77, 194,
  212, 214, 218, 220, 226, 244, 243
Pirates of Penzance   195, 203,
                                  249
Piscator, Erwin   46
Playbook   75
Playboy of the Western
  World, The   200, 230
Play of Daniel, The   235
Plays   253
Players Theater   211, 236, 239,
                             240, 243
Playwright's Educator
  Theater   101
Playwright's Pro. Co.   17

Playwright's Theater   35, 181
Plough and the Stars,
  The   203, 214, 248
Pockriss, Lee   240
Polis, Daniel   201
Pollack, Ted   100
Pomex, Lee   173
Pony Cart, The   210
Popkin, H.   173
Porcelain, Sidney   43, 70, 193
Pormanteau Thea.   7
Porter, Cole   214
Porter, Katherine A.   228
Porter, Lawrence &
  Taylor   251
Porter, Stephen   225
Portofino,   228
Portrait in Black   204
Pot Boils, The   193
Pot of Fat, The   219
Pound, Ezra   243, 249
Pound on Deamand, A   213
Power & The Glory, The   155,
                             176, 234
Power of Dream, A   144, 229
Pratt, Wm. W.   207
Praise of Folly   205
Precedent   20, 21, 22
Precious Debutants, The   238
Premise, The   247, 250
President Theater   72, 101,
                124, 197, 198, 209, 218
Presby. Labor Temple   139
Prevue Theater   124
Priestley, J.B.   194, 199, 214,
                             218, 220
Princess & The Pea, The   157
Princess Ida, The   249
Private Life of the Master
  Race, The   219, 225
Private Secretary, The   196
Proctor, James   198
Prodigal, The   164, 174, 241
Prof. Baker's Yale Work-
  shop   22
Progressive Stage
  Society   1, 2

Provincetown Players   4
Provincetown Theater   1, 2, 3,
   4, 5, 6, 15, 20, 21, 22, 25, 30, 31,
      35, 50, 72, 120, 124, 193, 219,
224, 228, 229, 232, 236, 238, 250
Pruneau, Phillip   225
Pryce-Jones, Alan   170
Public Theater   18
Purple Dust   225, 231

Quare Fellow, The   177,
                      230, 237
Queen After Death   220
Queen's Gambit, The   221
Quintero, Joaquin A.   238
Quintero, José   99, 127, 231
Quintero the Fortuitous   108

Racine, Jean   204
Rain   199
Ramsey, Robert   39
Randall, Charles   84
Rand, Ayn   204
Raposa, Joe   251
Rattigan, Terrence   237
Ravenscroft   226
Raw Meat   20
Recital 63rd St.   18
Rectenborn, Guenter   244
Red Barn Theater   41
Red Eye of Love, The 247, 250
Red Roses For Me   253
Red Turf   8
Redemptor, The   158, 233
Reed, John   3
Rehearsal, The   199
Reid, James Allen   240
Relative Strangers   61
Rella, Ettore   91, 96, 229
Renard, Julee   221
Renata Theater   226, 227, 228,
                 230, 234, 239, 240
Rendevouz in Wien   225
Respectful Prostitute, The 36
Restless Flame, The   197

Revolt of the Beavers, The 17
Rice, Elmer   17, 213, 236, 239
Rice, Vernon   108, 109
Richard III   235
Richard, Stanley   202, 205
Richards, John   198
Richards, Lexford   48, 71
Richardson & Berney   231
Richardson, Jack   164, 174,
                      241, 246
Richelieu Conspiracy, The 222
Riders of Dreams, The   10
Riders to the Sea   226
Ride the Right Bus   198
Ridgely, Torrence   10
Riegen, Deric   62, 70, 74, 95,
                          209
Riggs, Lynn   199
Right You Are   226
Right You Are If You Think
   You Are Right   194
Rigmarole   229
Rita Allen Theater   237
Rivals, The   203, 253
Robard, Jason, Jr.   99
Robbins, Harold   210
Robbins, Jean   243
Roberts, Leona   18
Roberts, Meade   103, 142, 150,
                 171, 176, 228, 233
Robins, Sam   241
Robinson, Earl 74, 86, 96, 209
Rodale, J.I.   253
Rodgers, Mary   157, 158, 173,
                      233, 234, 240
Roland, Georges   242
Romain, Jules   244
Romance   11
Romancers, The   238
Romano, Arthur   117, 131
Rome, Harold J.   28
Romeo & Juliet   219, 224
Roncsak, Irene, Mrs.   xi
Roof of the Hotel Sutton   18
Rooftop Theater 215, 218, 223,
                      226, 230, 231
Roots in Wasteland   192

Rope   200
Rope Dancers, The   236
Rose Marie   163
Rosemary and the Alligators
                             241, 246
Rosmersholm   279
Rosenthal, Andrew   136, 171,
                             215, 223
Ross, George M.   249
Ross, Robert   18
Rostand, Edmond   238
Roughton, A.I.   232
Rover, Dominic   221
Royal Gambit, The   239
Royal Playhouse   120, 139,
               160, 215, 220, 226, 237
Rules of the Game, The   244
Russell, Bertrand   48
Rustic Rivalry   220
Ryan, Robert   114

Sacred Flame   203
Safari   209
Sailors of Cattaro   26
Saint Joan   213, 227
Saintliness of Margery
   Kempe, The   158, 159, 233
Salacrou, Armand   61
Salad Days   236
Salinger, J.D.   238
Salome,   214
Salome and the Florentine
   Tragedy   221
Salt, Waldo   74, 96, 86, 209
Salvation On A String   211
Sambatian   202
Sandhog   69, 74, 76, 86, 87, 94,
                         96, 98, 209
Sands of the Negev   214
Sap of Life, The   250
Sappho   240
Saroyan, William   221, 222,
                                  252
Sartre, Jean Paul   196, 203,
                                  225

Saturday Night   10
Saturday Night Kid, The   229
Saturday Night Theater
   Club   235
Sauerkraut Seeds   35
Save the Pieces   35
Scarecrow, The   53, 204
Scars & Stripes   216
Schiller   235
Schleifer, Marc D   173
Schmidt, Harvey   125, 241,
                             246, 250
Schneider, Alan   230
Schnitzler   200, 212, 218, 243
School for Scandal, The   204
School for Social Research
                                   18
Scollay, Fred J.   149, 176, 233
Scott, Raymond   236
Scribe, Eugene   204, 221
Scudder, George   27
Sea Gull, The   203, 208, 224
Sea Serpent, The   198
Season in Hell   48, 192
Season of Choice   233
Second Mrs. Tanqueray
   The   208
Secon, Paul   197
Second Ave. Theater   18
Secret Concubine, The   167,
                                  241
Secret Summit, The   250
See How They Run   210, 215
Segal, Erich   251
Segal, Lynda   241
Sendesu, Jules   221
Separate Tables   236
Serafin   238
Servant of Two Masters
   The   232
Seven Ages of Man, The   253
Seven Lively Arts   38
Seymour, Ann   139
Shadow and Substance   243
Shadow of a Gunman   199
Shadow of the Glen,   219

Shadow Years, The   223
Shadows of Heroes   252
Shaeffer, Louis   108
Shake Hands With The
  Devil   37
Shakespeare, Wm.   194, 195,
  199, 207, 211, 212, 213, 214,
  217, 218, 219, 220, 222, 224,
  225, 230, 231, 235, 243, 244,
  245, 248, 249, 253
Shakespearean Theater   217,
  218, 220, 224, 225, 230, 244
Shakuntala   242
Shalmir, Moshe   209, 213, 218
Share My Lettuce   242
Sharon's Grave   253
Shaw, George Bernard   194,
  195, 199, 203, 204, 207, 211,
  212, 213, 218, 219, 225, 226,
  227, 230, 232, 235, 236, 237,
  238, 239, 242, 244, 247, 249,
  252, 253
Sheldon, Edward   11
Shelton, James   210
Sheridan   203, 204
Sheridan Square Playhouse
             133, 237, 249, 252
Sherman, Henry   213
Sherwood, Robt.   17, 34, 220,
                                  226
She Shall Have Music   236
She Stoops To Conquer   213,
             213, 218, 249, 252
Shewing-Up of Blanco
  Posnet, The   219
Shield for Murder   234
Shipley, Joseph   110
Shire, David   204
Shirokov Family   204
Shoemaker and the
  Peddler, The   241, 246
Shoestring '57   223
Shoestring Revue   209
Shrike, The   232
Shudraka   204
Shurtleff, Michael   169, 246
Shy and the Lonely, The   212

Shyre, John   172
Shyre, Paul   172, 244
Side Show   222
Sidney Howard Story-
  letter   73
Sierras, The   99, 217
Sign of Jonah, The   245
Sign of Winter   76, 91, 92, 94,
                        96, 166, 229
Signs Along the Cynic
  Route   251
Silbersher, Marvin   193
Silver Cord, The   212
Silverman, Ernest   240
Silver Tassie, The   195
Simon   10
Simone   242
Simpleton of the Unexpected
  Isle, The   207
Simply Heavenly   144, 223
Simpson, N. F.   249, 252
Sing Me No Lullaby   62, 63, 64,
                        69, 74, 98, 210
Sing Muse!   251
Single Man At A Party   234
Sisterhood, The   232
Sisyphe et la Mort   227
Six Characters In Search
  Of An Author   214, 218
Sklar, George   17, 22, 24, 26
Sklar & Peters   17
Sky High   192, 193
Sleep of Prisoners, A   209
Slightly Delinquent   209
Smith, E. V.   242
Smith, E. W.   237
Smith, O.   249
Smith, Winifred   213
Smokeweaver's
  Daughter   156, 233
Sokoloff, Ivan   18
Something Unspoken   233
Someone from Assisi   253
Something Unspoken   228
Son-In-Law of Mr. Pear   221
Song Out of Sorrow   210
Song of Walt Whitman   177

Sophocles   197, 208, 213, 218,
             222, 235, 236, 243, 249
Sound of Hunting, A   34
Speak to Me, Sam   228
Spewack, Sam & Bella   212
                       217, 245
Spicer, James   70, 110, 175,
                            187
Spippin House   198
Sprigge, Elizabeth   225
Spring's Awakening   213, 217
Squaring the Circle   17
Sr. Dramatic Workshop   220,
                            234
St. James Theater   157
St. John Theater   218, 225
St. Marks Playhouse   128, 129,
                  237, 241, 243, 252
Stalag 17   195
Stanley, Kim   36, 164
Star Minded   51, 72
Starfish   51, 198
Stark, Sheldon   55, 73, 89
Stavis, Barry   152, 172, 233
Steele, Wilbur D.   3
Steele, Owen   37
Steinbeck, John   99, 195
Steinberg, Mollie B   30
Stein, Gertrude   36, 70, 195,
                  199, 201, 213
Stephens, Peter John   144, 229
Stern, Harold   42, 71, 95, 109
Steuer, Arthur   65, 74, 210
Stevedore   17, 26
Stevens, Jerry   36
Stevens, Leslie   59, 30, 73
Stevens, Roger L   124, 127
Stevenson, Richard   8, 22
Stewart, Horace W   193
Stewart, Mary   78
Stewart, Robt, Jr.   72, 74, 109
Stewart, Tanjo   176
Stewed Prunes   241
Stockade   205
Stockdale, Joseph G.   198
Stoddard, Haila   239
Stone for Danny Fisher, A   210

Story Teller   198
Stradlcy, John D.   126, 240
Stranger, The   9
Strauss   220
Street Scene   236
Streetcar Named Desire,
   A   211, 236
Streets of New York, The   195
Strindberg, August   195, 204,
207, 219, 225, 227, 244, 245, 248,
                            253
Strong Feeling, The   197
Stronger, The   219
Strovo, Sidney   18
Stuart, Donald   78, 209
Sudden End of Anne
   Cinquefoil, The   241
Suddenly Last Summer   145,
                  146, 228, 233
Sullivan St. Playhouse   119,
120, 144, 229, 231, 239, 241, 243,
                            246
Summer & Smoke   69, 99, 112,
                183, 185, 195, 203
Summer Pygmies, The   241
Sundegaard, Arnold   203
Sundegaard & Connoly   198
Sun & I, The   152
Sunny Morning, A   238
Supper for the Dead   211
Supplement au Voyage
   de Cook   226
Suppressed Desire   3
Surprise Package   197, 202
Sutton Theater   18
Swayne, Viola   209
Sweeney Agonsites   199
Switch In Time, A   66, 70, 76,
                    82, 84, 209
Sword Without, The   215
Sydow, Jack   82, 228
Sylvester, Robert   111
Sylvia, Kenneth   216, 223
Synge, J. M.   219, 226, 230,
                       237, 242
Szeman, John   xi
Szeman, Julia Hegedus   v

Szogyi, Alex   243

Tabori, Geo.   58, 63, 73, 205
Tagore, Rabindranath   248
Take A Giant Step   226
Take 3 Theater   250
Talbot Story   234, 238
Talking To You   252
Tallmer, Jerry   75, 173, 175,
                    176, 177, 181
Taming of the Shrew, The 244
Tank, Herb   46, 101
Tattooed Countess, The   246
Taylor, Clarice   223
Taylor, Samuel   204
Teach Me To Cry   62, 63, 69,
                        74, 210
Tempo Thea. Pro.   213, 217,
                        224, 226
Ten Nights in a Barroom 207
Terrible Swift Sword,
   The   65, 74, 210
Tethered Sheep   8
Tevya And His Daughters 229
The 7 At Dawn   246
Theater One   240
Theater 74   232
Theater "108"   46
Theater Collective   24
Theater De Lys   59, 68, 124,
   204, 205, 206, 207, 209, 210,
   211, 230, 250
Theater East   225, 228, 230,
                            244
Theater Guild   7, 158
Theater League   2
Theater Marque   227, 231, 234,
                    241, 250, 253
Theater Union   24, 25, 26
Theater of Action   15
Theater of the Soul   204, 238
There Is No End   46, 101
There Shall Be No Night   34
There's Always A
   Murder   50, 70, 71
Tempest, The   244

Thesmophoriazusae   218
Thespis   201, 203
They Shall Not Die   184
Thieve's Carnival   100, 211
Third Person   136, 171, 215,
                            223
Thirteenth God, The   193
This Way To Me   39
Thomas, Dylan   208, 248
Thomas, Leo   209
Thompson, Jay   157, 234, 240
Thor, With Angels   224
Thorntons, The   137, 216
Thracian Horses, The   249
Three By Two   102
Three In One   51, 202
Threepenny Opera   207, 217,
                 230, 242, 248, 252
Three Sisters   211, 214, 243
Three Sisters Who Are Not
   Sisters   213
Throckmorton, Cleon   6
Thunder Rock   219
Ticklish Acrobat, The   66, 67,
                             75
Tiller, Ted   198
Time of Storm, A   55, 73, 76,
                     89, 90, 94, 205
Time of the Cuckoo, The 236
Time of Your Life, The   34
Time of Vengeance   244
Tinker's Wedding, The   226
Titus Andronicus   225
Tis Pity She's A Whore   114
Tobacco Road   17, 168
Today Is Friday   212
Toinette   253
Tompkins Sq. Playhouse   220
Tom Thumb, The Great   215
Tom Sawyer   223
Tonight We Improvise   212,
                        243, 244
Too Many Thumbs   36, 66, 67
Torn, Jesse   247
Torrence, Ridgely   10
Tortoise and the Hare,
   The   234

Totheroh, Dan   10   U.S.A.   147,241
Tower Beyond Tragedy   213   Utopia, Ltd.   227
Tragical History of Dr.
  Faustus, The   203
Transposed Heads, The   228   Valency, Maurice   249
Trazciuski, Edmund   195   Valentino, Rudolph   148
Treadwell, Sophie   243   Van Dam Theater   250
Treister, Leizer   217   Vasilisa Melentyeva   204
Trial, The   213, 217   Vechten, van, Carl   246
Trial By Jury   195, 203, 224   Veiller, Bayard   217
Trial of Dmitri Karamazoo,   Vein, Norman   205
  The   228   Venice Preserv'd   214,
Trial of Mary Dugan, The   217   218
Triangle Players   46   Victim, The   197
Trip to Bountiful, A   100,   Victor, Ben   201
                           231, 237   Victorious Island, The   227
Triumvirate   5   Vide, Larry   216
Trojan Women, The   227   Village Rep. Prod.   224
Trouble In July   37   Village Wooing   212, 218
Trouble in Mind   210, 215, 223   Vinaver, Stephen   233
Truce of the Bear   229   Vincent   240
Tumarin, Boris   228   Violar, Paul   228
Turkel, Pauline H   6   Voice of the Turtle   207
Turgeniev   222   Volner, Ruth   84
Turner, Lily   84   Volpone 125, 181, 182, 207, 226
Turnstile   193   Voulez Vous Jouer Avec
Twelfth Night   186, 211   Moi?   239
Two By Four Prod.   60
Two Fans and a Candle-
  stick   7   Wage Earners' Theater   2
Two For Fun   82   Wagstaff, Harry   216
Two Gentlemen of Verona   218   Waiting for Godot   160
Two Masks   177   Waldorf, Wilella   31
Two On An Island   213   Waldron, Jack   247
Typewritter, The   213, 217   Walker, Gerald   170
                                       Walker, Stuart   7
                                       Wallach, Ira   62, 74, 210
Ubu Roi   44, 70, 189, 194   Wallack's Theater   195
Ukranian Dramatic Circle   23   Waltz of the Toreadors,
Ulysses   231   The   237, 242
Ulysses in a Nightgown   177,   Want to be a Little Angel   134
                               231   Ward, Theodore   35
Uncle Vanya   106, 214, 219   Warren, Robt. Penn   196, 242
Under Milkwood   208, 248, 252   Warrior's Return, The   36,
Under the Sycamore Tree   245   103, 193
Une Ombre   228   Warwick, James   193
Urbont, Jack   223   Wash. Playhouse Studio   234

Washington Sq. Players   1, 6,
                    7, 234, 237, 238
Wasserman, Charles   244
Watts, Richard Jr.   147, 172
Way Before Spring, The   34
Way of the World, The   100,
                    106, 211, 214
Way the Cat Jumps, The   197
Wayside   126
We Present   124
We Will Dream Again   35
Weales, Gerald   134, 173
Webster, John   225, 226
Webster, Margaret   38, 211
Wedding, The   249
Wedding in Japan   101
Wedding March, The   218
Wedding Present, The   205
Wedekind, Frank   177, 194,
                          213
Weill, Kurt   217, 220, 221, 224,
                 230, 236, 248, 252
Weinstein, Arnold 234, 247, 250
Weintraub, Milton   118, 132
Weiss, Fred   205
Welles, Orson   28
Well of the Saints, The   237
Welsh, Gene   122
Werdman Studio   57
West Wind Blows   234
Wharf Theater   3
What A Killing!   247
What Every Woman Knows   36
When the Bow Breaks   209
Which Way Is Home   201
Whisper to Me   246
White Devil, The   211
White, George   245
White, Gordon   103
25 White Hat, The   234
Whiting, John   244
Whitney, George   215
Who'll Save the Plowboy? 251
Why Marry?   11
Widowers' Houses   203, 237
Wild Birds   10
Wild Birds   8

Wilde, Oscar   8, 167, 204, 214,
                     221, 227
Wilder, Thornton   154, 222,
                 230, 237, 242, 253
Wild Duck   231
Will and the Way, The   230
Willems, Paul   192
Williams, Jesse Lynch   11
Williams, Pauline   36
Williams, Rex   240
Williams, Tennessee 99, 124,
        144, 145, 150, 172, 180, 195,
        203, 204, 208, 211, 217, 220,
        228, 233, 236, 243
Williams, William Carlos   70,
                      104, 250
Willingham, Calder   54, 65,
                          205
Wilmot, Pat   227
Wilson, Charles M.   197
Wilson, Frank   193
Wilson, Sandy   237, 242
Wincelberg, Shimon   214
Wings of the Dove   142
Winkleberg   143
Winners & Losers   35
Winter Bound   6
Winter Garden   157
Winterset   179, 203
Wise Have Not Spoken
    The   207
Wiswell, Clark   215
Within the Gates   204
With Love and Squalor   238
Wittfogel, Karl   24
Wodehouse, P.G.   237, 242,
                          248
Wohl, de, Louis   197
Wolfson, Victor   205
Women, The   245
Women of Trachis, The   215
                      243, 249
Wonderful Town   124
Wood, G.   223
Workers Drama League   23
Workers Lab. Theater   24
Workhouse Ward, The   239

World, The   100
World Full of Men, A   201,
                          219
World of Sholom, The   207
World's My Oyster   223
Wright, Barbara   70
Wright Bros.   148
Wulp, John   158, 233

Yablonovitz, Nahum   219
Yablonsky, Harold   209
Year of Pillar, The   199
Year Round, The   202
Yeats, W.B. 212, 214, 218, 235
Yelvington, Ramsey   229
Yerma   39, 204
Yes Is For A Very Young
    Man   36
York Theater   118, 238, 244,
                246, 252, 253
You Can't Take It With You 29
You Never Can Tell   203, 230
You Twisted My Arm   192
Yours Till Yesterday   198
Young and the Beautiful,
    The   238
Young Disciple, The 104, 189,
                          221
Young, Effie   209
Young Go First, The   27
Young, Marshall   166
Young Provincials, The   177,
                          234
Yvrerinov, Nikolayevich   204

Ziegfield Follies   2
Zoom!   205
Zoo Story, The   125, 247
Zorachs, The   3